About the Author

Born in Germany, Edgar Rothermich studied music and sound engineering at the prestigious Tonmeister program at the University of Arts in Berlin where he graduated in 1989 with a Master's Degree. He worked as a composer and music producer in Berlin and moved to Los Angeles in 1991 where he continued his work on numerous projects in the music and film industry ("The Celestine Prophecy", "Outer Limits", "Babylon 5", "What the Bleep do we know", "Fuel", "Big Money Rustlas").

For the past 20 years Edgar has had a successful musical partnership with electronic music pioneer and founding Tangerine Dream member Christopher Franke. Recently in addition to his collaboration with Christopher, Edgar has been working with other artists as well as on his own projects.

In 2010 he started to release his solo records in the "Why Not ..." series with different styles and genres. The current releases are "Why Not Solo Piano", "Why Not Electronica", "Why Not Electronica Again", and "Why Not 90s Electronica". This previously unreleased album was produced in 1991/1992 by Christopher Franke. All albums are available on Amazon and iTunes including the 2012 release, the re-recording of the Blade Runner Soundtrack.

In addition to composing music, Edgar Rothermich is writing technical manuals with a unique style, focusing on rich graphics and diagrams to explain concepts and functionality of software applications under his popular GEM series (Graphically Enhanced Manuals). His bestselling titles are available as printed books on Amazon, as Multi-Touch eBooks on the iBookstore and as pdf downloads from his website. (languages: English, Deutsch, Español, 简体中文)

www.DingDingMusic.com   GEM@DingDingMusic.com

About the GEM (Graphically Enhanced Manuals)

UNDERSTAND, not just LEARN

What are Graphically Enhanced Manuals? They're a new type of manual with a visual approach that helps you UNDERSTAND a program, not just LEARN it. No need to read through 500 of pages of dry text explanations. Rich graphics and diagrams help you to get that "aha" effect and make it easy to comprehend difficult concepts. The Graphically Enhanced Manuals help you master a program much faster with a much deeper understanding of concepts, features and workflows in a very intuitive way that is easy to understand.

About the Formatting

Green colored text indicates keyboard shortcuts. I use the following abbreviations: **sh** (shift key), **ctr** (control key), **opt** (option key), **cmd** (command key). A plus (+) between the keys means that you have to press all those keys at the same time. **sh+opt+K** means: hold the shift and the option and the K key at the same time.

Brown colored text indicates Menu Commands with a greater sign (➤) indicating submenus.
Edit ➤ Source Media ➤ All means Click on the Edit Menu, scroll down to Source Media and select "All" from the submenu.

Blue arrows indicate what happens if you click on an item or popup menu ●——→

About the Editor

Many thanks to Chas Ferry for editing and proofreading my manuals. www.hollywoodtrax.com

The manual is based on GarageBand 11 v6.05
Manual: Print Version 2013-0808
ISBN-13: 978-1478236962
ISBN-10: 1478236965
Copyright © 2013 Edgar Rothermich
All rights reserved

Table of Contents

1 - Introduction

The Approach

Welcome to my Graphically Enhanced Manuals (GEM) about GarageBand. If you've never read any of my other books and you are not familiar with my GEM series, let me explain my approach. As I mentioned at the beginning, my motto is

"UNDERSTAND, not just LEARN"

Most manuals (original documentations or third party books) simply teach you a quick way to: "*press here and then click there, then that will happen, now click over there and something else will happen*". This will go on for the next couple hundred of pages and all you'll do is memorize lots of steps without understanding the reason for doing them in the first place. Even more problematic is that you are stuck when you try to perform a procedure and the promised outcome doesn't happen. You will have no understanding why it didn't happen and, most importantly, what to do in order to make it happen.

Don't get me wrong, I'll also explain all the necessary procedures, but beyond that, the understanding of the underlying concept so you'll know the reason why you have to click here or there. Teaching you "why" develops a much deeper understanding of the application that later enables you to react to "unexpected" situations based on your knowledge and, ultimately, master the application.

And how do I provide that understanding of GarageBand? Definitely not by giving you more dry text to read. The key element is the visual approach, presenting easy to understand diagrams that describe an underlying concept better than five pages of description.

Here are the three levels of learning, understanding and finally mastering a software application.

☑ **Foundation**

This is the level that everything is built on. You have to learn and understand the basics of the specific field (in this case, Music Production) and how it is applied to the specific software application (in this case, GarageBand). That involves the application's user interface with all of its commands and tools.

☑ **Content**

Many software packages, and GarageBand is no exception, come with a ton of content. That content, in the form of effects, sounds, instruments etc requires additional time to explore and get familiar with.

☑ **Practice**

The last step is just practice and experience, applying all the knowledge, learning tricks and workflows to become a true master.

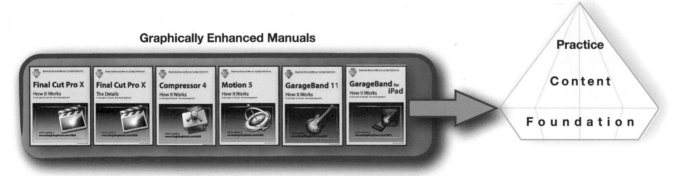

In my Graphically Enhanced Manuals, I'm concentrating on the first level, trying to build the solid foundation that everything else depend on. This requires a proper understanding of the software application (GarageBand), how it functions and how to use it, but also the necessary understanding of the field the application is built for (Music Production).

Learning the additional content in GarageBand means exploring it by applying the newly gained knowledge. After that, it is practice. You search for additional insights, tips and tricks, for which material is widely available. You exchange workflows with others, sharing your experience in forums etc leads to the last step of the life long learning process.

The Challenge

When writing a book, there is always the question of who is the audience. In the case of an instructional manual, the question is, who are the students, and especially at what level are the students.

When teaching a high end application designed for professionals, the author can assume that the target audience is somewhat familiar with the material and the field it was created for (music production, video editing, animation, etc). For example:

- You cannot pick up a manual for a fighter jet airplane, read it and then climb in the cockpit and blast off into the sunset. It might require a little background knowledge about aviation and airplanes. If you are a pilot of a Jumbo Jet, or even if you are only a hobby pilot that has flown just a little propellor airplane before, then you might understand the manual.
- How about picking up a manual to create your first iPhone app. If you have no experience in writing Objective-C or any other computer programming code, you might have a hard time understanding what the manual is talking about if it assumes that you have basic programming skills.

Most applications require a background in the field they cover (i.e. aviation, programming). A manual either assumes that the reader has that necessary background knowledge and targets an experienced user, or it has to provide that basic background knowledge along with the teaching of the app if the potential user is a beginner.

In that regard, GarageBand faces the following challenges:

➡ *Challenge 1*

- GarageBand is easy to use - perfect for **beginners**
- GarageBand is also powerful - usable for **professionals**

So you, the reader of this manual could be experienced, with some background in music production or a complete beginner who wants to get into the field with no prior knowledge or experience. But there is a second challenge.

➡ *Challenge 2*

As we will see in a minute, GarageBand is an app for music production. So what is the underlying field for this app? There is a challenge in that learning GarageBand requires an expertise in not one, but two different fields:

- Being a Musician
- Being a Sound Engineer

So on one side you have the musician (plus the composer) who create and play the music. The skill level can vary quite a bit from some teenager rocking away with his buddies in their garage up to a symphony orchestra with its professional musicians. However when they want to record their music, they have to go to a recording studio and rely on an experienced sound engineer who practiced his own skills for many years to become a professional in his own field.

The trend in music production in the last 10-20 years created a type of tool that combined those two fields into one, the DAW (Digital Audio Workstation). There are software applications like GarageBand, that merge those two fields:

Playing Music (Musician) - Recording Music (Sound Engineer)

➡ *The Solution*

So be aware of that when using GarageBand. You have to put on two hats:

- ☑ Being a Musician
- ☑ Being a Sound Engineer

Musician

Previously, you had to spend a lot of time practicing your instruments to be a musician regardless if it was the violin or the piano in the classical field or rocking away in your basement with the electric guitar or the drum set. This level of commitment however was often the turn-off right there. With "toys" like Guitar Hero, Smule and other easy to use music making devices, the bar was lowered in recent years and a new generation of kids started to "make" music and not just "consume" it. The good news is that for many it could be the gateway to pick up a real instrument later on, but it is still ok if the game/fun level of engagement is enough.

GarageBand (and especially GarageBand for the iPad) is positioned right there at the crossroad. It is a great tool for musicians who already play an instrument but also easy enough for anybody who likes to make music but doesn't have the necessary musical skills (yet).

But even with a more playful approach to making music, you will encounter some basic music terminology in GarageBand. If any procedure in this program requires the understanding of those underlying musical terms, I will of course explain it. (the eBook version of this manual for the iPad is perfect for this, because I'll include interactivity with Glossary terms).

Sound Engineer

The same applies to the second field in GarageBand, Sound Engineering. I will explain any term or concept that might require background knowledge in order to understand why to click on a button for example.

As we will see in the next chapter, GarageBand, as well as all the other Digital Audio Workstations (DAW) simulate a recording studio. Although all those different DAWs (GarageBand, Logic, ProTools, Cubase, etc) emulate the same elements and procedures, they use different ways to do so. For example, different user interfaces, different terminologies, different "specialties".

New Terminology vs different Terminology

Learning GarageBand as your first music production application has its advantage. You start with a clean slate, you are learning new terminology, a new interface. However, if you have experience with other music production applications already (ProTools, Logic or other PC based DAWs), then you are facing one common problem. You might have to re-learn or un-learn terminology or procedures. The underlying concepts and procedures of the various music production applications are pretty much the same, but different apps have different ways of presenting the same thing, use different terms, icons or just different layouts. GarageBand has its own unique way too. This re-learning of terms and workflows is sometimes more difficult than learning something new because with something new you don't have a specific expectation of how things work.

No Dumbing Down

One last thought.

It is difficult to write an app that requires a lot of skills but still make it accessible for an unskilled user. You might have to take it down a notch, make it easy to understand, make it accessible and maybe leave some (too complicated) stuff out. However, I think GarageBand has some areas where the creators went too far. Instead of making it easier, they "dumbed it down" which I think is unnecessary and more importantly, might create confusion and difficulty instead of making it simple and easy.

Throughout the manual I will point out those areas where I suggest different (in my opinion better) terminology and explain why. Using the proper terminology is not difficult if explained correctly. In addition, this will also help you later if you want to move to a different or a more pro oriented music production app like Logic or ProTools.

The Learning Path

So with all that in mind and being aware of the double duties we are performing as a Musician and Sound Engineer, lets dive into GarageBand.

Here is the outline of how I will teach GarageBand. The order I will go through the material is very important because each chapter is providing the understanding for the next steps in the following sections. Of course if your experience level is that of the former mentioned fighter jet pilot, then you might speed through some "basic" chapters a little bit faster.

I also included some sections that go a little bit further. I labeled them "advanced". They are not necessary for the basic use and understanding of GarageBand, but if you are curious, it will provide you with a deeper understanding of the topic.

Some topics I touch on might require some further reading beyond the scope of this manual. I mark them with "WIKI-MOMENT". Think of them as suggestions to Google around or study on Wikipedia to get an even deeper understanding.

Here are the chapters:

0 - Introduction

That's the chapter you are reading right now.

1 - What is GarageBand

Get the basic understanding what GarageBand is, with an introduction of the recording procedure.

2 - Hardware Setup

What preparation is needed to hook up external devices to play and record with GarageBand.

3 - Project

GarageBand is a software application dealing with files. So where are they on my computer.

4 - The Interface

The GarageBand window, finding all the elements on the screen and knowing what they're for.

5 - Tracks

Learning the most important element in GarageBand - the Tracks.

6 - Regions

Learning the second most important element in GarageBand - the Regions.

7 - Editing Regions ... in the Timolino

Basic editing techniques for your music - organize your stuff.

8 - Editing Regions ... in the Editor Pane

Detailed editing techniques for your music - everything goes.

9 - Apple Loops

A closer look at Loops and how to master them.

10 - Advanced Features

Taking it to the next level - for the nerd (I mean pro) inside of you.

11 - Share

Get your mix ready, export it and head for the iTunes Charts.

12 - Additional Feature

More cool features that come with GarageBand.

2 - What is GarageBand

A DAW

 I answered this question already in the introduction. GarageBand is a software application for producing music. However, this is a very generic description that can include a lot of things. I also mentioned that these types of applications are called "Digital Audio Workstations" or just DAW. Let's look at this term first:

- **Digital**: This means that we are working in the digital domain, using a computer. The opposite would be "analog" with analog tape machines, mixing consoles and effect racks, all connected with wires carrying analog signals. (WIKI-MOMENT: Analog vs Digital)
- **Audio**: This word means that we are working in the audio field, dealing with music and sound and not taking pictures or making a movie, although you can add video to your GarageBand Project to work on the audio aspect (create a soundtrack).
- **Workstation**: This word hints at the "swiss army knife" aspect of the program. DAWs can usually perform a wide variety of tasks (recording, editing, mixing, mastering). This also means that there is a lot to learn.

DAW

I also mentioned that there are other DAWs like Logic Pro, ProTools, Cubase, Live and a wide variety of DAWs on the PC side that are mostly unknown to the Mac user. Basically, they all provide the same tools for producing music. Their main difference is their feature set, different user interface and specific workflows.

Feature Set

The question about how much "stuff" a software application provides comes down to how much stuff the user actually needs. You might not need a full blown word processor like Word to just write a few notes or a letter and you might not need the full version of Photoshop when a magic "enhance" button is enough to make your picture look better.

It is the same thing with DAWs. ProTools or Logic might be too much for a user since all of their features and tools require a lot of time to learn and understand.

This is where GarageBand comes into the picture. It is a consumer product (with a consumer price tag), designed for the entry level user. It has a stripped down feature set, limited in many areas. A lot of things you could do with a professional product like Logic or ProTools can not be done with GarageBand. The big advantage however is its ease of use.

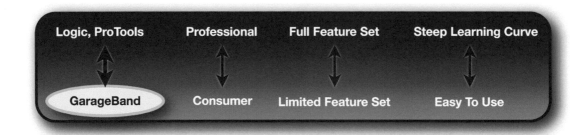

However, although GarageBand is made for the consumer and the entry level user, it turns out that despite its limitation, it is also useful for the professional user.

- Many musicians use it on their MacBook at home or on the road to record their material. Its ease of use lets you get stuff done very quickly.
- Some of GarageBand's features are not even available on professional systems.
- The iPad version of GarageBand makes it even more appealing with its portability and intuitive interface.

Here is a list of the main features in GarageBand with some of them not found in a professional DAW:

- ☑ Record your music with microphones, electric guitars or MIDI keyboards
- ☑ Mix your music and add loop based audio files
- ☑ Print music notation
- ☑ Create Ringtones
- ☑ Create Podcasts
- ☑ Use it as a synthesizer instrument (sound module)
- ☑ Use it as a guitar amp with stompboxes to play your guitar
- ☑ Create a soundtrack for your video
- ☑ Learn how to play Guitar and Piano with included Lessons
- ☑ Play along (jam) with a virtual Band, the Magic GarageBand

The Concept

Let's start with the main feature of GarageBand (and any DAW) - **Record and mix music**.

These are the two basic processes in every music production. A DAW simulates those processes which include all the equipment found in a recording studio. It emulates them with a software application so you can perform virtually all those tasks "inside the box", your computer. GarageBand is above all - your virtual recording studio.

GarageBand is your virtual Recording Studio

That is great. However, remember the fighter jet? What good is it if you have a fighter jet plane but don't know how to fly it. Same thing with a Recording Studio, you have to know how to operate it. There are two scenarios:

💡 **You know how to use the equipment in a recording studio:**

> In that case, you just look around in GarageBand to find the familiar components. It is like walking into a new recording studio. You check what console they have, what kind of recording equipment and outboard gears, etc. and you just need a little time to adjust before hitting the record button. (The ironic part is that many recording studios nowadays have only one piece of equipment, a DAW, which emulates a recording studio.)

💡 **You haven't any idea what all this stuff is for:**

> In that case, you have the feeling that someone put you in the fighter jet plane, handed you the ignition key (do they have one?) and told you "ready for take off". It can be a little bit overwhelming.

Because GarageBand is a consumer application and most users fit in scenario two, I will spend a little time explaining the components in a recording studio before diving into the details of GarageBand.

I will introduce the main components in a recording studio with a short description to develop a basic understanding of what elements are needed to record and mix your music. This will have an advantage later in the book in that when we look at GarageBand, we will recognize those components and will have a basic understanding which part belongs to what.

This may sound trivial but it is very important in the learning process. Don't get stuck in the detail with a single button or a menu. Always look at it in the context of the big picture.

Record Music

⚙ Tape Machine

This is the central element in a Recording Studio, the device that you record your music on. Some big studios still have the original type of device a "Tape Recorder", that thing with the two reels and magnetic tape moving across. These are mostly analog tape machines that changed into cassette based tape recorders using digital recording techniques. But all those separate hardware devices are replaced nowadays by a computer that records your music onto a big hard drive (using a DAW).

Although the mechanics and the functionality of a computer based recording device like GarageBand are quite different, the interface, the terminology and its operation are based on those old Tape Machines.

⚙ Transport/Navigation Control

Every kind of recording device has to have controls, the so called Transport Controls or Navigation Controls. With tape-based devices, they let you move the tape to the desired position. Even though there is no tape moved around on a hard drive (or no parts at all with SSD drives), the control buttons are the same as in the old days.

⚙ Reader, LCD Display

The essential part in a Navigation system is the read out that tells you where you are on the tape. When you want to record the second verse of your song, you have to be sure that you are at the 2nd Verse. Original Tape Machines had a simple time reader (sometimes even mechanical). Nowadays, you have some sort of digital LCD clock. Professional systems use the industry standard called SMPTE time to display time (WIKI MOMENT: SMPTE Time).

⚙ Playhead

A Playhead on an original Tape Machine was a special magnet that picked up the recording in form of magnetic fields from the tape that rolled by. This Playhead is now represented by a vertical line that represents the position where you play or record your music. That position relates to the number displayed in the LCD Display.

⚙ Tracks

One of the main characteristics of a Tape Recorder is the number of Tracks it can record. A track was originally the horizontal space on the tape where the Playhead reads the recorded information. The wider the tape (1/2 inch, 1 inch, 2 inch) the more separate tracks could fit on that tape. The more tracks a tape recorder provides, the more instruments you can record separately at the same time location. This has the advantage of recording them one after another (overdub) and also feed those separate tracks to separate channels on a mixing board to treat those tracks (instruments) differently. Often you could see the number of available tracks on a machine by the amount of separate Meters on the machine.

Modern DAWs are not restricted by the width of a tape anymore. The number of tracks is determined by the software and often just limited by the capabilities of the computer and the speed of your drive you are recording to.

⚙ Input

This element can be easily overlooked but it might be the most important one. If you can't get any signal (instrument) into the recording device then you cannot record anything, simple as that. A tape machine is usually hooked up to the mixing console and you record through it.

On a DAW the "first point of entry" is your computer and very often this is the first point of frustration if you cannot get your signal into it. This doesn't have much to do with the understanding of traditional recording devices, but more with modern computers and their input devices. To eliminate that frustration, I will spend the next chapter on this important aspect.

Mix Music

● Mixing Console

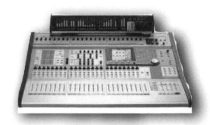

The second most important element in a recording studio is the mixing console, or mixer. This is the tool you use to mix your recording. Although it is also used for the recording part, its main purpose is to create the final mix of your recorded song.

In modern DAWs, the mixing console is transferred into a visual replica of a mixer so sound engineers feel right at home. But here we are again with the fighter jet plane. If you are not a sound engineer then it doesn't do you any good if the software mixer looks and functions the same as a real life mixing console. You wouldn't know what to do with it in either case.

That's why consumer DAW's like GarageBand try to simplify the part of the user interface that represents the mixing console. That could create a problem if you learned how to use a regular mixing board but now have to re-learn the "simplified" version, which you might find strange.

● Channels (Tracks)

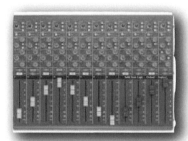

The main elements of a mixing console are its Channels, or Channel Strips. These are the identical looking strips with a long fader and all kinds of knobs. The size of a mixer is usually determined by how many physical channel strips it has (8, 32, 64, ...). The signal of each of your recorded Tracks from the recording machine is sent (routed) to their own channel strip so you can treat each instrument differently to achieve the right sound for your song.

A modern DAW often has virtually an unlimited amount of those Channel Strips, although somehow limited again by the capability of the computer. Because the Track from the recorder is related to the Channel on the mixer, both terms are often used to describe the same element.

● Channel Controls

The available Controls on a Channel Strip determine how you can alter the sound of the Instrument that is assigned to it (runs through that channel). The main controls are the Fader (change the volume), Pan (change the stereo position left-to-right), Mute (turn it off), Solo (listen only to that instrument), Meter (check the signal level). Depending on the mixing console (or DAW), the Channel Strips can provide even more controls.

● Outboard Effects

The basic step of mixing different Instruments (tracks) to get a great sounding song is to get the balance right. You set the correct volume for each instrument and position them in the stereo field, i.e. make the guitar come out of the left speaker and the keyboard from the right speaker. The singer comes from both speakers and therefore appears to come from the center (WIKI MOMENT: sound mixing techniques).

The interesting part of mixing however starts when you add effects to an instrument like delay or distortion. It would not be practical to build all those effects into a channel strip. There are too many of them and you might need them only on a few instruments. The channel strip would be too long and too expensive. This is where the outboard effects come in. A recording studio usually has a separate rack of effect modules that the engineer could use on specific channel strips.

A similar principle is used in a DAW which often provides a set of effect plugins (or you can add additional third party effects to your system). You can "use" those effects on an individual channel that you want an effect applied to. We will learn how to "add" those effects to your Channel in GarageBand, but the way to use (or misuse) them would require a complete manual (WIKI MOMENT: How to use Equalizer, Compressor, Delay, etc).

● Master Channel

While each Channel Strip affects only the instrument it is assigned to, there is one additional Channel Strip on each Mixing Console and that is the Master Channel. The signals of all the Channels (and their instruments) are added together and go through that Master Channel. This Master Channel is used to do some last final treatment to the mix, i.e. lower the overall volume or compress the mix to make it sound louder.

GarageBand also has that Master Channel, but it is called the Master Track.

3 - Hardware Setup

Now we have a basic understanding of what elements are needed in a Recording Studio. Step by step, we will "discover" those elements in GarageBand, our virtual Recording Studio. In this chapter we will look at the components that can be connected to our virtual studio.

How to get stuff in and out of GarageBand.

Signal Flow

Connecting devices together is usually not that difficult. For example, you have a guitar that you plug into an amp and the amp connects to the speaker and off you go. If there is no sound, then you check the cables and volume and that's about how complex it gets.

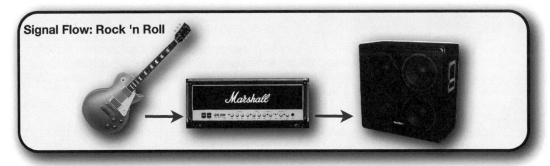

Setting up a DAW is a totally different kind of beast. Look at the following example which is a very simplified (!) diagram of how to get in and out of GarageBand. As you can see, the signal goes through different layers and at every step something could go wrong. On top of that, each layer, like the hardware or the operating system, contains its own level of complexity.

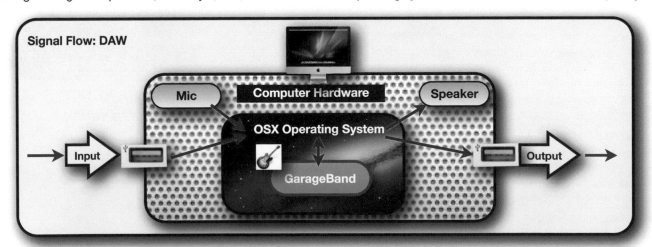

However, this diagram shouldn't scare you. You will find out that it is fairly simple as long you understand the basic components and keep the big picture in mind. That is what I try to teach in this book. Ultimately you'll spend more time making music instead of traveling to Apple's Genius Bar for help.

Before explaining **how** to get stuff in and out of GarageBand, let's look first at **what** stuff that could be.

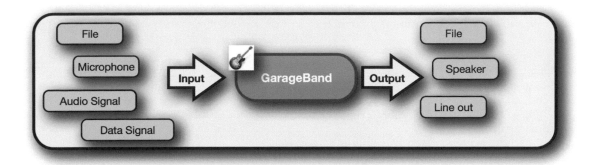

Here is a short explanation of various Input and Output Sources to get a general overview of the available components. I will discuss the configuration in the next section.

➡ *Input (Source)*

The Input determines what the possible Sources are for GarageBand. What can you put into ("feed") GarageBand in order to create your Song.

🎙 File

This is the case where you don't "record" anything in GarageBand. You don't have to play any instrument but you can still use GarageBand to create a song. Instead, you can use pre-recorded material in the form of Apple Loops or any existing audio files (that are supported by GarageBand). So instead of recording, you are importing stuff to create and/or mix a song.

There is no extra setup needed for this kind of input. As we will see later, GarageBand allows two ways to import those audio files:

- Drag an audio file directly from the Finder onto your GarageBand Project.
- Use a special window in GarageBand (Media Browser and Loop Browser) to conveniently access and import audio files that are available on your drive.

🎙 Internal Microphone

Most of Apple's computers have a built-in microphone. Although not necessarily the sound quality you want for your song, it provides a quick way to record any acoustic signal into GarageBand. No cables and no hardware hook-up required.

🎙 Audio In (Line In)

All of Apple's computers are also equipped with an Audio-In jack, the so called Line-in. This lets you connect virtually any audio signal directly to your Mac without additional hardware configuration. You can plug an electric piano, an electric guitar or the output of an audio player directly into your Mac and record that signal in GarageBand.

Most Macs are equipped with a mini-jack as the Line Input. The newer laptops have only one jack that functions as a switchable audio input/output (to be selected in the System Preferences ➤ Sound).

Audio Interface (input)

This type of Input requires an extra piece of hardware, the Audio Interface. It also might require a bit more prep work to set it up. The disadvantage of using the computer's built-in inputs is its average audio quality. Using a separate Audio Interface lets you choose from different models and manufacturers ranging from better quality to the best possible quality (with the highest possible price tag). Besides the quality, those Audio Interfaces often provide more features, i.e. more inputs for recording multiple sources at the same time (multi-track recording).

Many audio interfaces require the installation of additional software, so-called Drivers. They tell the Operating System (OS X) on the computer how to communicate with the external hardware device and how to use all those additional features it provides.

Please note that those Audio Interfaces will not be connected to the audio inputs of the computer. They are connected to the standard computer jacks, mostly USB nowadays. All of your Input sources that produce an audio signal (electric guitar, electric piano, microphone, etc) are now connected to the Audio Interface and GarageBand records those audio input sources through the Audio Interface. There are even USB Microphones that have the audio interface built-in, so you can connect the mic directly to the USB port of the computer.

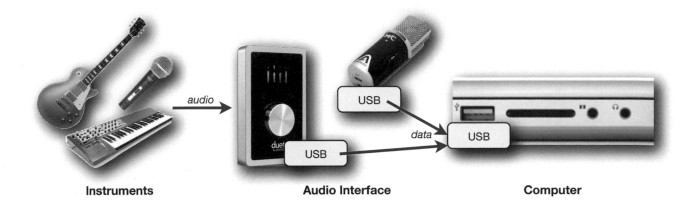

Instruments **Audio Interface** **Computer**

MIDI Interface (data)

This is the first time I mention the term MIDI. I will go into more details about it later. For now, all we have to know is that MIDI is a standard that defines how to send music information as a special Data Signal and not as an Audio Signal.

For example, you can connect the audio output of an Electric Piano to your speaker system and you will hear the music you are playing, with the sound it produces. If that electric piano has a MIDI out jack and you would connect that output signal to a speaker system, you would hear just noise. The reason is that the notes you are playing on the keyboard are transferred as a data signal. The data includes a "description" of what you are playing (what note, how loud, etc). How the music is translated into data is specified by the MIDI standard (WIKI MOMENT: MIDI).

A MIDI keyboard that generates MIDI data can send the signal via a MIDI cable to a device that "understands" the MIDI data. This can be either a sound module that "plays" the music or a computer that can record the MIDI signal and also plays the MIDI signal with its built-in sound modules (like GarageBand).

MIDI was originally connected through a standard 8-pin DIN connector but new devices use the standard USB connection. The good news is that the operating system running on your Mac (OS X) "speaks the MIDI language". You just need to connect your MIDI keyboard to the USB port on your Mac and GarageBand automatically "sees" that keyboard and lets you select it as a MIDI Input Source. I'll discuss the configuration in the Track Chapter.

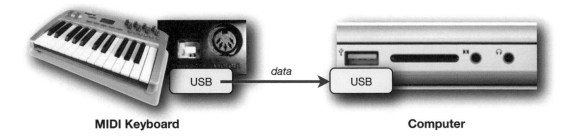

MIDI Keyboard **Computer**

➡ Output (Destination)

The Output in GarageBand determines what the destination is for your song, where you "send" it to.

☻ File

This is most likely the final destination when you export your complete mix of your song as a new audio file that you can play in iTunes, email to your fans or post on the internet.

☻ Internal Speaker

All Apple computers have a built-in speaker, a crappy one but a speaker nonetheless. The advantage of course, no extra hookup of additional hardware devices is needed.

☻ Audio Out (Line out)

All Apple computers have at least one audio output jack. This provides you with two options. You can plug in headphones or connect it to a speaker system.

Audio Out

☻ Audio Interface

Among other advantages, a dedicated Audio Interface for the output delivers a better sound quality than connecting speakers directly to your Mac.

Please note that many of the Audio Interfaces perform a double duty. You use only one (USB) cable to connect the Audio Interface to your computer, but that Audio Interface itself often provides audio connections for the input (connect Microphones and Guitars) and connections for the output (connect it to a speaker system or headphones).

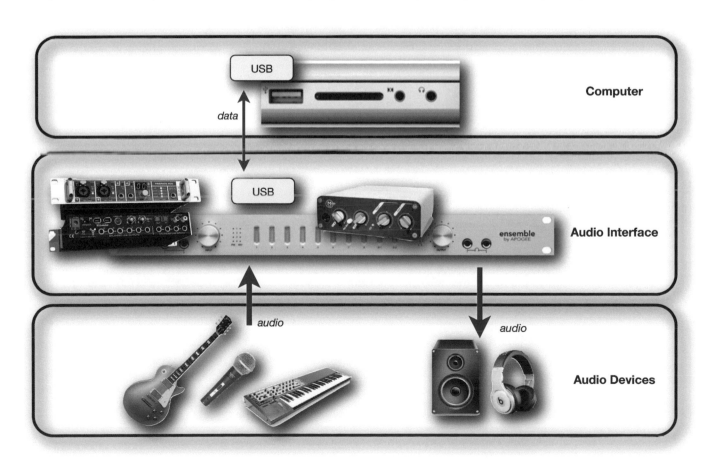

Think about it

"Why is all that source and destination stuff so important and why do I have to know that? I just want to record music."

Like in any recording studio, in order to start your session, you have to setup everything before you can hit the record button. Think about it, this is a big difference if you compare GarageBand to other software applications you might use. For example, editing some pictures in iPhoto or Photoshop and even making a movie with iMovie or Final Cut doesn't require this kind of setup before your start working. The reason is that those apps work mainly with files that are ready to use. The files are created outside that application using a different device, i.e. a picture camera or a video camera.

A music production application like GarageBand serves both tasks. Yes, it also lets you do the postproduction, which is called editing and mixing, but here is the main difference. A DAW performs the first half of the process too, capturing the music. In the photography and video world you don't have your camera hooked up to iPhoto or iMovie while you are capturing your material. Usually, you do that separately on a camera first and later import the material as files to your software application.

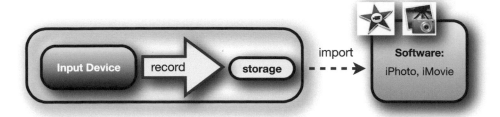

With a DAW you're capturing (recording) directly into the software application (GarageBand). And this requires the extra configuration at the beginning to get the "source devices" like microphones, guitars and MIDI keyboards into the program. Of course, it also requires the right output destination to listen to your song.

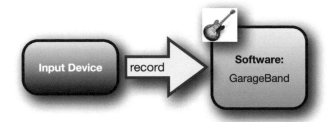

Input - Output

For the rest of the manual, I will regroup all those input and output options into three categories:

Files - Audio - MIDI

🔘 Files

Although files are one form of "stuff" that needs to get in and out of your GarageBand project, this group belongs to file management and is not considered a signal in that context. I cover that aspect of file management later.

🔘 Audio

This category includes everything that carries sound or transforms sound. This could be in any acoustic form like a speaker, a microphone (recording a singer or a drum setup) or any sound in electric form like the signal from an electric guitar, the audio output from any electric instrument (synthesizer, drum pads, etc) or an mp3 player.

🔘 MIDI

This is a very specific category of an electric signal that is carried over a cable from your MIDI keyboard into GarageBand. The difference, as I just mentioned, is that this signal, the MIDI signal, doesn't carry music as sound information, it carries music as data, specific information about the notes your are playing on your MIDI keyboard.

Devices (advanced)

Warning, this section dives a little bit deeper into the configuration discussion. It is not necessarily required for using GarageBand, but if you are up for the task, you will understand the basics about audio in OSX better. If it is too geeky, don't worry, skip to the next section.

Remember that scary diagram in the previous section about the signal diagram in a DAW?

Unlike a straight forward "Rock 'n Roll" setup where you plug your guitar into an amp, connecting a DAW involves various layers. Once you are aware of those layers, it becomes easy to troubleshoot potential problems like "I can't hear anything".

Whatever you are doing on your Mac that involves audio (including GarageBand), touches 4 components. Only one of them, the actual Device, is a hardware component, the other three are software components.

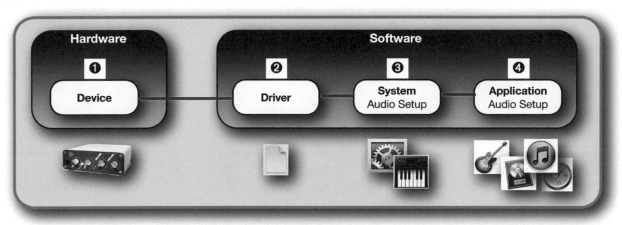

❶ Device

This is the actual physical device in form of the hardware components that your computer software uses. For example, this can be an external Audio Interface that you connect via USB to your computer. Please note that a Device can also be an internal hardware device inside your computer like the built-in microphone or the speaker inside your computer.

❷ Driver

A driver is a little file on your hard disk that functions as the interpreter between the hardware and the software side. It tells your operating system how to communicate with a connected hardware device. Many hardware devices are plug-and-play, meaning OSX knows how to communicate with them because the manufacturer who built that device followed basic OSX guidelines. Other Audio Devices however function in a way that the operating system doesn't know. Those devices require that you install additional software, including a driver that tells OSX how to recognize the device and how to use it. Those drivers are placed somewhere "under the hood" of your OSX system and you don't have to deal with them (unless they require an update). So keep in mind, whatever Audio Device you want to use with GarageBand, has to have a proper driver installed. If that piece is missing then you won't "see" that device in GarageBand and therefore cannot use it.

❸ System - Audio Setup

There are two special applications in OSX, the "System Preferences" and the "Audio MIDI Setup" utility. They provide the user interface to configure the hardware Devices with the help of their Drivers. The two applications let you choose which Device you want to use on your computer (built-in audio, external audio, etc) and how to use it (control the level, mute, balance, etc).

❹ Application - Audio Setup

And finally the application itself. There are two categories of applications that use sound input and/or output.

- Applications that rely on the settings of the System audio settings. Those apps don't have their own configuration window for audio. For example iTunes, Safari and even the Finder that plays the startup chime or alert sounds.

- Applications that provide their own audio settings window. They can talk directly to the driver (choose, control) without using the System audio setting. GarageBand falls into that category.

Who's controlling What

Here is another diagram with the same 4 layers that demonstrates the concept:

- Whatever audio application you are using ❹, has to "reach" the Audio Device ❶ to play or record through it.

- An application can "see" and control the Audio Device only if a proper Driver ❷ is available/installed on your system for that Device.

- Some applications cannot choose or control an Audio Device's Driver directly. They rely on the System Audio settings ❸.

- The System Audio settings can be configured in two applications, the *System Preferences* or the *Audio MIDI Setup* utility. Here you set globally for all audio applications that use the system settings, which Driver (Audio Device) will be used and how it is configured.

- Many applications however provide their own audio configuration window where you can choose a Driver directly instead of using the selection from the System Audio. These are not only audio applications like GarageBand or Logic, other apps like Skype, Quicktime or VLC let you also choose the Audio Device directly.

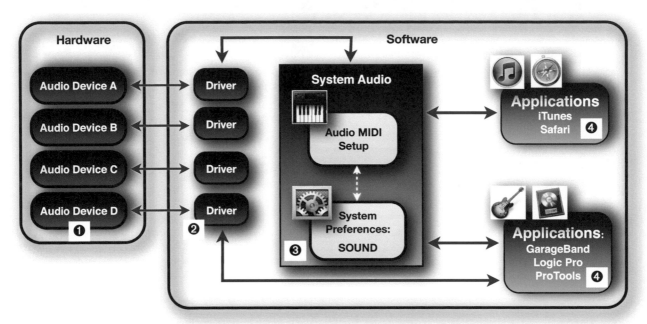

While we are already so deep into this, let me point out one aspect that could cause confusion: The red arrows in the diagram that point to the Drivers could mean two things, "choose that Driver (Device)" and also "control the Driver's setting". Most applications just let you choose the Device which is not a problem because many applications can play through the same Device. The problem is when two applications both provide Device controls that let you configure the Device. In that case, it is important which app functions as the "master control", potentially disabling (ignoring) the controls of the other app.

Troubleshooting

One advantage for understanding this basic concept of how audio works on your computer is for troubleshooting. Like a check list, you can go through each layer to see if everything is set up correctly.

- ☑ In the case of an external Audio Device ❶, it has to be connected to the computer of course.

- ☑ If you connect a new Audio Device, it might require the installation of a Driver ❷ or an updated driver in case you have updated your operating system which doesn't work with your old Driver anymore.

- ☑ The Device you want to use has to be listed in the System Preferences or the Audio MIDI Setup utility ❸. If it is not there, then your system doesn't "see" the device and you cannot use it in any of your applications. Check the previous two steps.

- ☑ Check the System Audio settings if the configurations for the Driver are set correctly.

- ☑ If your audio application ❹ provides a separate audio configuration window, make sure to select the right Device and configure it accordingly.

Here is a quick look at the two applications that configure the System Audio and MIDI:

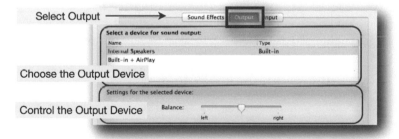
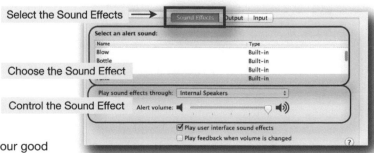
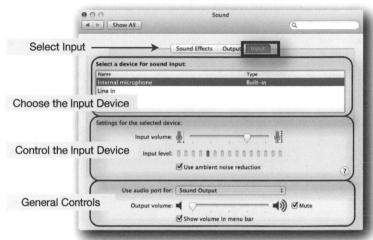

 System Preferences - Sound

System Preferences

Open the System Preferences window from `Apple Menu` ➤ `System Preferences...` and click on the speaker icon to open the Sound window.

This will display the System Sound Preferences window which has three different window views. You switch between them by clicking on one of the three tabs at the top:

Please note that these are settings for the System. This means that different computers and operating systems might have slightly different controls. The layout of the window with its sections however stays the same.

Input

☑ Select the Input Tab to switch to the input view.

☑ The list below will display all the Devices that the System "sees" (connected Audio Device with a proper Driver). Choose the one you want to use as the input Device for the System (and all the applications that use the System Audio setting).

☑ The next section displays the controls for the selected Audio Device. Here you can set the input volume for that Device. It is like reaching into the Device through its Driver to control its level. The LED meter gives you a visual feedback to tell you (monitor) if your input level is too low or too high.

☑ The section at the bottom of the window stays the same regardless which window view you've selected.

Output

☑ Select the Output Tab to switch to the Output view.

☑ The list displays all the valid Audio Devices that have an audio output. Choose the one you want to use.

☑ The next sections again lets you control the selected Device. In this case the left-right balance of your stereo signal.

Sound Effects

This window view gives you a separate control over the system's various Alert sounds, which are all those annoying but helpful sounds that let you know if you clicked something wrong, a task is finished, or just the startup chimes.

Besides selecting your favorite sound, you can choose a separate output Device. For example, have them routed to the crappy internal speaker while the rest of your System Audio plays through your good speakers connected to your external Audio Device.

Audio MIDI Setup - Audio Devices

The *System Preferences - Sound* window is usually enough for configuring the system audio. However, there is another application that provides more controls. Please keep in mind that both apps have the same functionality in regards to the system audio, they just use a different user interface and different control sets.

The *Audio MIDI Setup* app is stored in the Utilities folder inside your Applications folder `Applications/Utilities/Audio MIDI Setup`.

As its name implies, the app performs a double duty. It lets you configure the Audio side and the MIDI side on your system. There is a separate window for each task that can be open with the menu command `Window` ➤ `Show Audio Window`

Here is a look at the Audio Devices window.

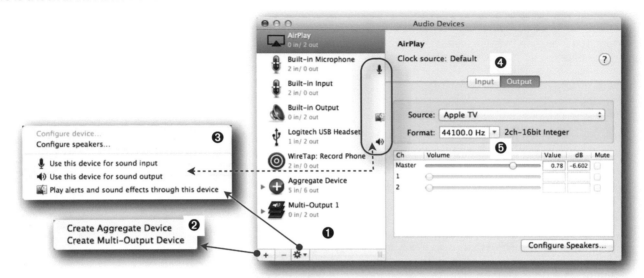

❶ On the left is the list with all the Audio Devices available on your computer. Please note that this includes not only the hardware Devices. You can also create virtual Audio Devices. Below the name of each device is an indication how many input and output channels that Device provides.

❷ OSX lets you create two types of virtual Audio Devices. Click on the plus button at the bottom to create them:

- **Aggregate Device**: The OSX system and most audio apps only let you select one Audio Device. An Aggregate Device circumvents that limitation. Here you can combine two or more hardware Audio Devices into one virtual Device. Choosing that Device in your audio app makes all the inputs and outputs of all those "combined" Devices available.

- **Multi-Output Device**: This is a new feature in Mountain Lion. It is similar to the Aggregate Device but uses only the outputs of all the combined devices. This can be very useful in combination with the Airplay feature in OSX that lets you send audio over WiFi to an Apple TV or Airport Base Station. For example, you can set it up to send the output of GarageBand to your local Audio Device in your studio and through Airplay to the recording booth or your living room.

❸ Select an Audio Device as the System input and output. In the System Preferences window, you selected the device from each window's list. Here, you have all the Devices displayed in one list. You define them as a system Devices in two ways:

 Ctr+click on the Device and choose from the Shortcut Menu.

 Select the Device first and click on the "Gear" icon at the bottom. This opens the same Shortcut Menu.

You can choose a Device to be the System sound input, output and also use it as the output for the alerts and sound effects. Here you can see that the Audio MIDI Setup app and the System Preferences settings are just different user interfaces which can configure the same controls. Whatever selection you make here will change the selection in the System Preferences and vice versa.

❹ The right window pane has two tabs that switch the view between the input and output controls. A tab is grayed out if there are no controls for either the input or output for the selected device on the list.

❺ This section displays the various controls for the Device. Again, think of those controls as "remote controls" that configure a specific Device. This can be either your built-in Devices (speaker, microphone) or an external Device that you hooked up via a USB cable. As a casual user, you won't need to adjust any of those controls. However, if you need to find out why you don't here a sound when playing GarageBand, this might be worth a peek. If you see that the Mute button is checked or the volume slider is all the way down, this might be the reason.

Audio MIDI Setup - MIDI Devices

The second window in the Audio MIDI Setup utility lets you configure the MIDI Devices on your system. To open this window, the MIDI Studio window, use the menu command Window ➤ Show MIDI Window.

The basic principles with MIDI Devices are the same as with Audio Devices:

❶ You connect the hardware (the MIDI Device) to your computer via USB.

❷ OSX has to have a software Driver for that MIDI Device installed. Same procedure here. If the manufacturer for your MIDI keyboard follows OSX protocol, then the standard OSX MIDI driver will work to recognize it. If not, then you need to install its own software Driver (for that MIDI device) so OSX can "see" it.

❸ The system setup for MIDI devices can only be configured in the Audio MIDI Setup utility (not in the System Preferences) in its own "MIDI Studio" window. If your MIDI Device doesn't show up here, then you have a Driver or a Hardware issue.

❹ All those MIDI Devices that are displayed in the MIDI Studio window will automatically be available in GarageBand, or any other application that supports MIDI.

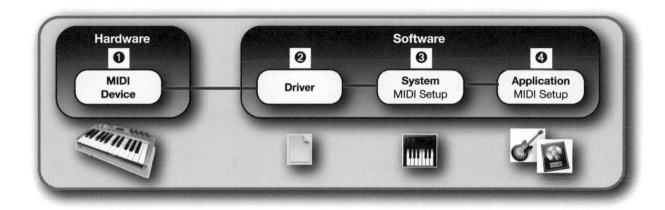

For the basic MIDI recording in GarageBand, it is enough that you see your MIDI device in the MIDI Studio window (active, not dimmed). This means that your OSX recognizes the MIDI Keyboard and you can use it with your MIDI applications.

I don't want to go into further details about the MIDI configuration, just a few points:

- The MIDI Studio window displays all the MIDI Devices (you can re-arrange them) plus a customizable toolbar at the top.

- There are two special MIDI Devices listed in addition to your connected Hardware MIDI Device:
  - **Network**: This lets you configure Devices that receive their MIDI information over the network (when working with a multi-computer setup).
  - **IAC Driver**: This device enables you to send MIDI information directly between applications. IAC stands for "Inter Application Communication").

- **Double-click** on any Device icon to open its detailed configuration window.

- You can save and recall different Configurations you made.

GarageBand Configuration

By now, you might understand the reason why I don't start the manual by telling you where to click in order to play your first loop. We are already deep into this book and finally we are about to launch GarageBand. But I still won't tell you where to click to play your first loop. Instead, the first window I will introduce you to in GarageBand is the "exciting" Preferences window. Even if I show you were to click to play your first loop, you won't hear it if the Preferences window isn't configured correctly. So please hang in there.

➡ Preferences: Audio/MIDI

But wait a minute, I'm about to tell you how to configure GarageBand in its Preferences window, but I didn't even explain how to open GarageBand in the first place. This is the old chicken and egg problem - what comes first? If you don't know how to open GarageBand yet, just continue to read to get the basic understanding for the setup and revisit this section again later. If you are running GarageBand already, use any of those two commands to open the GarageBand Preferences window and click on the Audio/MIDI icon in its header:

 Menu Command GarageBand ➤ Preferences

 Key Command **cmd+,** (the comma key)

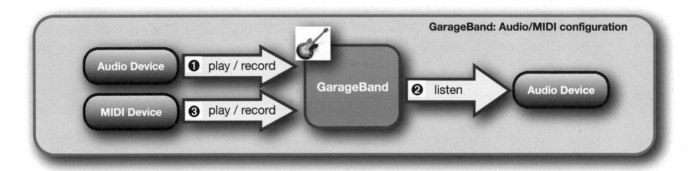

GarageBand: Audio/MIDI configuration

The window pane has only a few but very important settings:

☑️ **Audio Output ❶**: From the popup menu, select any of the available Devices to use as the output of GarageBand. The menu varies, depending on what output Devices are available (connected) on your system. If you read the previous section, then you should fully understand what you see here in the popup menu. You have two options:

Preferences ➤ Audio/MIDI

- You can choose any of the output Audio Devices that GarageBand "recognizes". These are the same Audio Devices the System sees (listed in the System Preferences).

- If you select "System Setting", then GarageBand uses whatever Output Device was selected in the System Preferences window. Also keep in mind, whenever you open up GarageBand again, make sure that you haven't changed those audio settings in the System Preferences.

☑️ **Audio Input ❷**: From the popup menu, select any available Device that you want to "feed" into GarageBand". This is what GarageBand uses as the source to record from. The same rules apply regarding the popup menu selections.

☑️ **MIDI Status ❸**: This line only tells you how many MIDI Devices GarageBand has detected. These are your MIDI Keyboards that are connected to your computer. If you connected a MIDI Keyboard to your computer but the MIDI Status reads "0 MIDI input(s) detected" then you have to check your MIDI connections or drivers.

☑️ **Keyboard Sensitivity ❹**: This slider lets you adjust how GarageBand interprets the range of your key stroke strength (how soft or how hard you hit the keys on the MIDI keyboard) and how it translates that into the dynamic range of the instrument you are playing (from soft to loud).

GarageBand will update its MIDI status whenever you connect or disconnect a MIDI device. It will open an Alert window notifying you about those changes. It is not necessary to restart the app.

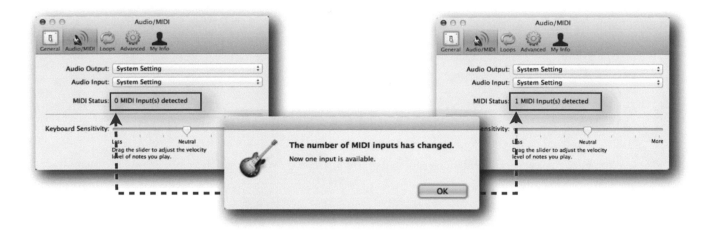

Please note that this MIDI status is the only setup available for MIDI in GarageBand. Unlike other DAWs, GarageBand won't allow the selection of a specific MIDI Keyboard as a recording input if you have more than one MIDI keyboard connected. All the connected MIDI keyboards (MIDI inputs) will be available as a MIDI recording source.

Audio Quality

There is one more setting regarding the audio configuration that you should be aware of before starting to record your audio. When dealing with audio on a computer (which means in digital form) you always have a trade off: "The higher the audio quality of a file, the bigger the file size". Usually the decision should be towards better audio quality, but if you are dealing with limited storage space on you computer or limited upload/download speed when transferring your audio files, then you might accept a compromise.

There are three basic parameters that determine the audio quality of an audio file:

💡 **Uncompressed/Compressed**

Audio files can be compressed to make the file size smaller. For example, mp3 is a compressed audio format with a lower audio quality than aiff or wav, which are typical uncompressed audio formats.

➡ GarageBand uses the uncompressed aiff file format to record and to export audio files (as a default).

💡 **Sample Rate:**

This value (usually ranging from 32 ... 48 kHz) determines what the highest possible frequency for that audio file can be:

➡ GarageBand always records in 44.1kHz

💡 **Bit Depth**

This value determines the dynamic range of your audio file, the range of the softest to the loudest signal (usually 16 ... 32bit) without any noise.

➡ GarageBand lets you configure that in the window
Preferences ➤ Advanced ➤ Audio Resolution

- *Good*: Record and Export in 16bit.
- *Better*: Record in 24bit, Export in 16bit.
- *Best*: Record and Export in 24bit.

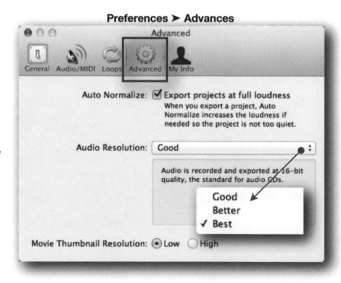

4 - Project

Finally we are well prepared with the basic setup and can now start to dive into GarageBand.

There are many ways to launch the GarageBand application:

 Use the **Finder**: Go to your Applications folder on the top level of your boot drive and **double-click** the GarageBand app.

 Use **Spotlight**: Press **cmd+space** to open the Spotlight menu in the upper right corner of your screen. Type in "GarageBand"A and hit enter.

 Use **LaunchPad**: Open Launchpad and **click** on the GarageBand icon.

 Use the **File**: You can **double-click** on an existing GarageBand Project file which opens GarageBand with that Project.

Project Chooser

The very first thing you see when you open GarageBand is a window called the *Project Chooser*. This could already be a bit overwhelming with all those available options.

Let's look at the window elements of the interface first. You have three sections, sometimes referred to as *Window Panes*.

1 - Sidebar: This is similar to the Sidebar in your Finder window which is a list of items that you can select. Think of those items as folders. When you select one, the window section next to it will display its Content.

2 - Content: This window pane displays the content of the selected item in the Sidebar.

3 - Bottom: The bottom bar contains three buttons for quick access to often used commands that are almost self explanatory.

- *Quit*: This will close the Project Chooser and quit GarageBand.

- *Open an Existing File...*: This also closes the Project Chooser but opens the Open Dialog instead which lets you navigate directly to a GarageBand Project file on your Finder and open it without using the Project Chooser.

- *Choose*: This opens the selected item in the window. Of course you could also **double-click** on that item.

But what do all those items and icons mean? Because we are looking at the Project Chooser, we have first to be clear on the term "Project" and what it means in GarageBand.

A "Project" is the term that is used for what you are working on in GarageBand. This can be a song, a ringtone, a podcast or even a movie score. It is similar to working on a document in a word processor. The document exists in your application while you are working on it and is saved as a file to your drive.

This is the same concept in GarageBand. In GarageBand you are working on a Project which is saved to your hard drive as a Project File that includes all the components of your current Project. Later you can open that Project file in GarageBand and everything is right there where you left it.

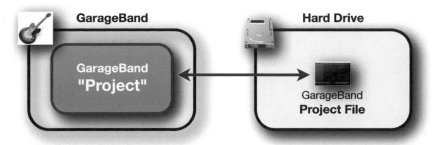

Here is what you have to know about a Project:

- A Project is the song that you are working on in GarageBand.
- You can only work on one single Project at a time (have only one Project open in GarageBand).
- A GarageBand Project is saved to the drive as a GarageBand Project File.
- When you launch GarageBand, you can either open an existing Project from a Project File or create a new Project.
- The name of the current Project you are working on is displayed at the top of your GarageBand window, the header.
- The default location for GarageBand Projects is the GarageBand folder inside your Music folder.

New Project

The following diagram shows the four steps that are required when creating a new Project in GarageBand.

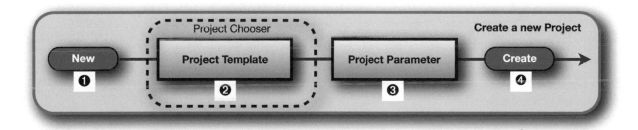

❶ New

Every new Project starts with the command "New", telling GarageBand that you want to create a new Project. This command always opens the Project Chooser window

❷ Project Template

You cannot start with a blank Project. You have to choose a Project Template from the Project Chooser. That's why the Project Chooser always pops up when you use the New command.

❸ Project Parameter

There is a second step involved after choosing a Project Template. You have to configure the main parameters for that new Project: Tempo, Time Signature and Key Signature in addition to its name and location.

❹ Create

After those mandatory steps, you can finally click the "Create" button to create your new Project.

Let's have a closer look at those four steps:

➡ *New*

The method of initiating the New command depends on whether or not GarageBand is already running.

- GarageBand is not launched yet:
  - Launch GarageBand which will always automatically open the Project Chooser first.
- GarageBand is already launched (but the Project Chooser window is not visible)
  - Use the Menu Command File ➤ New
  - Use the Key Command **cmd+C**

The main purpose of the New command is to open the Project Chooser to select a Project Template.

➡ *Project Template*

Now we are in the Project Chooser. This window provides the various Project Templates to choose from. Beyond that, it provides other features that we'll discuss later.

The concept of the Template is similar to a template in a word processor. For example, when you write letters, you may soon realize that you generally type the same elements in every new letter (company logo, company address, your signature, etc.). In order to speed things up, you could create an "almost blank" document that contains all those elements already typed in. The next time you want to write a letter, you can open that *template* and start right away with the letter while all the redundant elements are already there.

And that's the same concept with Project Templates in GarageBand. They already include some pre-configuration to give you a head start. For example, a track is already created and an instrument is assigned to it, so when you open the Template Project, you can start to play/record right away. And, as with a word processor where you might use different Templates for different kinds of letters (company, personal, etc). GarageBand offers different Templates for the types of Projects you might want to create. For example a Project based on loops, based on acoustic recording or a simple MIDI project.

The process of selecting a Project Template in the Project Chooser window involves three steps:

❶ Selecting a Project type form the Sidebar

The Sidebar lists two items that contain Projects.

 New Project: When selecting this item, nine different Project Templates will be displayed in the window pane next to it.

 iPhone Ringtone: When selecting this item, three Project Templates will be displayed that have the same icon as in the New Project selection. However, the Project Templates are made especially for the requirements when creating Ringtones.

❷ Selecting a Template

The name of the Project Templates and their icons indicate what type of Project you want to create. The pre-configuration for the newly created Project is based on those parameters.

❸ Confirm the selection

The last step in this section is to confirm the selection. You can do this in two ways.

 Double-click on the Project Template icon.

 Click the Choose button at the right lower corner after you selected your Project Template.

➡ *Project Parameter*

This configuration window that opens after you chose your Project Template is actually a Save Dialog with the additional section to set the parameters.

- 🔵 The upper portion of the Dialog window contains the three standard controls of a Save Dialog (the window that opens up after you use the Save command).

  ❶ **Name**: Next to the "Save As" is a text entry box where you can type in a name for your New Project.

  ❷ **Location**: The next line defines "where" you want to store the Project file. The popup menu contains a list of destination folders including the GarageBand folder which is pre-selected. GarageBand automatically creates that folder inside your Music folder.

  ❸ **Disclosure Button**: The GarageBand folder is usually the place where you want to store your Project file. However if you want to navigate to a different folder (on a different connected drive), you have to switch to the full Save Dialog view. You can toggle the view with this button.

- 🔵 The lower portion of the window contains the main parameters for your new Project. These are the default parameters, but keep in mind that you can change them later in your Project.

  ❹ **Tempo**: To set the Tempo, you can either drag the Tempo Slider or type the tempo in the value box next to the "bpm" (beats per minutes). You can set the tempo between 40 - 240 bpm.

  ❺ **Time Signature**: The popup menu provides eleven different Time Signatures to choose from.

  ❻ **Key Signature**: The Key Signature provides two popup menus. The first one lets you select any of the twelve keys while the second one gives you the choice between "major" and "minor". The Key is important if you want to view or print a musical score but it also controls the transposition of any Apple Loops in your Project. More details about that in the Apple Loops Chapter of this manual.

  WIKI MOMENT: These three parameters are the foundation of every song in western music and that's why GarageBand ask you to configure them before starting your song. If you didn't have a chance to learn them in music class, please look it up to understand their purpose.

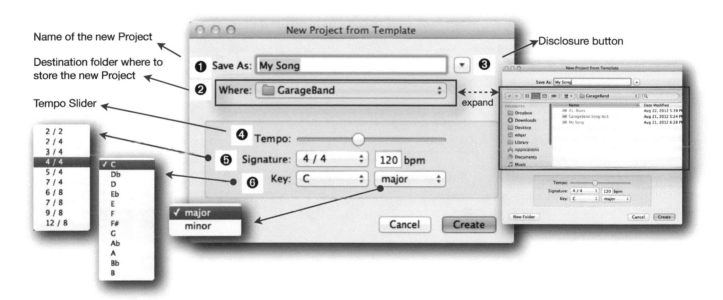

➡ *Create*

After you've configured all those parameters, click on the Create button (or hit return) and GarageBand creates that new Project. It actually is doing two things.

- ☑️ The new Project is saved as a Project file to the location you just specified.
- ☑️ The new Project will be opened in GarageBand. Using the Save command while you are working on that Project, will save the changes to the Project file it just created on the drive.

Project File

➡ File Menu

All the commands that relate to your Project File are listed under the File Menu. These are the standard file commands. Please note that GarageBand 11 does not support the new Auto-Save procedure and Versioning which was introduced in OSX 10.7 Lion.

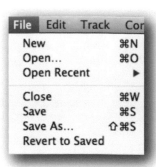

- **New**: This will open the Project Chooser to select a Project Template.
- **Open**: Opens the Open Dialog to select an existing GarageBand Project on your drive.
- **Open Recent ➤**: The submenu displays a list of recently opened GarageBand Projects that you can choose from. This is convenient in that you don't have to navigate to the folder where it is stored.
- **Close**: Closes the currently open Project and displays the Project Chooser to start a new Project. This command will quit GarageBand if the Project Chooser window is open.
- **Save**: Saves the current Project to its Project File.
- **Save As**: Opens the Save Dialog that lets you save the current Project under a different name and continues with that Project.
- **Revert to Saved**: This discards all the changes you made in your current Project since the last time you used the Save command and re-opens that saved version of your Project again.

➡ Open Existing Projects

Let's have another look at the Project Chooser.

❶ Recent Projects

When selecting this item in the Sidebar, all the Projects that you had recently opened will be displayed in the Window Pane next to it. It doesn't matter where those Project Files are stored on your disk. Each Project is represented by a snapshot of the actual Project as it appeared when you had it open in GarageBand.

The displayed Projects are the same as those listed in the submenu when you choose the "Open Recent" command from the File Menu.

❷ Open an Existing File

This button at the left lower corner of the Project Chooser window is identical to the "Open" command from the File Menu. It opens the Open Dialog window to navigate to any existing Project File on your drive.

Please note that while most of the Menu Commands in GarageBand are grayed out when the Project Chooser window is open, those commands in the File Menu are still active ❸.

Project Chooser

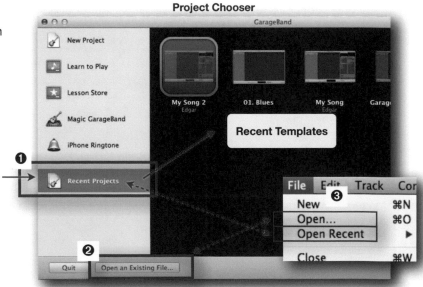

Project File (advanced)

Geek alert! The following section is a discussion of some details regarding the Project Files that are not required for the basic understanding of GarageBand.

➡ Project File Extension

Every Application uses a unique File Extension to identify what type of file it is. These extensions are three or more characters long and are automatically added at the end of the filename after a period. You have the option to display or hide those extension in the Finder.

GarageBand uses the extension "**.band**" for its Project Files.

➡ Project File Icon

OSX introduced a feature a while ago that displays a file in the Finder not just with a generic file icon but with a custom image so you can see in the Finder window what type of file it is.

Whenever you save your GarageBand Project, a snapshot image is taken of your current GarageBand window, and that is used as the File Icon (but not only in the Finder).

❶ The Project Chooser uses those File Icons when displaying the Recent Projects.

❷ The Finder in Icon View uses the File Icon and if you enlarge the Icon, you can actually see your Project very well.

❸ The Finder displays the File Icon in all the other view options (List, Columns, CoverFlow), even the tiny icon in List View displays that image.

❹ The File Info window in the Finder (ctr+click on a file and select "Get Info" from the Shortcut Menu) also displays the icon together with the main Parameters of that Project ❺ (under "More Info").

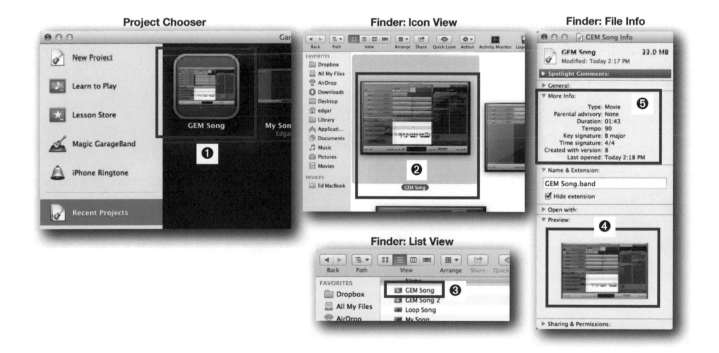

➡ *Project Preview*

Every time you close your Project (after you made changes and saved those changes), GarageBand first brings up an Alert window asking you if you want to save your Project with an iLife preview.

Remember, GarageBand is an application that ultimately creates a media file, most likely an audio file. However, the GarageBand Project File is not an audio file, it cannot be played in iTunes, on your iPhone or any other music application. The GarageBand Project File only works with GarageBand itself. Until you export your song as an audio file (mp3, aiff), no other app can "play" it (except in Logic Pro).

And that is where the "Preview" feature comes in:

If you click "Yes" on the Alert window, GarageBand will export your song in the current state as an audio file and embed it in your GarageBand Project File. Now, any application that knows where to find that Preview sound file inside the Project File can play it. Although the text in the Alert window explains that it is used in other iLife applications, this Preview sound file can be used in more places:

❶ QuickLook: This is an OSX feature that lets you preview a wide variety of files directly in the Finder without opening the application that created the file like audio, video, pdf, etc. If your GarageBand has that Preview sound file embedded, then opening QuickLook will display a Navigation Control at the bottom of the QuickLook window that lets you play the file.

Use QuickLook by selecting a file and hit the Space key or choose "QuickLook" from the file's Shortcut Menu (ctr+click on the file).

❷ The Info window of a file (ctr+click on a file and select "Get Info" from the Shortcut Menu) displays a Play button over the icon in the Preview section if the Project File contains a Preview sound file. Just click on it to play it.

❸ Any of Apple's iLife applications that contain a Media Browser to access audio, video or images (iMovie, Keynote, etc) also can access the Preview file in a GarageBand Project File. Not only can you listen to the file, you can also import it into that application. The screenshot below is from iMovie. Please note the different GarageBand icons. Only the file with the Guitar icon has an embedded Preview sound file.

QuickLook Window	File Info	iMovie: Media Browser

➡ Package File

When you look at a GarageBand Project File, it looks like any other file in the Finder, a text file, an audio or movie file. However, what looks like an ordinary file is actually a folder disguised as a file, a so called "Package File". Unlike a folder that you can open by double-clicking it, these Package Files require a special command to "open them up" and display their content (double-clicking on a package file would just launch GarageBand with that file).

Ctrl-click on the Project File and select the command "Show Package Content" from the Shortcut Menu. This functions as an "open folder" command, displaying the content inside. The files and folders inside can be viewed and navigated with the standard Finder commands.

Assets

Package Files are a very elegant solution in a file system. They provide the ease of use of a single file in the Finder while packaging a lot of stuff inside like a folder. It also keeps that stuff out of reach of the user to keep it simple and also maintain the data integrity by not letting the user mess around with the content.

Another reason to use those Package Files are the required "Assets" in your GarageBand Project. These are all the additional media files that you may use in your GarageBand Project, mainly audio files in form of loops or your own recordings. Images and Videos can also be used in GarageBand for Podcast and Movie score Projects.

- 💡 **Pro**: To guarantee that all the assets stay with your Project, everything should be embedded in your Project File. Every file you import into your Project that you want to use should be copied into the Project File. This also makes it easy to move the Project File around (either on your machine or when moving it to a friend's computer to continue to work on your Project).

- 💡 **Cons**: The problem however is that the size of your Project File could increase dramatically.

The Archive feature in GarageBand provides a suitable compromise.

➡ Archive Projects

The more you work in GarageBand and the more serious your work is, the more important is the question about the Assets. You don't want to end up with missing elements the next time you open up your Project. Here is what will be saved with your Project using the "*Save As*" command

- 💡 **Saved with your Project Files**
  - ☑ Recorded Data (MIDI, mix, etc)
  - ☑ Recorded Audio in GarageBand
  - ☑ Imported Audio (excluded Loops)
  - ☑ Imported Video (only the audio portion)
- 💡 **Additionally saved with your Project Files if checked as Archive**
  - ☑ Imported Apple Loops from the Loop Browser
  - ☑ Imported Movie file
- 💡 **Never Saved with your Project**
  - ☑ Software Instruments including the ones that are based on audio samples

The "Compact Project" checkbox tells GarageBand to convert all audio files to smaller compressed audio file format. You can choose from three options. Of course the smaller the size the lower the resulting audio quality of the audio files.

➡ *Delete Project.*

Of course you can delete the Project File if you don't need the Project anymore (or if you have archived it). Just delete the file in the Finder. All the Assets inside the Project File will also be deleted.

Remember, it is still in the Trash bin until you empty the Trash.

Summary

Here is a diagram with an overview of the commands and procedures that are involved between the Project and the Project File.

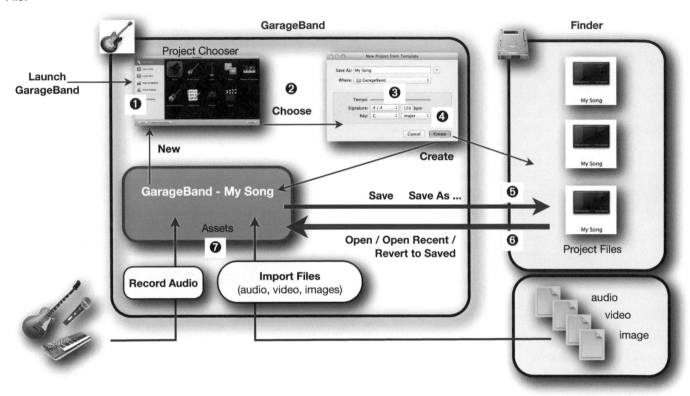

❶ A new Project always starts from the Project Chooser, either by launching GarageBand or by using the *New* command from the open GarageBand.

❷ You have to Choose a Project Template as the starting point for a new Project.

❸ A new Project has to be configured with its main parameters.

❹ Creating a new Project will save it as a Project File and opens it in GarageBand.

❺ Any save command will update the Project File or save it as a new File when using the "Save As" command.

❻ Any existing Project File on the drive can be opened in GarageBand.

❼ Media Files will be either recorded (audio) or imported. They become the asset of your Project that are saved with the Project File.

5 - Interface

Window Elements

GarageBand has a very clean and simple Graphical User Interface (GUI). First of all, you can have only one Project open at a time and that Project is represented by a single window. There are just a few smaller floating windows that are not part of the main window.

❶ Project Window:

This is the main single window frame (with the wooden side panels) that represents your GarageBand Project. You can change the size of that window in three ways:

- **Resize**: Resize the window by dragging any of its corners or sides.
- **Zoom Button**: Press the green bullet in the upper left corner of the screen to resize the window to its biggest size possible on your computer screen. Click again to return to its previous size. Please note that this is not the same as Full Screen Mode.
- **Full Screen**: When switching to Full Screen Mode, the window will take over the whole computer screen. The Main Menu also disappears but moving the mouse to the top of your screen will temporarily slide out the Main Menu to access the Menu Commands. You can toggle Full Screen Mode in two ways:
  - Use Menu Command Window ➤ Enter Full Screen Mode / Exit Full Screen Mode
  - Click on the double arrow in the upper right corner of the Project Window. To exit Full Screen Mode, move your mouse to the upper right corner of your screen to click on the now blue double arrow in the Main Menu (that slides out). Or you can just click the Esc key to exit Full Screen Mode.

 Enter Full Screen Mode   Exit Full Screen Mode

The Project window has two main areas that are always visible: The Arrange window and the Control Bar at the bottom.

❷ Arrange Window: This is the area where you create and "arrange" all the elements of your song.

❸ Control Bar: This is similar to the dashboard on a car where you find all the controls and displays to navigate and control your Project.

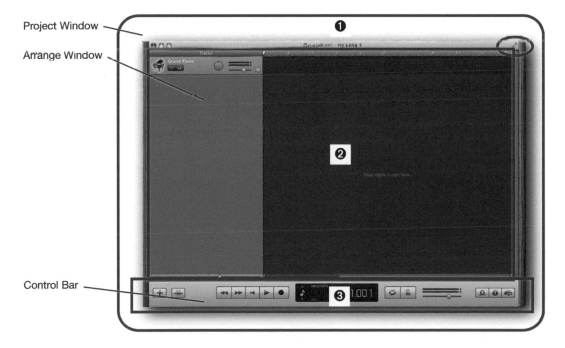

Window Panes

Unlike the Control Bar, the Arrange Window has to share its available size with two other windows. This is a typical interface concept also used in other applications. Instead of having additional windows pop up that clutter your screen, GarageBand slides additional windows in and out of the Arrange Window, thereby resizing the Arrange Window. Please note, the size of the Project Window (wooden frame) is not affected by this.

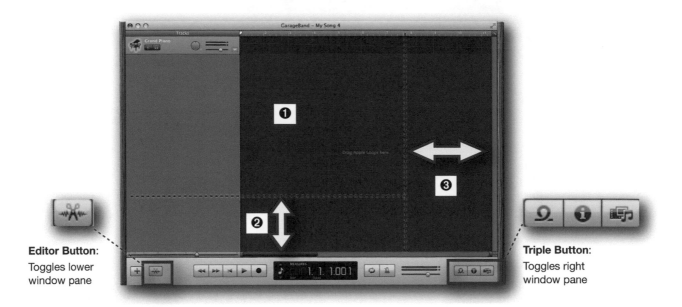

Editor Button:
Toggles lower window pane

Triple Button:
Toggles right window pane

❶ This is the Arrange Window. Its content is always visible.

❷ Editor Window: This window segment or window pane can be toggled with any of the three commands

 Editor

- Click on the scissor button in the lower left corner. The scissor turns blue when the window is visible.
- Use the Key Command **cmd+E**
- Use the Main Menu Command Control ➤ Show Editor / Hide Editor

    The divider line at the top of the Editor window can be dragged up or down to resize the window height and, of course, by doing so affecting the height of the Arrange Window.

❸ "Triple-function" Window: This window pane is used to display any of the following three windows

Track Info - Loop Browser - Media Browser

This window pane has a fixed width and its height depends on the available size of the Project Window. Clicking any of the following buttons will toggle the window. Clicking on a different button while the window pane is visible, will switch to that window. Each button has its own Key Command and Menu Command. I will go into more details a little bit later.

 Track Info

This should actually be the first button based on its importance. It is an Inspector window, which is a common window element in content-creation applications. It displays and lets you edit a selected Object in another window, in this case the Tracks in the Arrange Window.

Loop Browser

This window displays all the Audio Loops on your computer and lets you drag them onto a Track in the Arrange Window.

 Media Browser

This is another browser window that displays all the media files on your computer and lets you drag them onto the Arrange Window.

Arrange Window

Before getting into the details about those extra window panes, let's explore the Arrange window a little bit further. As I mentioned before, the Arrange window is where you will spend most of your time in GarageBand, creating your song. It is also the main window in every DAW (consumer or professional) and they all look pretty much alike. So let's have a closer look to understand the basic elements and what they represent.

The Arrange window has two main areas:

❶ Track Area:

This area represents the various sound sources in your Project. You can think of it as the different musicians in a band that would perform your song. For Example, 4 musicians and a DJ, that would mean 5 people, or 5 Tracks.

❷ Timeline Area:

This area is a horizontal extension of the Track area. Here is where you tell each musician (each Track) **WHAT** to play and **WHEN** to play it.

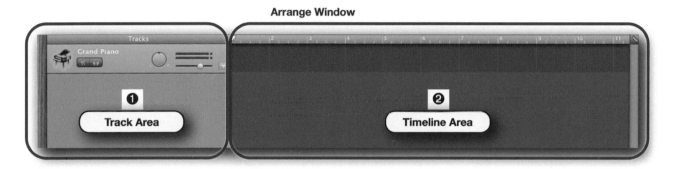

Arrange Window

Here is a diagram of the Arrange window. It bears a similarity to a spreadsheet.

Each row represents a single Track in your Project (Track 1, Track 2, etc). The first column, the Track List, lists all the Track Headers with the main controls for that Track. The second column is empty when you start a new Project. This is where you place/record your music on the individual Track's Track Lane, the extension of the Track Header.

❸ Time Ruler

An important part of the Arrange Area is its header. This is the Time Ruler (or timeline), a time axis that can display time in "Absolute Time" as minutes:seconds:milliseconds or display it in "Musical Time" with bars and beats.

This is the time axis of your song, starting at 0 minutes and 0 seconds which represents bar 1. Wherever you place/record your music on a specific Track Lane, the Time Ruler functions as a vertical time reference to tell you where in your song you are playing/recording your music.

Track Header and Track Lane

Let me go one step further and provide another diagram to explain the function and relationship of the Track Header and Track Lane

❶ Track Area - The Band:

Each Track has to be assigned to a sound source that can play whatever is on its Track Lane. All those Tracks make up your final Band. The more tracks you create in your Project, the more band members you have available.

❷ Timeline Area - The Music

Regardless how many tracks you've got, if you don't give the sound sources (your band member) anything to play, then there is no song. You have to tell each player what to play. In real life, that could be some verbal instructions ("play some blues riffs over Eb minor") or you can hand over some sheet music or a written score. In GarageBand (as with any other DAW), those "music instructions" are called Regions. These are the building blocks of your song.

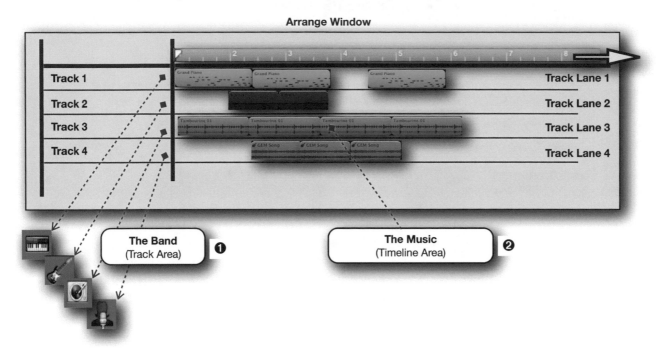

Arrange Window

If you think about it, your whole song comes down to three basic questions:

What to play?

The content of a Region is the audio or MIDI data inside. These are the "instructions," what the region will play. Does the region contain just plain chords, a melody or the rhythm part for the drums?

Who is playing it?

This is the part where you decide to which musician (Track) you give the Region. For example, should the solo be played by the guitar player or the synth player. You make that decision by placing the Region on the Track Lane of the Instrument that is assigned to that Track.

When to play it?

Of course, telling the guitar player to play a melody is only half the story. You have to tell him when to play it. That is determined by where you place the Region on the Track Lane. And here is where the Time Ruler comes in. It gives you the time reference where you place the Region along the Track Lane. The Time Ruler can display that reference in Absolute Time (minutes and seconds) or in Musical Time (bars and beats).

5 - Interface

If you think that the concept of the Arrange window in a DAW is something new, then think again. Here are two examples that show where the idea might come from.

💡 Exhibit A

If you come from a musical background and are familiar with reading musical notations, look at the following diagram. The Arrange window is nothing other than a representation of a musical score with the same basic elements. The same three questions about What-Who-When also applies to a score.

💡 Exhibit B

If you come from a recording engineer background and are familiar with tape machines, look at the following diagram. The Arrange window is nothing other than a representation of a Tape Machine. The Track Area is the playback head that has a specified number of tracks it can record and play back (8, 16, 24, 32). Each Track is used to record and play back one band member. This is the assignment. The Track Lane is the actual magnetic tape where the music is recorded on in electro-magnetic form. Think about, the time axis is your tape that is wounded up on a reel.

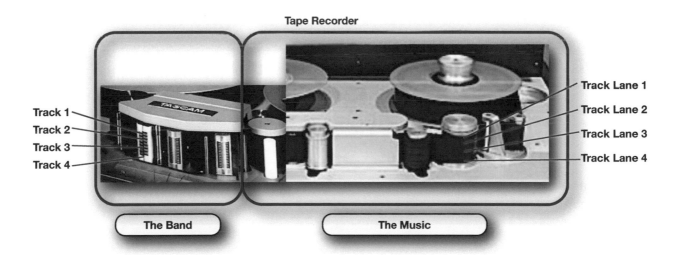

That should be enough to get the basic idea of the Arrange window, of its elements and their function.

Control Bar

Now lets have a look at the second window element in GarageBand which is always visible at the bottom of the Project window, the Control Bar. First a quick overview of the various control elements:

Control Bar

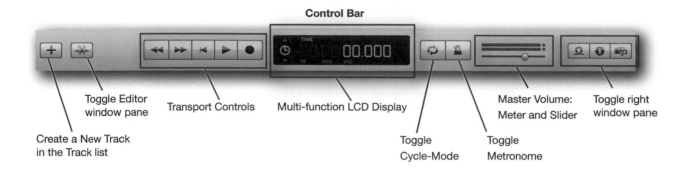

Create a New Track in the Track list
Toggle Editor window pane
Transport Controls
Multi-function LCD Display
Toggle Cycle-Mode
Toggle Metronome
Master Volume: Meter and Slider
Toggle right window pane

Transport Controls

The buttons on the Transport Controls are similar on every tape machine and DAW. However, the exact functionality is always a little bit different. Here are the five buttons in GarageBand. Please note that the third button changes its appearance and function. The Play and Record button changes color when active and the other buttons change color when pressed down.

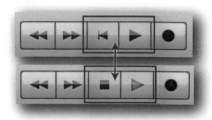

 Play

This button toggles between Start and Stop. Clicking while the song is in stop mode starts the song and clicking while it plays will stop it.

Alternatively, use the Key Command Space.

Record

The behavior depends on what the current play mode is. Alternatively, use the Key Command R.

- Click while in stop mode: Starts recording.
- Click while playing: Changes from playing to recording.
- Click while recording: Disables recording but continues playing.

Stop

The stop button is only visible when GarageBand is playing or recording. Otherwise it is "Back to Beginning".

Alternatively, use the Key Command Space which toggles between play and stop.

Back to Beginning

Moves the Playhead to the beginning of the Song at bat 1, or time 0:00

Alternatively, use the Key Command Z or Home or Return.

Rewind

Moves the playback position back by one bar.

Forward

Moves the playback position forward by one bar.

Navigation Controls / Navigation Display

Please be aware that the Transport Controls have two elements:

⚉ **Navigation Controls:**

> This is the actual instruction that tells GarageBand where and how to move in your song or not to move at all (stop).

⚉ **Navigation Displays:**

> This is the visual feedback that tells you the current position in the song you are moving to or parked at.

> The following diagram shows you the four types of Navigation Controls available in GarageBand:
> - ☑ Transport Buttons
> - ☑ Key Commands
> - ☑ Playhead
> - ☑ Time Display

> Two of those Navigation Controls function also as Navigation Displays
> - ☑ Playhead
> - ☑ Time Display

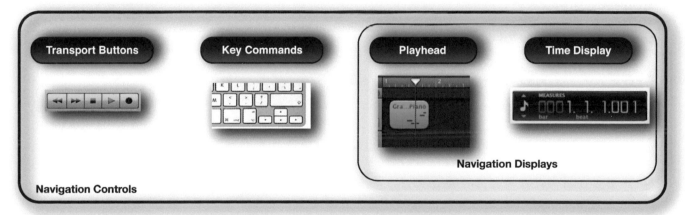

➡ *Transport Buttons*

That section, I just explained on the previous page.

➡ *Key Commands*

GarageBand provides a lot of Key Commands that exceed the functionality of the transport controls buttons. Of course, you have to remember those commands, but if you use GarageBand a lot, you will find that they will speed up your workflow tremendously when navigating around your project.

Use the Main Menu Command Help ➤ Keyboard Shortcuts to open the HelpViewer window with a list of all the available Shortcuts.

➡ *Playhead*

As we have just seen, the visual representation of your song is the Timeline Area in the Arrange window similar to a musical score. The ruler on top functions as the time axis that provides the orientation to see which elements of your song (the Regions) are placed at what section of your song. Now when you hit the play button, you want to know from what position GarageBand is playing your song.

This "play position indicator" is called the Playhead. It is a white triangle on the Time Ruler that marks the exact play position on the Ruler and extends as a vertical red line across the Track Lanes in the Arrange Area.

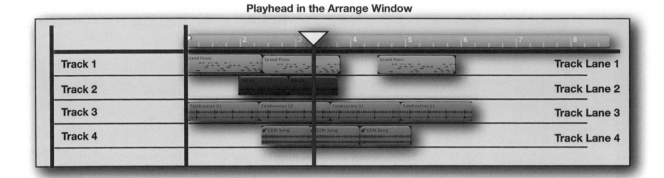

Playhead in the Arrange Window

Here is the basic functionality:

- **GarageBand is not playing**: The Playhead shows the position from where GarageBand will play your song when you hit the Play button, or start recording when you hit the Record button (if cycle mode is off).
- **GarageBand is playing (or recording)**: The Playhead moves across the Timeline Area so you can see exactly which part of your song is playing.
- **Other Navigation**: Using the Forward, Rewind or other navigation commands will move the Playhead accordingly.

As we have seen on the previous page, the Playhead functions as a (passive) Navigation Display as well as an (active) Navigation Control.

This is how you use it as an active Navigation Control:

- **Click-drag** the white triangle of the Playhead along the ruler to move the Playhead to a different position.
- **Click** on any position in the ruler to move the Playhead to that position (see "Snap to Grid").
- **Double-click** on any position in the Time Ruler to move the Playhead to that position and start playing.

You have to pay attention to two factors that influence the visibility and the behavior of the Playhead.

🔮 Snap to Grid

Clicking on the Time Ruler lets you freely position the Playhead. However, you can restrict the position to an invisible grid that the Playhead snaps to. That grid is set in the menu that opens when you click on the Grid Button in the upper right corner of the Project window.

Grid Button

Toggle the function with the Menu Command Control ➤ Snap to Grid or the Key Command **cmd+G**.

This Snap function works only if the Time Ruler displays bars:beats and not absolute time. I cover that functionality and the menu later in more detail.

🔮 Zoom

If you are zoomed in horizontally, then the Timeline Area shows only a portion of your song. In that case, the Playhead might not be visible. However, starting to play or record will scroll the Arrange Area automatically to the Playhead position.

GarageBand provides an additional feature called "Scroll in Play" or "Auto Scroll" that locks the Playhead in the middle of the Timeline Area and continuously scrolls the Arrange Area underneath the (fixed) Playhead. See the "Scroll - Zoom" section

➡ Time Display

On old tape machines, this display was a simple mechanical number display. Nowadays, it is a digital display and in GarageBand, it is called the LCD Display where LCD stands for "Liquid Crystal Display", which is a common type of a digital display. Here, the LCD is a multi-function display that can be switched between four different screens. The first two screens function as the Navigation Control and Display.

Change the Display mode with any of the following commands:

 ❶ Click on the left icon in the LCD Display to open a popup menu

❷ Use the Menu Commands from the Control menu

❸ Use the assigned Key Commands

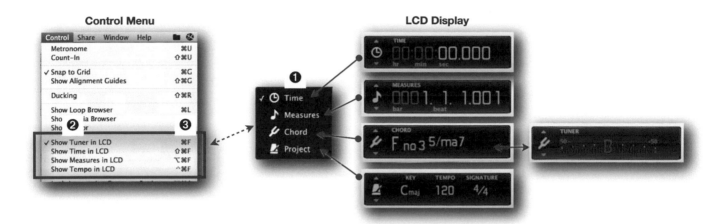

- 💡 **Timer:** This shows the current position of the song as absolute time in *hours:minutes:second.milliseconds*.

- 💡 **Measures:** This shows the current position of the song as musical time in *bars* and *beats* (the third number value is a 1/16 division, 4 per quarter beat and the fourth number value provides another division of 240 ticks per 1/16, resulting in a resolution of 960 ticks per beat).

- 💡 **Chords:** This display mode shows either the currently played chord when you play a MIDI keyboard or it shows a Tuner if your currently selected Track is a Guitar Track.

- 💡 **Project:** This displays the basic settings that you chose when you created your song, the Key (Key Signature), Tempo and Signature (Time Signature). You can click on the values to change them.

💡 Navigation Display

The role of the Navigation Display is easy to understand. Whatever position the LCD displays, in either absolute or musical time, is the position of the Playhead. If the Playhead moves, the LCD will update its display accordingly. It is like the Playhead and the LCD time display are linked together.

💡 Navigation Control

Because the LCD time display and the Playhead are linked, you can use the LCD also as a Navigation Control to move the Playhead position. You can do this in two ways:

Numerical input

Click on any number value in the LCD and it starts to flash. This means it is in input mode. Type a numeric value and hit return. Please note that you can enter only a single place value at a time, i.e. minutes, seconds, bars. You cannot enter a full address like 3min:22sec at once.

Sliding values

You can click-drag a place value up or down (slide) to change its value. This is similar to dragging the Playhead left or right. You can only slide one place value at a time which has actually an advantage. Dragging the minutes moves the Playhead in big steps, while sliding the seconds or the smaller values moves the Playhead in smaller (finer) steps.

Cycle Mode

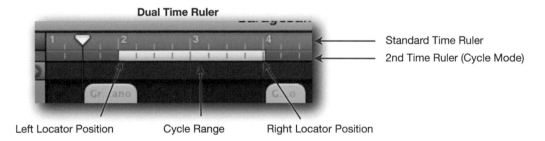

Cycle Mode Button

The button next to the LCD screen is the Cycle Mode button. This is a common transport function in DAWs with a simple concept.

- ☑ You activate Cycle Mode.
- ☑ You define a Left Locator Position, a time value on the Time Ruler.
- ☑ You define a Right Locator Position, a second time value on the Time Ruler.

Now when the Playhead reaches the Right Locator Position while playing or recording, it jumps back to the Left Locator Position continuing to play or record. Once it reaches the Right Locator Position again, it jumps back to the Left Locator Position and continues to repeat that section until you hit stop or position the Playhead outside that Cycle Range with any other navigation command.

Activate Cycle Mode

 You can toggle the Cycle Mode by clicking on the Cycle Mode Button in the Control Bar (it turns blue if activated) or by using the Key Command C. (you can also drag the yellow Cycle Range up, to turn off Cycle Mode)

When you turn on Cycle Mode, two things will happen in the Timeline Area:
- The single Time Ruler on the top becomes a double Time Ruler.
- On the second Time Ruler a yellow bar appears that marks the Cycle Range.

Dual Time Ruler

Standard Time Ruler
2nd Time Ruler (Cycle Mode)

Left Locator Position   Cycle Range   Right Locator Position

Modify Cycle Range

- Click-drag on the yellow Cycle Range to move it along the Time Ruler. This changes its position while maintaining its relative length.
- Click-drag the left or the right edge of the yellow Cycle Range to change the position of the Left Locator or Right Locator. If you drag the right edge towards the left beyond the left edge, then the Right Locator becomes the Left Locator. Play with it and you'll quickly get the hang of it.

Please note:
- You can change the Cycle Range only if the yellow bar is visible, which is, when Cycle Mode is activated.
- The Snap to Grid function, if activated, applies to the dragging of the Cycle Range.
- When you start to play or record while the Cycle Mode is active, then GarageBand will not start at the current Playhead position but moves the Playhead position to the beginning of the Cycle Range first. GarageBand doesn't have any memory locator, so you could use this behavior as a "Play from Left Locator" function. Just press the C key before hitting the Space key.
- The Cycle Range is also used to define a specific range when exporting the song.

Metronome

Next to the Cycle Mode button is the Metronome button. When activated, this plays a click based on the tempo of your Song on every beat, any time you are in play or recording mode.

Activate Metronome

You can toggle the Metronome with any of these three commands:

- **Click** on the Metronome button in the Control Bar (it turns blue if activated).
- Use the Key Command **cmd+U**.
- Use the Menu Command `Control` ➤ `Metronome`.

Please note

- You can't change the sound of the Click.
- You can't change the volume of the Metronome separately.
- Although the Metronome is played through the Master output, it will not be part (audible) when you export your song.

➡ *Count-In*

This feature is a special Metronome function used for recording. Think of it as the conductor, the band leader or the drummer that counts in the song. The behavior of this function is slightly different depending on the circumstances. So make sure you understand the rules which might be different from what you are expecting or accustomed to from other DAWs:

- The Count-in is only used (audible) when you hit the record button.
- The count-in is independent from the Metronome. If the Metronome is off, then you will hear the click only during the Count-in. Then it stops.
- The Count-in plays the beats for one bar, always starting with the first beat of a bar (never in the middle of a bar). Of course, the amount of beats depends on the Time Signature setting of your Song. If you selected 7/4, then you will hear 7 quarter note clicks and if you selected 6/8, then you will hear 6 eighth note clicks.
- If your Playhead is parked at the beginning of the song, then the Count-in plays one bar before the GarageBand starts your song on bar 1.
- If your Playhead is parked anywhere in the song, then GarageBand starts to record at that position while playing the metronome for the first bar. This behavior is arguably not a Count-In because it starts to record right away without a Count-In. This feature should be called "*start recording and play with a click, but play the click for only one bar*".
- When Cycle Mode is activated, the behavior is again different. GarageBand starts to play at least one bar ahead of the Left Locator Position of the Cycle Range. More details on the recording procedure in the Regions Chapter.

As you can see, there are different options and behaviors. You have to play with it and use it in order to get used to it.

The GarageBand Interface provides two elements to move around your song more efficiently, the scroll and zoom functionality. They are similar to other applications.

Scroll

You can scroll in the Arrange Window vertically or horizontally.

- **Horizontally**: If your song is longer than what is displayed in the Timeline Area, then you can scroll left and right. Your orientation is of course the Time Ruler that moves along as the time reference of your song. The Track Area is not affected by the horizontal scroll.
- **Vertically**: If your song has more Tracks (Band Members) than the Arrange Window can display vertically, then you can scroll up and down. As we have learned earlier, the Track Header and the Track Lane are connected as single rows, they move together up and down.

You can scroll with the standard tools:

- **Scroll Bar**: Click-drag the Scroll Bars which are only visible if there is more visible area available, horizontally or vertically
- **Gesture**: If you have a trackpad, you can use the standard Swipe Gestures for scrolling
- **Auto-scrolling (Locked Playhead)**: If the Timeline Area shows only a portion of your song's length, then the Playhead will "disappear" when it reaches the right edge of the Project. You then have to manually scroll the Timeline Area to view that section. To avoid this constant interaction, GarageBand provides a feature called "Auto-scrolling". Now when you play your song, the Playhead stays fixed at the center of the Timeline Area and the Time Ruler with all the Track Lanes scrolls underneath the fixed Playhead. The little double-arrow icon in the lower right corner of the Arrange window lets you toggle between Auto-scrolling on and off.

Auto-scrolling On

Auto-scrolling Off

A neat little feature is the overlay window during scrolling, that displays the current time or bar position at the left edge of the Timeline Area. Depending on the LCD setting and what is displayed in the Time Ruler, it displays either the absolute time in min:sec or the musical time as a bar number.

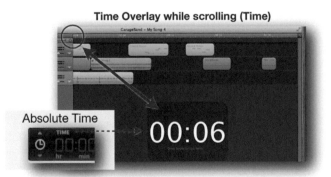

Time Overlay while scrolling (Time)

Absolute Time

00:06

Time Overlay while scrolling (Measure)

Bar

4

Zoom

Zoom Slider

GarageBand allows you to zoom in and out horizontally (but not vertically). That means, the height of the Track Lane (and Track Header) is fixed. You can zoom in and out only on the time axis, the Time Ruler.

You can zoom in two ways:

- **Zoom Slider**: This is the slider at the bottom of the Track Header.
- **Gesture**: If you have a trackpad, you can use the standard Pinch Gesture to zoom in and out.

6 - Tracks

By now, we've encountered the term "Track" already. In this chapter we will have a closer look to fully understand what it is and how to work with it.

Let's recap what we've learned so far:

- From a pure layout standpoint, a Track is represented by a row in the Arrange window. Each additional row represents another Track.
- Each row has two segments: The Track Header ❶ which expands into the Track Lane ❷.
- You can think of each Track (each row) as a member of the band that performs your song.
- So if we look at the Arrange Window, we have the Track Area on the left which lists all the "Band Members" and the Timeline Area on the right that contains the musical information that each "Band Member" has to play.

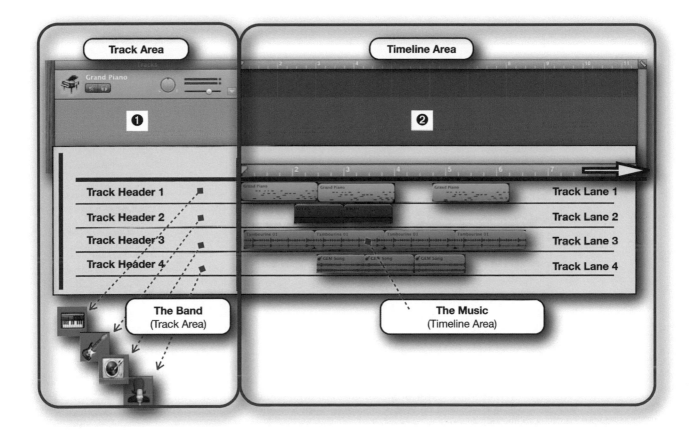

Who's in the Band

As in real life, before you start to make music, you have to form your band. For that, you ask two basic questions.

- ☑ "How many musicians" - in GarageBand terms that means "how many Tracks".
- ☑ "What kind of musicians" - in GarageBand terms that means "what type of Tracks".

The question about the number of musicians makes sense. You can create a piece of music for a one-man band in the form of a solo pianist (needs only one Track in GarageBand) or for a full Orchestra (needs many Tracks in GarageBand).

The second question about the type of musician or type of Track is not so obvious and that's where we have to look a little deeper.

At the beginning of this manual, I introduced GarageBand as an entry-level consumer application which "simplifies" some functions and concepts of a DAW to make it easy for the casual user to operate and understand. However, I think Apple went off a little bit how they implemented Tracks in GarageBand. It is obvious that they tried to simplify it but I think, in the end this could lead to more confusion.

The concept of different types of tracks is not that complicated after all. I'll try to explain that simple foundation first and then show how it is implemented in GarageBand and what kind of (questionable) terminology is used.

How to "record" Music

There are two basic methods of recording music.

💡 **Method 1: Describe how to Play the Music**

This is a traditional form of recording music. You use instructions, most likely in the form of written notes. You write down your song in a commonly understood language, i.e. western music notation. A composer can write down a symphony, and every orchestra can play that piece of music. Or a musician writes down sheet music or a chord chart and every Jazz Band then can play that tune.

Music	described (written down)	as Notation

💀 **Method 2: Capture the Sound of Played Music**

With the invention of the gramophone in the 20th century, music could be recorded right there when it was performed. You can come up with a great song and instead of writing it down, you would just play it on your instrument and record that performed music. A recording device captures the audio, the sound of the music from a musician, a band or an orchestra. Now instead of describing the music, you capture the audio and store it on a disc or an mp3 file.

Music	played and captured (recorded)	as Audio File

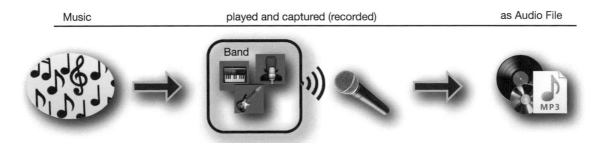

But what does that have to do with Tracks? Pretty much everything. Every DAW on the market has both abilities to record music and that is linked to the two common terms:

☑ Record and play a description of music (Method 1) - **MIDI Track**
☑ Record and play the sound of performed music (Method 2) - **Audio Track**

➡ *MIDI Track*

First we look at a so called "MIDI Track". Let's hold on to the previous analogy that the various Tracks in your Project represent the band members that perform your song.

A "MIDI Track band member" would be the one that can read music. This would be Method 1 of capturing music in some form of description. Think of it this way. You come to the rehearsal and hand out your sheet music to your fellow band members. However, in a DAW, you cannot feed the computer your sheet music. You must use a different form of "music description". The common language of describing music in a DAW is MIDI.

I briefly explained MIDI in the chapter about the Hardware Setup. The MIDI standard defines how to translate (convert) music into computer language (a series of zeros and ones). For example, when you play the notes "c-e-g" on a MIDI keyboard, it will translate the information about those notes and how you played them into the MIDI language which can be transmitted over a cable from the keyboard to the computer that hosts the DAW. The DAW on the other side "speaks" the MIDI language and understands that specific description of music. It can store the notes (record them) and also play them, which means sending the notes "c-e-g" to a sound module (part of the DAW) and you will hear the music "c-e-g".

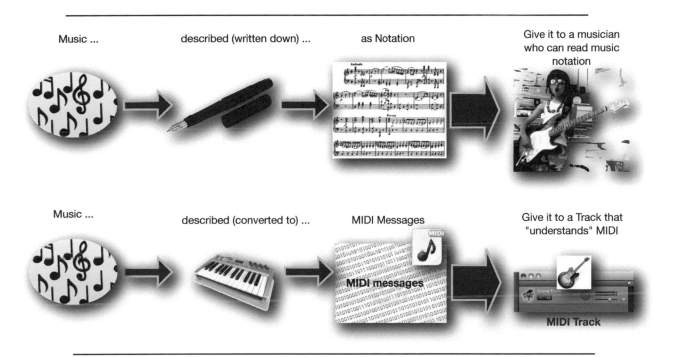

So the important thing is that on a MIDI Track, the DAW records and stores music as a description in the form of a specific music language called MIDI. There are two advantages to recording music as MIDI.

💡 Change the music
At any time, you can edit your music. The DAW presents the stored MIDI information in various graphical forms that you can read and understand (even in standard musical notation). This is like taking your sheet music to the rehearsal and there make some corrections in your score.

💡 Change the performer
The same way as you can take the sheet music from the guitar player during rehearsal and give it to the sax player because it sounds better, you can assign different sound modules to your stored MIDI information. This provides a great deal of flexibility when it comes to arranging your song.

➡ *Audio Track*

Besides the MIDI Track, the other type of Track is the "Audio Track". This would be Method 2 of capturing music. As I explained, it is a sound recording which is quite different from a MIDI recording.

Back to the rehearsal room. All the musicians in our band are like MIDI Tracks that can read or understand "described" music. So who would represent the Audio Track? How about the DJ. Many bands now also have a DJ that scratches some records (let's not get into the discussion of wether a DJ is considered a musician and spinning records is considered playing an instrument). In our model, the DJ is a perfect representation of the Audio Track. He doesn't have to read music in order to play it on his instrument (turn table). Instead, you would hand him a recorded piece of music as a record or an audio file. This is basically what happens on an Audio Track. There you place an existing audio file or you record a new audio file from a sound source in form of an acoustic signal (microphone) or an electric signal (electric guitar, synth). The Audio Track can then play back that audio recording as part of your song.

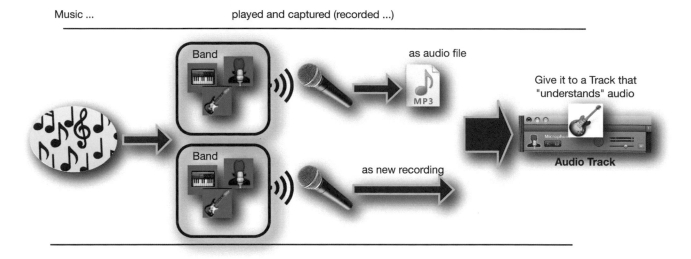

The main advantage you can see from the table below is that MIDI Tracks provide the most flexibility when it comes to editing (changing) anything while you are working on your song. For example, when you record a melody as an audio file from a guitar player, you cannot change the melody or go ahead and change it to sax player later. However, technology advanced tremendously the last couple of years and there are now tools available that let you change many parameters of an otherwise fixed audio file (tempo, pitch, timing). Some of those tools are available in GarageBand and we will cover them later in the book.

The main advantage of an audio recording is that you capture the performance of a musician with all the nuances of his instrument. Also recording vocals doesn't work well with MIDI instruments.

	MIDI Track	Audio Track
Band Member Analogy	guitarist, pianist, drummer	DJ
Records what	Music description (MIDI)	Music performance
Change music content	Freely editable	Very limited
Change instrument	Any available electronic instruments	Not possible
Change Song Parameters	Not a problem	very limited
Performance	Restricted to electronic instruments	Record any live instrument

New Tracks in GarageBand

Now we will check GarageBand and see where we find those two track types, MIDI Tracks and Audio Tracks.

We learned in the Project chapter that you have to select a Project Template when you want to create a new Project. Any of those Project Templates opens with at least one Track in their Project. Let's ignore those Tracks for a moment and go ahead and create a new Track. This is the best way to understand the concept of Tracks in GarageBand.

You can create a new Track, "add a new band member", with any of the following three commands:

- **Click** on the Plus button in the left lower corner of the Control Bar
- Use the Menu Command Track ➤ New Track ... (or ➤ New Basic Track)
- Use the Key Command **opt+cmd+N**

Control Bar

Add a new Track

Before a new row with a Track will be created, a big dialog window opens up.

Based on the explanation of the two track types, you would expect a window with two options:

Create new MIDI Track   Create new Audio Track

But instead, the window gives you three different options:

Software Instrument   Real Instrument   Electric Guitar

Are you confused already? No mention of Tracks or Track type at all. Instead you have the option to choose different Instrument types along with an explanation.

New Track Dialog Window

Software Instrument
For Instrument sounds created by GarageBand and playable using a USB, MIDI, or onscreen keyboard.

Real Instrument
For audio recordings such as voice, guitar, bass, or any instrument that can be captured by a microphone.

Electric Guitar
For audio recordings of electric guitar using built-in GarageBand amps and stompbox effects.

▶ Instrument Setup

And this is exactly what I find problematic with this "simplified" approach. It tries to avoid using the proper technical terms "MIDI Track" and "Audio Track". However, the "GarageBand" terminology of Software and Real Instrument along with the choice of "Electric Guitar" is not immediately obvious to many users. It also requires to learn the definition of new terms, so why not use the industry standard terms of MIDI Tracks and Audio Tracks. On top of that, GarageBand also uses in other places the term "Basic Track" for "Real Instrument" and "Guitar Track" for "Electric Guitar".

At the bottom of the window is a disclosure triangle that extends the window to display the Instrument Setup. Here you can choose the input and output for the newly created Track. I will discuss those settings later in this chapter.

Let's first translate those GarageBand specific terms into standard DAW terminology.

Software Instrument ⟶ **MIDI Track**

Explanation: *For Instrument sounds created by GarageBand and playable using a USB, MIDI, or onscreen keyboard*

This option creates a **MIDI Track**.

- "Playable using a USB, MIDI, or onscreen keyboard" means that these are input devices that create MIDI messages and those MIDI messages can be recorded on this MIDI Track (Software Instrument Track).
- The first half of the sentence "For Instrument sounds created by GarageBand" means that GarageBand has built-in sound modules (also know as Software Instruments) that can understand those MIDI messages (the musical descriptions) and "play" them with any sound you are selecting on those Software Instruments.

Real Instrument ⟶ **Audio Track**

It becomes clear that under these considerations the term "Real Instrument" could be misleading. Yes, it makes a distinction to the MIDI based "*Software* Instruments" but if you record the vocal track or some audio from an external device then "Real Instrument" doesn't sound quite right.

Explanation: *For audio recordings such as voice, guitar, bass, or any instrument that can be captured by a microphone*

This option creates an Audio Track.

- "For audio recordings" makes it at least clear that this is about capturing music as audio and not as MIDI, indicating that we are dealing with an **Audio Track.**
- "...any instrument that can be captured by a microphone" is only partially correct. You can capture (record) an audio signal from any of the audio inputs on your computer. The source can be the built-in microphone or line-in or anything that is connected to an external audio interface. This can be a microphone, but also the pickup from an electric guitar or even the signal from a CD player. I discussed this already in the Hardware chapter.

Electric Guitar ⟶ **Audio Track ***

Explanation: *For audio recording of electric guitar using built-in GarageBand amps and stompbox effects*

This option also creates an **Audio Track**.

- "For audio recording" gives us the hint again that we are dealing with an Audio Track, which is correct.
- "... using built-in GarageBand amps and stompbox effects" hints that this Track includes some special features. And that is exactly the case. When selecting this option, GarageBand creates and Audio Track that, in regards to the input configurations, behaves exactly like the Audio Track that you created when selecting the "Real Instrument" option.

Despite its name, you can feed/record any audio signal to that track, not only Electric Guitars. The available guitar amps and stompboxes on this special Audio Track makes it, of course, more suitable for Electric Guitars, but that doesn't mean that you cannot experiment with running other signals through those amps and effects.

Track Color Code

A selected Track in the Track Area is displayed in color. The interesting thing is that the "Software Instrument" track is green but a "Real Instrument" Track and a "Electric Guitar" Track both are displayed in the same blue color. Maybe that is the distinction between a MIDI Track (green) and an Audio Track (blue).

Selected Track: Software Instrument

Selected Track: Real Instrument

Selected Track: Electric Guitar

Other Tracks

The MIDI Tracks and Audio Tracks are where you record and arrange your music. But GarageBand has four additional types of Tracks. Those Tracks are always part of your Project, you just choose to Show or Hide them in the Track Area.

The commands for all four of those tracks are listed in the Track Menu that also displays their corresponding Key Command.

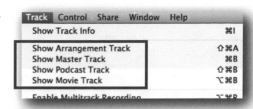

Here is a quick overview:

➡ Movie Track

The Movie Track lets you import a Quicktime video file to your Project to score a movie or video.

- The Movie Track is always located above any MIDI or Audio Tracks.
- If selected, the Track Header is displayed in purple.
- The Track Header provides no controls, only a thumbnail of the movie.

➡ Podcast Track

The Podcast Track provides the tools to create an enhanced Podcast with chapters and artwork (not a video Podcast).

- The Podcast Track is always located above any MIDI or Audio Tracks.
- You can display either the Movie Track or the Podcast Track. An Alert window will remind you if you have the other track already visible.
- The selected Track Header is also displayed in purple.
- The Track Header provides no controls, only an image of the artwork.
- More details in the Podcast chapter.

➡ Master Track

The Master Track provides all the controls similar to a Master Channel Strip on a mixing board. These are the main controls that affect your whole Project.

- The Master Track is always located at the bottom of the Track Area.
- The selected Track Header is also displayed in purple.

➡ Arrange Track

The Arrange Track is a special Track that lets you add visual Those markers are a visual guidance and can be used to edit whole sections in your Song.

- The Arrange Track is always located at the top of the Track Area.
- Add a Marker: Click the Plus button to create a Marker
- The first Marker always starts at the beginning of the song. Additional Markers will always snap to each other avoiding any gaps. The editing commands are as expected:
  - **Resize**: Click-drag the edge of a Marker.
  - **Move**: Click-drag on the Marker.
  - **Copy**: Opt+drag a Marker.
  - **Rename**: double-click on a Marker, enter a text and hit return.

Here is an overview of all the different types of Tracks in the Track Area of the GarageBand Project Window.

On the left side is a screenshot with an empty Track Area and on the right side a Track Area with one of each Track type.

Please note that the Arrange Track, the Movie/Podcast Track and the Master Track have a fixed location. The MIDI Tracks and Audio Tracks populate the middle section. Those individual Tracks can be moved up and down (click+drag) to re-arrange their order.

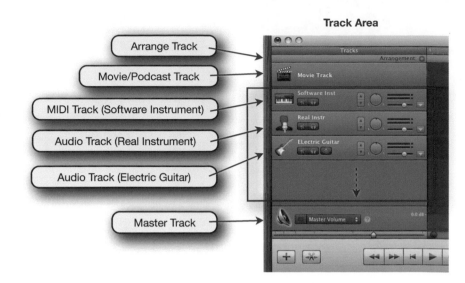

Track Commands

The Track Menu contains four more commands to manage Tracks.

🔘 New Track ...

This is the same command as clicking on the Plus button at the bottom of the Track Area. Key Command opt+cmd+N. It opens the Track Selector window we just discussed.

🔘 Delete Track

Select a Track first and use this command to delete it (only one at a time). Key Command cmd+delete. But be careful, you won't get an Alert that you are about to "kick out a band member". However you can bring him back with the Undo command (cmd+Z), "no hard feelings".

Deleting a Movie or Podcast Track will just hide it. The Master Track and Arrange Track cannot be deleted.

🔘 Duplicate Track

Duplicate any selected Tracks. This works only on a MIDI Track or Audio Track. This duplicates only the Track, but not its current content on the Track Lane. Key Command cmd+D.

🔘 New Basic Track

This is a special command that immediately creates an Audio Track (Real Instrument) without going through the Track Selector window. Key Command sh+cmd+N. This is an example of unnecessary confusion. I made my case already about the questionable term "Real Instruments" instead of using "Audio Track". But now, using a command with a new generic term "Basic Track" instead of established term "Real Instrument" Track makes no sense.

To fully understand how to edit the Tracks in GarageBand, it helps to know a little bit about the background. In the first chapter "What is GarageBand", I explained that GarageBand provides the two basic functions of a recording studio.

However, GarageBand has neither a tape machine nor a mixing board. Instead, GarageBand (and most other DAW) uses Tracks which provide both functionalities, the recording part and the mixing part.

Here is a diagram that shows the anatomy of a GarageBand Track. You can see the basic signal flow with all the main elements that are involved to provide the full functionality of a recording studio with a recording device and a mixing console.

How does a signal travel through a Track

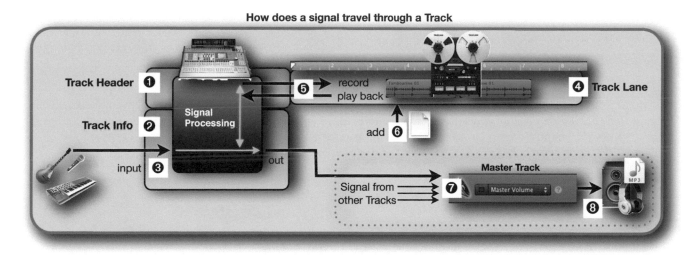

- The mixing part is represented by two elements: The always visible Track Header ❶ and the Track Info window ❷ that can be shown as an additional window pane in the Arrange Window. These two elements provide the typical controls of a channel strip on a mixing console. We will explore the Track Info window in a minute, but in the diagram you can already see that this is the place where you select which input ❸ is used for the Track.

- The Recording part is represented by the Track Lane ❹. This is where your music is laid out over time. Music is recorded onto the Track Lane and played back from the Track Lane ❺, which means the signal goes back through the signal processing part, the Channel Strip.

- A common feature in DAWs that is not possible with traditional recording devices is that you can add an existing audio file ❻ onto the Track Lane without "recording' it through the Track's input.

- The output of a Track together with the output of all the other Tracks in your Project will go to the Master Track ❼ for final adjustments before the mixed signal reaches the speaker or you export it to a new audio file ❽.

- When you follow the arrows, you can see how the signal is "flowing" through the components (hence the "signal flow").
  - The input signal can go straight to the Output without recording. This is the scenario when you plug-in your guitar to GarageBand and use it basically as a guitar amp or with a MIDI keyboard using it as a synth sound module.
  - The input signal also goes to the Track Lane so it can be recorded at any time as an audio signal (Audio Track) or a MIDI signal (MIDI Track).
  - When you are playing your song, any recorded music on the Track Lane travels through the signal processing (amp, sound module, effects)

Track Header

We just saw that the Track Header functions as a part of our virtual Mixing Console. Unlike the Track Info window which is a separate window pane that has to be "opened", the Track Header is always visible. That's why you'll find here the controls that are used the most on a Track.

Track Header

Track Icon   Track Name   Record Enable   Mute   Solo   Lock   Monitor   Panorama   Level Meter   Volume   Automation

Track Icon

You can assign an icon from a list in the Track Info window for easy visualization.

Track Name

The Track will inherit the name of the Instrument that is assigned to that Track. You can rename it by **double-clicking** on the name. The name appears highlighted and you can type in a new name.

The Track Name will be used later to name the Regions you record on that Track.

Record Enable

GarageBand doesn't require a button to enable a Track for recording. The currently selected Track is the one that will be recorded on. However you can switch to Multitrack Recording mode which allows you to record up to 8 Audio Tracks and 1 MIDI Track. The "Record Enable" button will appear on the Track Header only if this mode is enabled.

- Menu Command Track ➤ Enable/Disable Multitrack Recording
- Key Command **opt+cmd+R**

Mute

This button, when activated, disables the Track temporarily. Its signal to the output is interrupted.

Solo

This button, when activated, mutes all other tracks so you can listen to this isolated Track. You can also "solo" multiple Tracks. **Opt+click** any Solo button will un-solo all Solo buttons at once.

Lock

This button locks the Track for two practical reasons. One is that you cant' make any (accidental) changes to a Locked Track nor to the Tracks' Regions. The second reason is to "Freeze" the track which saves processing power on your computer when playing your Project. The button is hidden by default but you can toggle it with

- Menu Command Track ➤ Show/Hide Track Lock
- Key Command **opt+cmd+L**

The Lock button has three stages: Unlocked - Lock Enabled - Locked

After you enable the Lock on a Track, you have to let it play all the way through to start the locking procedure. Other DAWs call this "freeze a track". During that play, GarageBand records that "lock enabled" Track to a temporary audio file (including all its effects). Now when you play back a Locked Track, GarageBand just plays back that audio file which is less demanding on the computer than playing the original Track, especially if you have a lot of CPU intensive plugins used on that Track.

The Volume Slider and the Panorama Dial are not "frozen" on a Locked Track. You still can make those changes.

Monitor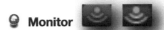

This is a popup button. When you click on it, a popup menu with three options will be displayed. I will discuss the function in detail in the next chapter.

This button is always visible for Electric Guitar Tracks, but can also be displayed for regular Audio Tracks (Real Instruments, Basic Tracks) with the following commands.

- Menu Command Track ➤ Show/Hide Monitoring for Real Instrument Tracks
- Key Command opt+cmd+I

 Panorama Dial

The dial lets you set the stereo balance, placing the signal on the stereo panorama between left and right speaker. Turning the dial all the way to the left will play the signal on the track only through the left speaker, dialing all the way to the right will play only through the right speaker. Placing the dial in the center will play it through both speakers. Or choose any position in between.

- Sh+drag the Dial for finer adjustments.
- opt+click to set the Dial to the center.

current value

A yellow Tool Tip will display the pan value (-64 ... +63).

 Level Meter

This Stereo Meter lets you monitor the level of the signal on this Track. It uses three colors for its segments (green to orange to red). A separate red Overload LED indicates when the signal is too strong.

- The meter will hold any peak signal for 2 seconds for better monitoring.
- The red Overload LED stays on (even after playback stops) until

  - you reset it by clicking on it.
  - you start playing your song again.

2 second peak hold   Overload LED

 Volume Slider

The Volume Slider lets you adjust the level of the signal on that Track to find the right balance when mixed with all the other Tracks in your Project. Please note that this level has no affect on the recorded input signal.

- Sh+drag the slider for finder adjustments.
- Opt+click to reset the slider to 0dB.

A yellow Tool Tip will display the value of the slider position (-144dB ... +6dB).

You can use the Rotate Gesture on a Trackpad to move the slider on a selected Track.

current value

What is dB? "dB" is an abbreviation for *decibel* which is used as a logarithmic unit for signal levels. 0dB on a fader is referred to as "unity gain", where the signal passes through without a level change. +6dB is usually the maximum level on a Fader. Moving the fader below 0dB will lower the signal all the way to the bottom with a maximum attenuation. This means the signal is basically muted.

 Automation

This is a disclosure button. It toggles the Automation Lane on and off, a section that slides out below the track. This is where you control the Track automation. See the Automation chapter for details.

 Groove Tracks

There is one additional element on the Track Header that I didn't show on the previous page. It is a star or a checkbox on the left side of the Track Header. This is only visible if you use the Groove Track feature which I cover in a separate chapter.

Track Info window

The Track Info window follows a standard interface convention known as "**Inspector**". In most content-creation applications like word processor or music and video production apps, you click on an Object and a separate Inspector window displays the parameters of that object and lets you edit them.

The Object

In the Track Info window, there is only one type of Object that can be selected in order to show and edit its parameters. That object is a Track. That's why the window is specifically called "Track Info window". You can have the Track Info window open and whatever Track you select, the window will change its content to display the parameters of the currently selected Track.

The Window

Many applications use a separate window but in GarageBand's single window interface, the Track Info window is a window pane that slides out from the right of the Arrange window. I already discussed in the Interface chapter that the content of this window pane can be switched between three different windows.

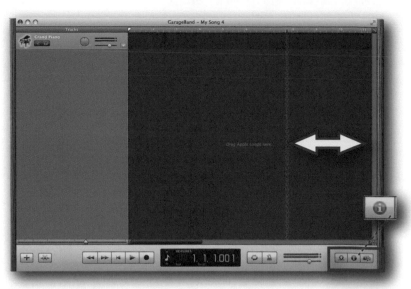

The Command

You toggle the Track Info window with any of these four commands:

- **Click** on the i-Button in the Control Bar on the lower right corner of the Project Window
- **Double-Click** on a Track Header
- Use the Menu Command Track ➤ Track Info
- Use the Key Command **cmd+I**

The Content

The content of each type of Track is different due to the different parameters (MIDI, audio). However the layout of the window is similar.

- Each window has two main tabs at the top. The first one is labeled after the type of Track and displays the parameters for the track in a specific layout. The second tab is always the "Master Track" tab. This functions as a shortcut to quickly switch to the Master Track Info window without selecting the Master Track in the Track Area first.

- All three Track windows (Software Instrument, Real Instrument, Electric Guitar) also have in common two secondary tabs. The first one is labeled "**Browse**" to select an Instrument Preset and a second tab is labeled "**Edit**" that switches the window view to display the parameters for editing.

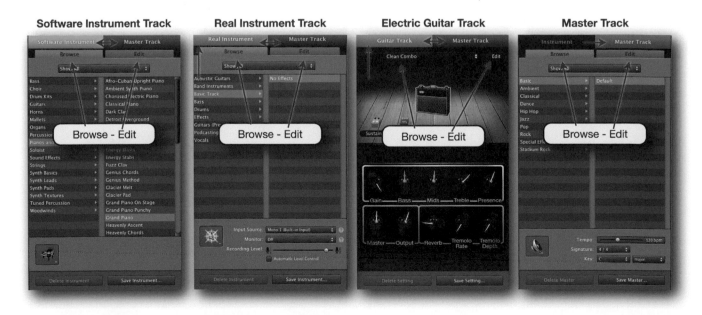

The next step would be to explain the different controls and features in the Track Info window. However, before that, I want to discuss some topics about a mixing console.

Virtual Mixer

There are different ways to re-create a mixing console in a software application. Visually, you can replicate the look of a hardware mixer so the interface elements look exactly like a real mixer and if you learned how to use one, you will feel at home right away with that virtual mixer. However it requires that you know how to operate a mixer and that you are familiar with the technology and terminology.

Because GarageBand is an entry level software application, Apple chose not to have a visual replication of a mixer. Instead, GarageBand replaces the look of a mixing console with a different interface that is based more on the layout of a typical computer application with windows, menus and controls. The underlying concept of a mixing console however is still there.

You can operate GarageBand by just making selections on various menus and adjusting controls on various windows without ever having seen a mixer or knowing how it operates. However, if you know a little bit about the underlying concept of Channel Strips, then you will be much more in control when working on your song. In this advanced section I explain the basic concept and functionality of a mixer and how it relates to the interface elements in GarageBand.

If you are new to this topic, then you will gain a solid foundation and a better understanding and if you know how to use a mixer, you will learn the GarageBand-way of a mixing console very fast by discovering the various mixer elements in GarageBand and its own (strange?) terminology.

I already provided an overview about the Mixer in the Introduction chapter with some of the basic functionality. For the preparation of the understanding of the Track Info window I will concentrate on the Signal Flow and the elements on a mixer's Channels Strip that are available in GarageBand.

At the beginning of the signal flow on a Channel Strip is the Input. Here you decide, which Signal you connect (feed) to the channel strip.

➡ *Input Source Selection*

❶ Depending on your setup, you have a variety of Instruments or Microphones connected to your computer input.

❷ Those Input Sources show up as Audio Input Devices in a menu where you select which one you choose to send to the Track (check the Hardware Setup chapter for details).

❸ The selected Input Source signal "travels" through that Track and you can treat it with anything that is available on that Track (volume, pan, effects, etc).

❹ Please note that the Input Signal is also sent to a second destination at the same time, like a splitter. It is available at the Track Lane for the purpose of recording it.

❺ Any recorded signal on the Track's Track Lane is "played back" through the Track once you hit the Play button in GarageBand creating a second input for the Track.

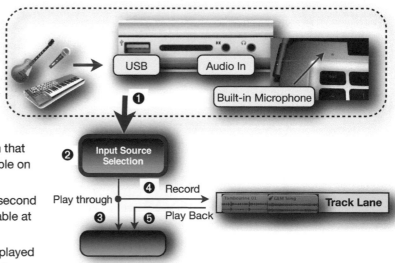

➡ Input Gain (Recording Level)

To record a signal in GarageBand you have to make sure that the level is right, not too low, or too high (which causes distortion.). The Input Gain (in GarageBand it is labeled "Recording Level") is the control that lets you adjust the level from the incoming signal that you feed into the Track (Channel Strip) and the Track Lane for recording. This might be necessary because different sources (microphone, electric guitar, synthesizer, etc) have different signal strength. Sometimes you can adjust the level with a separate gain control on the external Audio Interface before it "enters' GarageBand. Please note that the "Recording Level" slider in GarageBand is linked to the "Input level" slider in the System Preferences Sound window..

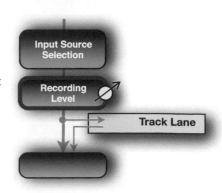

➡ Inserts (Effects)

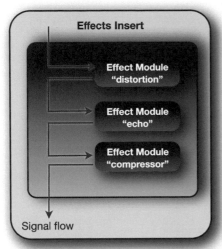

This section on a mixer's channel strip is called the "Inserts" or "Effect Inserts". The concept is that you use external signal processing modules that you insert into the signal flow. These modules are used to alter the signal in any kind of form or shape.

For example, add distortion, compress the signal, add echoes or reverb, etc. In a Studio, these modules (outboard gears arranged in an effects rack) are physically connected into the channel strip's signal flow with cables on a patchbay. Nowadays in DAWs, the effect modules are little software applications that are added by selecting them from a menu.

On a virtual mixer, you assign those effects to a slot and usually you have a limited amount of slots available on a Track. All the DAWs come with a wide variety of effect modules (also known as plug-ins) and you can install even more plug-ins on your system from third party vendors.

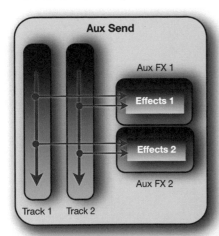

With hardware effect modules, you can use an effects module only for one Track but on a digital mixer you can "assign" a plugin to as many tracks you want. You are just adding a piece of computer code to the Project a and the only limitation on the number of effects you use is your computer's power.

➡ Aux Sends (Master Effect)

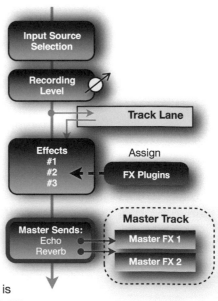

Another important section on a channel strip are the Aux Sends. GarageBand labels them "Master Echo" and "Master Reverb"

The original concept has a practical idea behind it. When you have an Effects Module for an Echo on a standard mixing console, then you can use it only for one Track if you use the insert method. Instead, you put the Echo Effect on a separate Track (an Aux Track) and enable other Tracks on your mixer to send a portion of their signal to that Aux track. All the Tracks that send their signal to that Aux Track will now have an echo effect. If you have 4 Tracks on your mixer that require that echo effect then instead of using 4 Echo effects units, you will need only 1 Echo effect on that Aux Track.

Each Audio and MIDI Track in GarageBand has two of those Sends. The actual effect is not hosted on an Aux Channel but is part of the Master Track. That's why those sends are called "Master ...". The concept however is the same.

➡ Pan - Volume

The rest of the controls are the easy ones to understand. They are located on the Track Header and I discussed them already in the previous section. The Pan determines where to place the signal on the stereo balance and the Volume slider determines the level of the signal.

➡ Mute - Solo

The Mute and Solo function, also located on the Track Header are switches. You can temporarily mute a specific channel if you want to hear your song without it. The Mute function can also be used as part of your arrangement. You could mute an Instrument on a Track during specific sections of your song, i.e. use the shaker only during the first and second verse, even you have recorded it through the whole song.

The Solo function works like an inverse mute button. Pressing the Solo button on one Track, mutes all other Tracks in your song.

➡ Output

Usually, at the end of the signal flow of a Channel Strip you have the option to select an output destination where you want to send the signal. This is similar to the Input, where you select an input source. GarageBand however, due to its simplicity doesn't need such a selection. Every Track sends its output signal automatically to the Master Track.

The separate Master Track in your song has similar control elements like Volume, Effects and the controls for the two Master Effects.

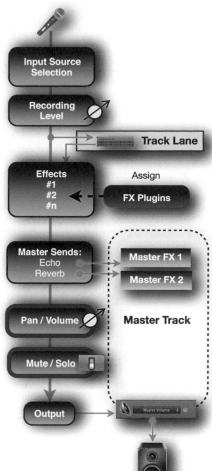

These are the main controls that you would find on a typical Channel Strip of a mixing console and are also available in GarageBand's Tracks. There is one more component and that has to do with the functionality of Monitoring and Metering.

Feedback

Usually, a recording studio has two rooms, the control room with the mixer and the big speakers and then a separate (sound proof) recording booth where the musicians are placed with the microphones. If you don't have a separate recording booth and place the microphone in the same room where the speakers are, then you're running into a potential problem - Feedback.

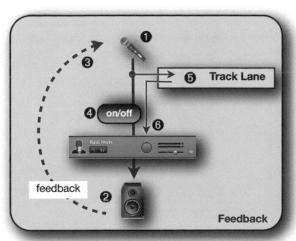

This is the phenomena when the sound waves coming from the (turned up) loud speaker are picked up from the microphone ❶, gets amplified, blasting through the speaker again ❷ and the microphone picks them up again ❸ and runs through the amplifier again, and so. The result is a loud high pitched noise that is often heard during live concerts when the singer on stage gets to close to the monitor speaker with his mic.

To avoid such a feedback, you could lower the speaker volume, use headphones or mute the signal ❹ that runs through the Channel Strip to the speakers. In order to record your singing from the microphone (or recording of an acoustic instrument) you don't have to hear yourself amplified through the speakers anyway. The signal only has to reach the Track Lane ❺, to record your part. Playing back the recorded parts from the Track Lane through the speakers is ok because that signal is not coming from the microphone anymore ❻.

➡ *Metering*

A Meter is a measurement instrument ❸. On a Channel Strip, it serves two main purposes. If you are doing trouble shooting because you can't hear an instrument on a Track, the meters can tell you if a signal is present in the signal path (maybe the speaker volume is turned down). The other purpose is to see how strong the signal is, maybe too strong which you can see by the red overload LEDs.

The important part however is, at what point of the signal path do you measure the level. In GarageBand, the Track Meters can show the level of the signal at two stages ❹. Which one depends on the transport controls.

❶ If GarageBand is in Play mode (and only then), the Meters will show the signal "at the end" of the Track before it gets send to the Master Track. This means that any element in the signal path (effects, volume, pan, mute) will effect the metered signal. For example, if you play GarageBand and you press the Mute button on a Track, its Meter won't show any signal.

❷ If GarageBand is in any other mode than Play (i.e. Stop or Record), the Meters will show the signal "at the beginning" of the Track, after the Recording Level control. This is very practical, because you can set the Recording Level while monitoring it on the Meters.

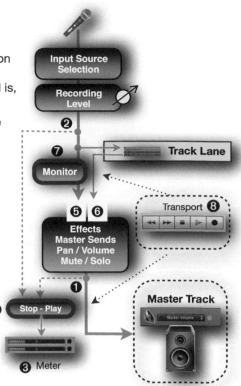

➡ *Monitoring*

While the Metering is the function of "what you see", the Monitoring is the function of "what you hear".

You know by now that there are two signals that enter the Channel Strip. Input Signal and Playback Signal.

❺ **Input Signal:** This is the original input signal that you select for the Track to "feed" into the Track. You can use GarageBand with that functionality to just play "through" the Track without recording at all. For example, use the built-in guitar amps to play your guitar or use the built-in sound modules to play piano or synth with your MIDI keyboard.

❻ **Playback Signal:** The second source is the material that you recorded or placed onto the Track's Track Lane. That signal is also fed into the signal chain running through all the elements of the Track.

Now the question is, do you hear both signals? That depends on two things:

☑ The Monitoring setting ❼
☑ The Transport controls ❽

Of course there are many different combinations, but the two simple rules are as follows:

- The Input Signal ❺ is running through the Track only if the Monitor is on. If Monitor is set to off then the Input Signal is muted at that point ❼. Please note that the Input Signal can still be recorded onto the Track Lane.

- The Playback Signal ❻ is running through the Track only if GarageBand is in Play mode. Of course, in Stop mode, nothing is playing and while recording, GarageBand is technically playing but any material that is on the Track Lane at that moment is replaced with the new Input Signal.

So technically, when you have Monitoring on and you play back the music on the Track's Track Lane, you will hear both signals. This is not a problem because you can listen and/or play without switching back and forth.

If you're recording with a microphone and have your speaker up in the same room you might want to turn off Monitoring to avoid Feedback. GarageBand however has a built-in safety net to protect your ears. If a Feedback occurs, It will turn the Monitor off and pops up an Alert Window ❾ where you can "rethink" your setting. If you want to live dangerously, choose the option "Monitor On" (no feedback protection).

Feedback Detection Alert Window

Track Info

Now that you have a basic understanding of the signal flow and the components on a Channel Strip, let's look at where those elements are located in GarageBand.

GarageBand spreads them over three window elements:

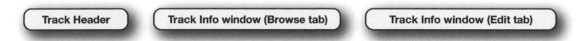

| Track Header | Track Info window (Browse tab) | Track Info window (Edit tab) |

Unfortunately the elements are not always at the same location for the various Track types.

Audio Track (aka Basic Track aka Real Instrument)

The signal flow of the Audio Track is the closest to that of a real console. A few things to pay attention to:

◉ The Input Source Selection and Record Level are located in the Browse tab ❶.

◉ The Monitor can be set in two locations, Browse tab ❷ and Track Header ❸ (if the button is made visible).

◉ The seven slots for the Effects ❹ and the two Master Effects ❺ are located in the Edit tab.

◉ The "Automatic Level Control" ❻ (available for some Audio Interfaces) lowers the level to prevent Feedback and raises the level if it is too low. Monitor has to be set to off.

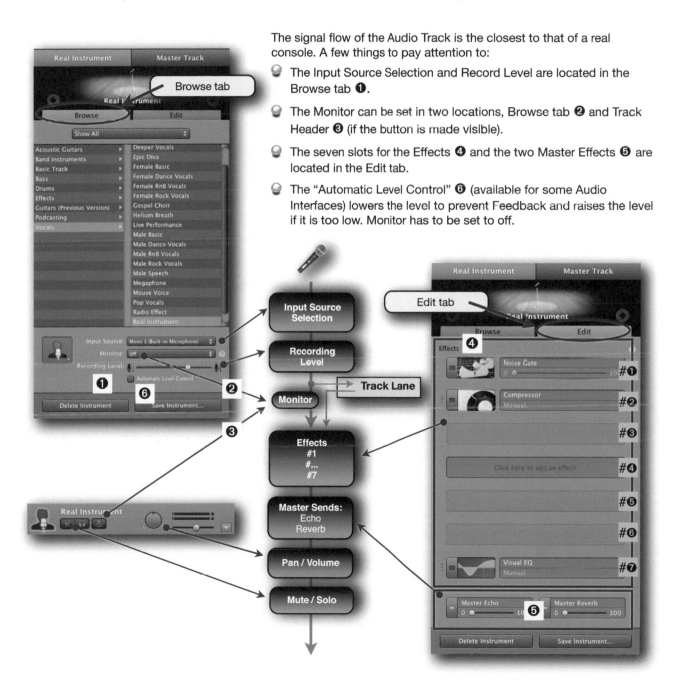

Audio Track (aka Guitar Track aka Electric Guitar)

As I mentioned earlier, the Electric Guitar Track is technically just another Audio Track. That's why the elements in the Track's signal flow are the same as with the regular Audio Track (Real Instrument). The difference lies in the layout of the Track Info window and the two additional components, amp simulation and stompboxes.

Instead of a Browse and Edit tab, the window can switch between 4 different displays.

- ► The first one is the "Front" view ❶ (the picture of the amp at the top shows the front of the amp).
    - ◎ Selecting the amp picture in Front view will display all the controls for that amp ❷ so you can adjust the sound.
    - ◎ Selecting any of the stompboxes in Front view will change the lower portion of the window to display that stompbox with its controls ❸ so you can adjust the effect.
- ► To switch to Rear view ❹ (you look at the back of the amp), **double-click** on the amp or the stomp box or click the *Edit* button in the upper right corner. To switch back to Front view, **double-click** on the amp or stompbox again or click the *Done* button in the upper right corner.
    - ◎ Now when you select the amp picture in Rear view, the window displays all the components ❺ of the Track's signal flow.
    - ◎ If you click on a stompbox in Rear view, the lower portion of the window will display all of GarageBand's stompboxes ❻ and you can drag them to any of the 5 stompbox slots below the amp.
- ◎ The first section of the Track's signal flow contains the components ❼ Input Source, Recording Level and Monitoring, which again is also available on the Track Header.
- ◎ The second section contains the menu for the Amp Model ❽ plus a slider for the noise gate. Just think about it as another Effects insert.
- ◎ The third section ❾ contains three slots for Effects plus the two Master Effects, Master Echo and Master Reverb.

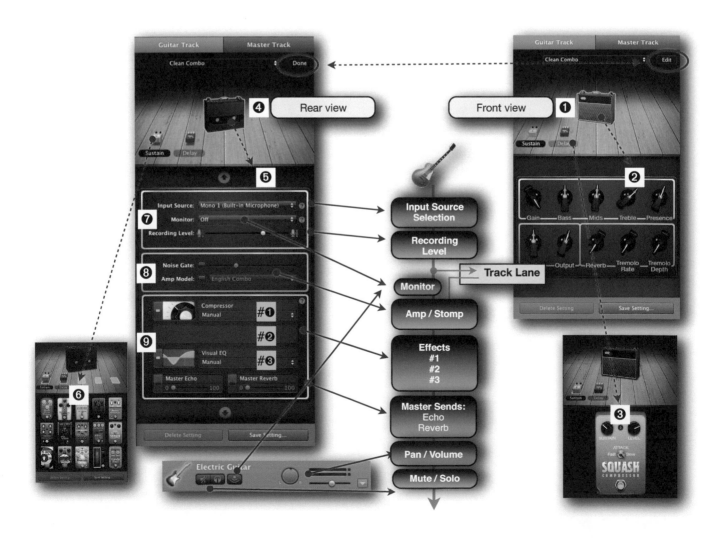

MIDI Track (Software Instrument)

What makes a MIDI Track different from an Audio Track is that you don't feed it an audio signal like a microphone or an electric guitar. Therefore, the first three components on the channel strip are missing (Input Source, Recording Level, Monitoring).

Instead, the input source for a MIDI Track is a MIDI input device like a MIDI Keyboard ❶ that generates MIDI messages. A MIDI message is a data stream representing a description of the music played on the keyboard.

> You don't have to select a MIDI Keyboard as an input source. GarageBand automatically detects any connected MIDI Input device and makes it available as a MIDI input source. Alternatively, you can use any of the two onscreen MIDI Keyboards: Musical Typing or Keyboard available from the Windows Menu.

That incoming MIDI data can be recorded on the MIDI Track's Track Lane ❷ and also reaches the first component of the channel strip. Here's the important part.

The first Effect in the signal chain of a MIDI Track is a dedicated "Sound Generator" Plugin ❸. That means the purpose of the first component is to take an incoming MIDI message and translate that into an audio signal with the selected sound.

After the Sound Generator, the Track behaves like a regular Audio Track.

- The Effects section ❹ provides 6 Effects slots.

- The Master Effects section ❺, as with all the other Track types, contains the Master Echo and Master Reverb.

- Because the MIDI Track handles an audio signal after the first Sound Generator component, the Track Header contains the usual elements ❻ like volume, pan, mute and solo. The Monitor button is not necessary because there is no danger of an audio feedback from the incoming MIDI signals.

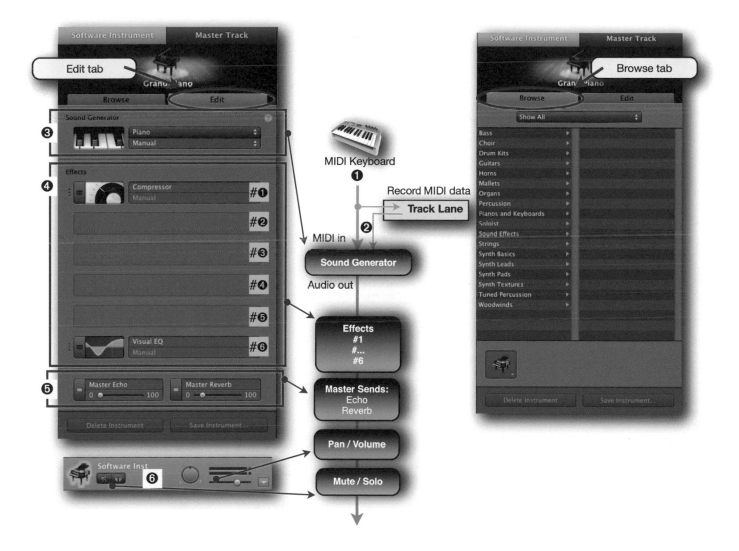

Concept

During the work on your Project, you might have created some great sounding effects or special configurations of an amp or sound generator. GarageBand lets you save those configurations as so called *Settings*, which you can recall later to use on a different Track or different Project. GarageBand also provides a wide variety of preconfigured Factory Settings that you can use in your Project.

There are two different types of Settings: Plug-In Settings and Track Settings.

➡ *Plug-In Setting*

A Plug-In Setting stores the configuration of a single Plugin. These are the single Effect Plugin settings in the Effects section as well as the Sound Generator Module settings on a MIDI Track.

- 💡 **Plug-Ins that "Generate Sounds": Modules**
- 💡 **Plug-Ins that "Process Sounds": Effects**

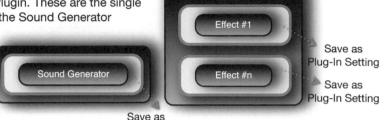

➡ *Track Settings*

A Track Setting stores everything on a Track that is responsible for how the signal is treated, except the volume and pan controls. It stores both, the information about what Plugin is assigned to which slot and how it is configured. It's like a snapshot of that whole channel strip section.

Here are the three types of Tracks with their components that indicate which section is included in a Setting.

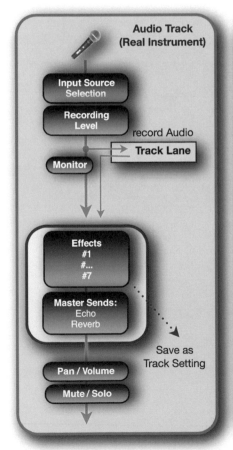
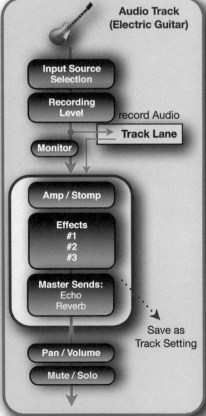
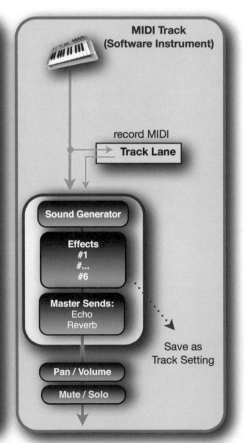

Structure (advanced)

➡ *Plug-In Setting*

In Theory

The available Plug-In Settings are organized on four levels

- 🔊 **Plugin Type:** GarageBand has two types of Plug-Ins. "Modules", which are the Sound Modules used on a MIDI Track and "Effects", like Effect Plugins that can be assigned to an Effect slot on a Track.

- 🔊 **Library:** Settings originate from two sources. These are considered the two Libraries. The settings you created (User Library) and the ones that come from Apple or other manufacturers (Factory Library).

- 🔊 **Format:** GarageBand supports two different Plugin formats, its own proprietary plugin format (GarageBand) which is only compatible with Logic Pro and the standard AU format (Audio Unit).

- 🔊 **Plugin:** This is the actual plugin for which a Setting is available. Settings saved from within one Plugin are only compatible with that Plugin. It wouldn't make sense to load a Setting from a Reverb plugin into a Flanger plugin which has completely different controls.

- 🔊 **Settings (Preset):** These are the actual Settings files that contain all the configuration data. Watch out for the inconsistency in the terminology. Plug-In Settings are also called "Presets".

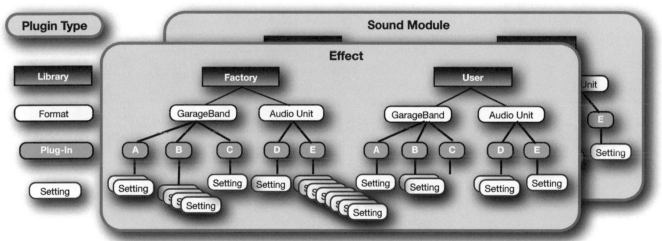

In the Finder

Each Plug-In Setting is represented by a small Settings file on your drive. The locations and the folder hierarchy might be a little bit confusing.

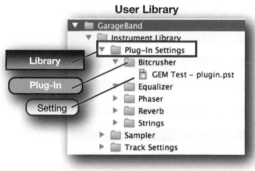

- 🔊 **Plugin Type:** The Finder makes no distinction between the Settings for an Effects Plugin or a Sound Module Plugin regarding the location.

- 🔊 **Library:** The Library determines the general location. The Factory Settings are stored in the System Library folder and the User Settings are stored in the User's Library folder.

- 🔊 **Format:** Here is an important fact. The Settings for GarageBand plugins and Audio Units plugins are stored in different locations inside each Library:

  - Audio Unit: `/Library/Audio/Presets/`
  - GarageBand: `/Library/Application Support/GarageBand/Instrument Library/Plug-In Settings`

- 🔊 **Plugin:** Each Plugin has its own folder, named after the plugin name. This is where the Settings are stored. The Audio Units have an additional folder, named after the manufacturer (i.e. Native Instruments, Spectrasonics, etc) to group all manufacturer specific Plugins together.

- 🔊 **Settings:** The Settings files have the file extension .pst (Preset Settings). They are compatible with Logic Pro.

You can organize (move, copy, delete) your Plug-In Settings files in the Finder and exchange those files with other users.

In GarageBand

All that background theory might be a little bit much but you don't necessarily have to deal with it. You can manage everything inside GarageBand. The user interface in GarageBand for Plug-In Settings is very easy and nicely done. It is the same for both Plugin Types, the Effects and the Sound Modules.

In this section I also discuss how to edit the Plug-Ins, so let's look at some basic rules first:

- 💡 Everything related to Plug-Ins is done in the Edit pane ❶ of the Track Info window.

- 💡 Plugins are assigned to slots ❷.

  - The Sound Generator slot ❸ (only on a MIDI Track) is always assigned and always on.

  - Some Effect slots are pre-assigned. They are missing the popup menu ❹ to choose a different plugin. However, you can select a different Setting and also edit the controls.

  - Add a new Effects plugin to an empty slot by clicking on that slot ❺ and select one from the popup menu.

- 💡 You can change the order of the Plugins by dragging the whole Plugin on the three dots on the left ❻.
  Please note that the audio signal runs from the top to the bottom on a channel strip and depending on the selected plugins, the order may affect the outcome of the resulting sound. Here again is the diagram that illustrates the concept of how a Plugin component is "inserted" or "plugged in" to the signal flow.

- 💡 To Edit a Plugin, click on its image which opens a separate free floating Edit window ❼. The GarageBand Plugins have specific images that hint at the functionality of the Plugin ❽. Audio Unit plugins only display the Audio Unit Logo ❾.

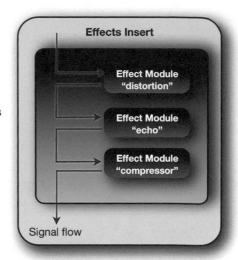

Plugin Edit Window

Plugin Slots (Track Info window)

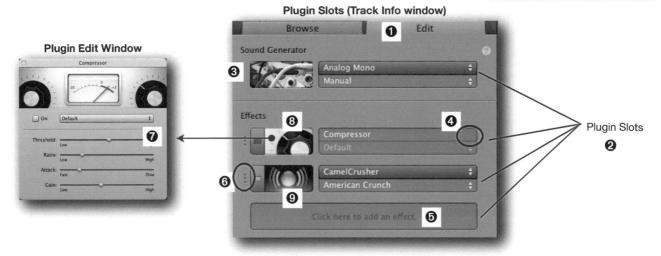

Amp Model

The Amp Model component on a Guitar Track is also a Plugin per definition. It is plugged into the signal flow before the Effects Plugins. Similar to the MIDI Track, where the Sound Module is a fixed Plugin, the Amp Model is also a fixed plugin. You can only change the amp model from the popup menu.

However, there are no Plug-In Settings available for the amp model. To save a specific sound that you created with the amp, you have to save it as a Track Setting with all the rest of the Track's Plug-Ins.

6 - Tracks

Here is how to interact with the Plug-In interface.

◉ The first line displays the selected Plugin ❶. Click on it to open a popup menu with a list of all the available Plugins.

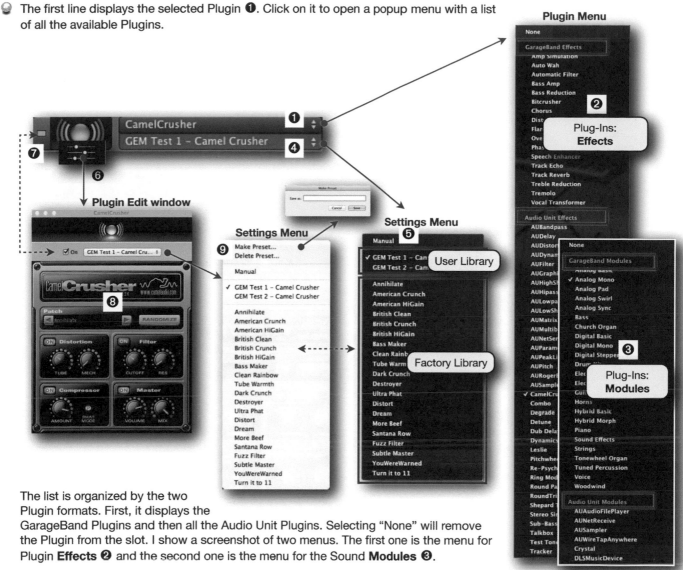

The list is organized by the two Plugin formats. First, it displays the GarageBand Plugins and then all the Audio Unit Plugins. Selecting "None" will remove the Plugin from the slot. I show a screenshot of two menus. The first one is the menu for Plugin **Effects** ❷ and the second one is the menu for the Sound **Modules** ❸.

◉ The second line displays the current Setting ❹ for that Plugin. It is also a popup menu with a list of all the available Settings for that specific Plugin. Many Plugins have no Factory Settings.

The list is also divided into two Libraries. The first Library represents the User Settings (if there are any) and the second Library shows all the Factory Settings (if there are any). The "Manual" ❺ Setting is a special Setting. Every time you change the controls from a loaded Setting, the Settings is stored to a RAM (a "temporary memory location"). You can even select a different Setting and go back to that Manual Setting which is still in memory until it is overwritten with a new change you make. "Default" indicates the default setting of that Plugin.

◉ The Plugin picture is an active button ❻ that opens the Edit window for the plugin. When you move your mouse over the picture, it will change to an image of three sliders, indicating that it will open the Edit window when you click on it.

◉ The green on-off button lets you bypass the Plugin, to listen to the Track without it. That button ❼ is linked to the "on" checkbox on the Plugin Edit window with the same functionality.

◉ The Plugin Edit window ❽ is a separate floating window, one of the few exceptions of GarageBand's single-window interface concept. It functions as an Inspector window, which means it switches its displayed content to whatever Plugin you select in the Track Info window.

◉ The Edit window also contains the popup menu for selecting a Setting for that Plugin. It has two additional commands at the top ❾. "*Make Preset...*" lets you create a User Settings of the current configuration. Please note the inconsistency in the terminology. Plugin Settings are referred to as "Presets", that's why it doesn't say "Make Settings". The "Delete Preset..." command is only visible if you currently have a User Settings selected.

In Theory

The Track Settings are organized on four levels. This is slightly different than the Plug-In Settings.

- 💡 **Track Type:** Each Track Type has its own type of settings. Think about it, it doesn't make sense to load a MIDI Track Setting into a Guitar Track Setting that doesn't have a Sound Generator Module.
- 💡 **Library:** Settings can originate from three places, the ones you create yourself, the ones that come with GarageBand and the so called "JamPacks" which are sold separately.
- 💡 **Category:** This level is just a way to group similar Settings together for specific purposes, i.e. vocals, guitar, drums.
- 💡 **Settings:** These are the actual Settings files that contain all the configuration data.

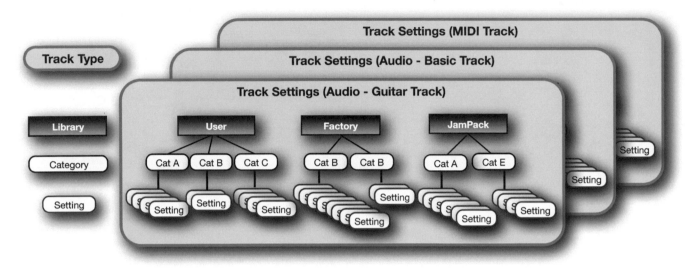

In the Finder

Each individual Track Setting is represented by a small Settings file on your drive. The location and the folder hierarchy follows the same structure.

- 💡 **Library:** The Library determines the general location. For example, the Factory and the additional JamPack Libraries are stored in the system folder and are off limits. The Settings that you create are stored in your home folder inside the following path: user/Library/Application Support/GarageBand/Instrument Library/Track Settings
- 💡 **Track Type:** The Track Types are represented by the folder "Basic Track" "Guitar Track" and Software".
- 💡 **Category:** Inside those Track folders are the Category folders.
- 💡 **Settings:** The various folders, named after a Category, contain the actual Track Settings files with the file extension .cst which stands for "channel strip settings" (remember, a Track in GarageBand represents the Channel Strip of a mixing console). This is a Logic Pro file type, compatible with GarageBand. That's why the GarageBand Track Settings are also displayed in Logic Pro and can be used there.

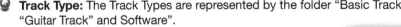

You can organize (move, copy, delete) your Track Settings files in the Finder and exchange those files with other users.

In GarageBand

And here is how to manage Track Settings in GarageBand. They are located under the Browse tab in the Track Info window. Let's look at the MIDI Track (Software Instrument) and Audio Track (Basic Track, Real Instrument) first because their interface is similar.

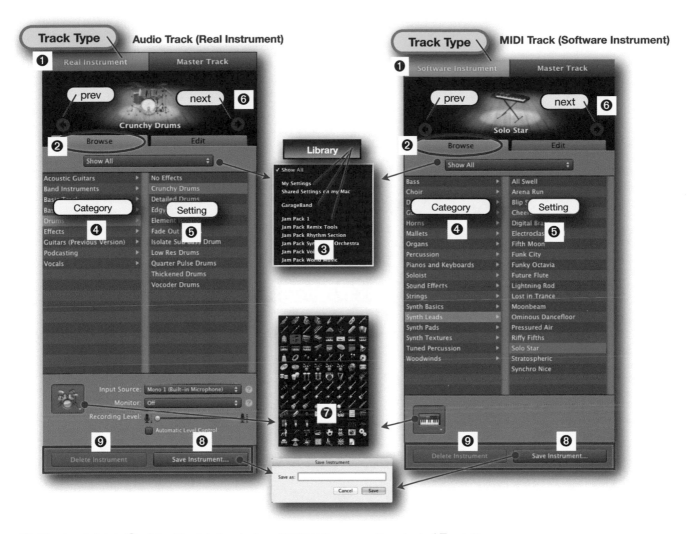

◉ The top left tab ❶ of the Track Info window displays the currently selected Track Type.

◉ The secondary tab "Browse" ❷ displays the window with the Settings controls.

◉ Underneath is a popup menu that displays all the Libraries ❸ that are available on your computer. If you don't have JamPacks installed, then you won't see those items in the menu. Select a specific Library or select "Show All".

◉ Underneath the popup menu are two columns. The left one displays all the Categories ❹ in the currently selected Library and the right column displays all the available Track Settings ❺ in the selected Category.

◉ You can also step through the Settings list with the left-right arrows ❻ in the top window segment that displays the instrument picture. Please note that this window segment is only visible if the Project window is big enough and the two arrows appear only if you move your mouse over that window segment.

◉ In the lower left corner is the popup button that displays a menu with all the available instrument icons ❼. The icon you select here will be displayed in the Track Header. You cannot add your own icons (without some serious hacking).

◉ At the bottom of the window are two big buttons. They are visible in both, the Browse and Edit tab:

- **Save Instrument...**❽: This opens a dialog window where you give your Setting a name. It will be saved to your user folder inside the currently selected Category (folder).

- **Delete Instrument** ❾: This button lets you delete the currently selected Setting (an Alert window gives you a warning before executing the command). Delete can only be used for User Settings and the button is grayed for all other Settings.

We already saw that the Track Info window for the Audio Track (Electric Guitar) looks different than the other two Track Types. This is also true for the Track Settings interface. Maybe because this Track Type was introduced in a later GarageBand version, it seems that Apple didn't use the already established terminology and interface conventions. Of course, this leads to potential confusion.

○ The main left tab ❶ of the Track Info Window displays the currently selected Track Type: Guitar Track

○ The secondary tab "Browse" is missing. Instead, there is a popup menu ❷ that is always visible in the Track Info window regardless if you display the Front view or Rear view of this Guitar Track Info window.

○ The popup menu contains a long list with all the Track Settings ❸. The darker font header on the menu is the name of the Library ❹, "My Settings" and "GarageBand". The My Settings will only be displayed if you have saved at least one Guitar Track Setting.

○ You can also step through the Settings list with the left-right arrows ❺ in the top window segment that shows the amp picture. Please note that this window segment is only visible if the Project window is big enough and the two arrows appear only if you move your mouse over that window segment.

○ The window doesn't provide a menu button to select different instrument icons. The icons are pre-selected, based on the chosen amp.

○ At the bottom of the window are the two big buttons, similar to the other Track Types. However, they use a different terminology, "Setting" instead of "Instrument".

  • **Save Setting... ❻**: This opens a dialog window where you give your Setting a name. It will be saved to your user folder inside the currently selected Category (folder).

  • **Delete Setting ❼**: This button lets you delete the currently selected Setting (an Alert window gives you a warning before executing the command). The Delete command can only be used for User Settings and the button is grayed for all other Settings.

Master Track

Before going over the available controls in the Track Info window for the Master Track, let's have first a quick look at the signal flow in the Master Track.

- The Master Track has three inputs that "enter" the Master Effects section.

    ❶ The output signals of all the Tracks in your Project.

    ❷ All the signals that were sent from each Track's Master Echo component.

    ❸ All the signals that were sent from each Track's Master Reverb component.

- The Track Echo Effect is a fixed Plugin ❹ that you cannot change to a different Effect. However you can change its configuration and save/recall them as Plug-In Settings. You can also bypass the whole Plugin.

- The Track Reverb Effect is also a fixed Plugin ❺ that you cannot change to a different Effect. You can change its configurations and save/recall them as Plugin Settings. You can also bypass the whole Plug-in.

- The Master Effects unit has four Plugin slots ❻. However, you can only choose the first one yourself, the other three Plugins are fixed. Changing the order is also not possible.

- The Track Header for the Master Track has no further controls ❼ except for the Automation (discussed in the Automation chapter).

- The Master Volume and the Meter ❽ for the Master output is located on the Control Bar. Please note that it is positioned in the signal flow after the Master Track Volume Automation and not controlled by that Automation.

- The output is going directly to the Output Audio Device ❾ that has been selected in the Preferences window. This is the same signal that will be exported as an audio file.

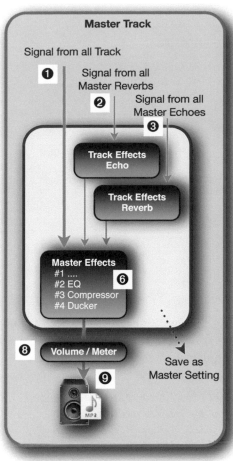

Master Track

Signal from all Track

❶ Signal from all Master Reverbs

❷ Signal from all Master Echoes

❸

Track Effects Echo

Track Effects Reverb

Master Effects
#1 ....
#2 EQ ❻
#3 Compressor
#4 Ducker

❽ Volume / Meter

Save as Master Setting

❾

Track Header

❼

Controls Bar

❽

Track Info Window

➡ Edit Tab

The Edit tab, like in the MIDI and Audio Track, contains the components of the signal flow.

The interface for the Plugins behaves the same as for the other Tracks.

➡ *Browse Tab*

You can also save the Setting of a Master Track as a "Master Setting" in the same way as you store the Settings for a MIDI Track or Audio Track. The interface is the same with the Library popup menu and the two columns ❶. The save button however at the bottom is now called "**Save Master...**" ❷

The Browse window also contains the main parameters for a Project ❸: Tempo, Time Signature, Key Signature. You can change them right there in addition to the LCD controls

LCD on the Control Bar

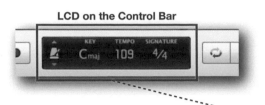

Movie Track - Podcast Track

The Track Info window is also used for the Movie Track and the Podcast Track. However, those Tracks don't represent a Channel Strip of an audio mixer, so no signal is running through them. Therefore, their Track Header ❹ contains no audio controls and the Track Info window only displays six text boxes ❺ to enter information about the Movie or Podcast.

For Both Tracks, you have the Master Track tab ❻ in the Track Info window, where you can switch the window to display the Master Track controls.

Track Header

Track Header

Track Info Window

Track Info Window

Now we move on to the second most important element in a DAW, the Regions. We learned in the previous chapter how to gather our band (represented by the Tracks). Now it is time we give them something to play, the Regions. Here is the simple concept.

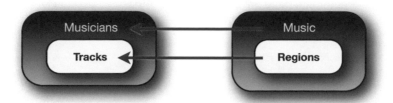

The Regions are the building blocks of your song, similar to a score or lead sheet that has the music content written on it. You hand them out to each musician in a band or orchestra so they know what to play. The same way you put the score for each musician on his or her music stand, you put the Regions for each Track on its Track Lane. This way you determine what Regions are played by which Track.

Arrange Window

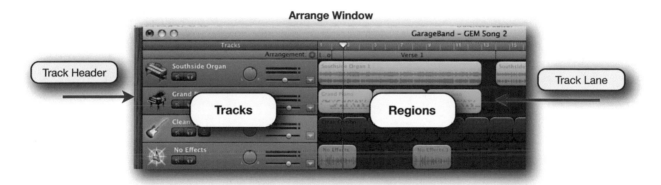

What is a Region

The basic concept and use of Regions is pretty much the same with all the DAWs. These are the basics:

- A Region is represented by a rectangle on the Track's Track Lane.
- You can think of the Region as a container that holds the information (music) for the Track, telling it what to play.
- Another model is to think of a Region as a music score with one long single piece of paper, reading the notes from left to right.
- The length of the Region defines the length of the "musical instruction" for the Track.
- The beginning of a Region doesn't necessarily mean that the Track starts to play right away. If the instruction says "pause for two bars" then you won't hear anything in the first two bars from the musician either.
- In the previous chapter I also compared the Track Lane to the tape of a tape recorder. Recording a guitar solo at 1 minute into the song would be the same as recording the guitar solo at 1 minute on the Track Lane in the form of an Audio Region. The advantage with a DAW however, is that you can move that Region later to any place in the song, something that isn't possible with tape based recording.
- The "musical instruction" for a Track can be one long Region or many shorter Regions that are placed on the Track Lane only at the position where the Track has to play something. This way, you get a visual representation of your arrangement where you can quickly see what Track is playing and when.
- The Regions are also color coded which provides an additional indication what kind of Regions are placed (and play) at what part of the song. The different colors hint at different purposes of the Region.
- The most important thing however is to understand that there are two fundamentally different types of Regions.

The Regions I'm focusing on in this section are the two types that contain the "musical information" in the form of MIDI or Audio.

We already learned in the Track chapter that there are two main types of Tracks, MIDI Tracks and Audio Tracks. The same distinction exists for Regions. There are MIDI Regions and Audio Regions.

Although they look and behave similarly in a lot of ways, there are some fundamental differences that need to be understood.

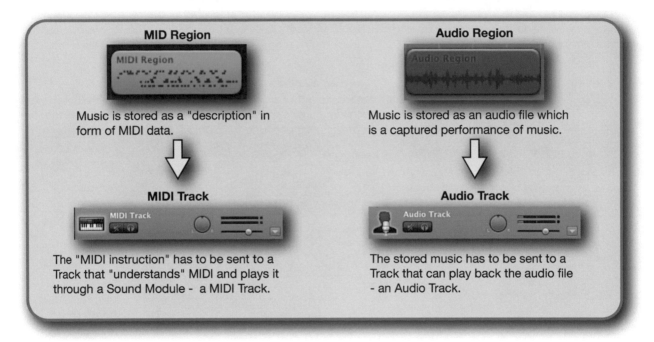

Maybe it's clear by now why I have a problem with the terminology that GarageBand uses for Tracks. If Apple would stick with the established terms "Audio" and "MIDI", the whole concept would be much more understandable even for the casual DAW user. You place MIDI Regions on MIDI Tracks and Audio Regions on Audio Tracks. It is that simple.

If you want simplicity, here is a simple analogy with trucks.

For example, a freight truck and a fuel truck are both trucks that carry content from A to B. They have many similarities but the content they carry is quite different and not really compatible. You cannot load fuel onto a freight truck or boxes onto a fuel truck. We will find out in a minute what the exact distinction between a MIDI Region and an Audio Region is.

Where do Regions come from?

We now understand that Regions are the building blocks of your song and contain musical information in the form of MIDI or Audio data. The next question is, who is creating the Regions and when are they created.

GarageBand creates a new Region whenever you ...

- **Record** something in GarageBand.
  - If you record a MIDI signal, then GarageBand creates a new MIDI Region for that.
  - If you record an Audio signal, then GarageBand creates a new Audio Region for that.
- **Drag** an existing file to your GarageBand project.
  - If you drag an existing MIDI File onto your Project, then GarageBand creates a new MIDI Region for that.
  - If you drag an existing Audio File onto your Project, then GarageBand creates a new Audio Region for that.

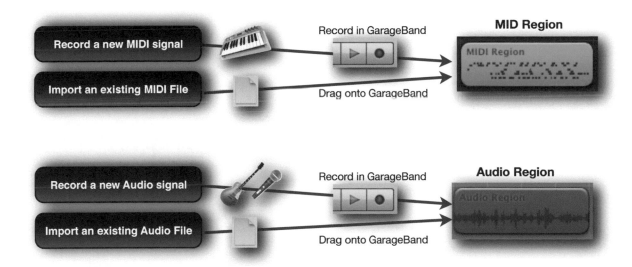

This is pretty simple and straight forward. The procedure for MIDI Regions and Audio Regions looks the same. MIDI Regions contain MIDI information and Audio Regions contain audio information, right?. No, this is not the case. There is a fundamental difference between those two types of Regions regarding what they represent and what they actually "store" inside. This misconception often leads to confusion. So let's look inside those Regions.

What's in a Region

⚬ MIDI Region

A MIDI Region in your Project functions like a container that holds MIDI data. This is the musical content we already talked about. Moving that Region on the Track Lane or copying it affects the Region as a whole and therefore moves or copies all its MIDI data inside with it. You can actually "see" the MIDI data on a Region as little dots that indicate (very vaguely) where MIDI data is present along the Regions timeline.

When you save your Project all that MIDI data (all your "MIDI music") is saved with the GarageBand Project File.

⚬ Audio Region

An Audio Region is also a container and it looks like that it contains the actual audio data. The Region is displaying the audio waveform of the audio inside. But this is misleading

An Audio Region does not contain audio data !

The audio data of that Region is stored in a separate audio file. The Audio Region contains only the instruction "where to start that audio file" and "how long to play that audio file" and of course the link to the actual audio file. Only this reference information is stored in an Audio Region. The visual audio waveform on the Audio Region displays that audio signal so you have a reference against the Timeline.

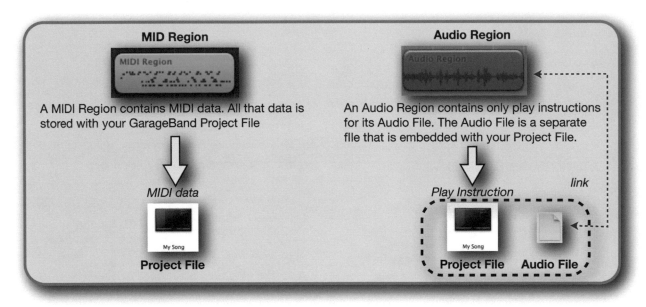

Here is another diagram that shows the connection between the Audio Region and the Audio File. Please note that you can have multiple Audio Regions linking to the same Audio File. The Regions might have different instructions for that audio file, i.e. play the first 30s or play the last 45s. GarageBand never touches (alters, changes) the Audio File. I cover that in the next chapter about Region editing.

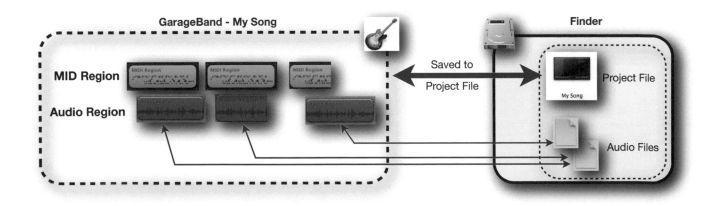

Getting Regions onto the Track Lane

Now let's go back to the two procedures that create Regions on the Track Lane.

☑ Use **existing** content - dragging Audio or MIDI files to your Project.

☑ Create **new** content - recording Audio or MIDI.

➡ *Use existing Content*

This is the easiest way to create a song because it doesn't require that you play any instrument. You can use existing files, audio files and MIDI files, that you just drag onto the Track Lane. The only thing you have to pay attention to is:

| Drag a MIDI File only onto a MIDI Track | Drag an Audio File only onto an Audio Track |

Arrange Window

To add an existing file to your Project, use any of these three sources:

❶ Drag a file from the Finder directly onto the Track Lane

❷ Drag a file from the Media Browser to the Track Lane

❸ Drag a file from the Loop Browser to the Track Lane

➡ *Create new Content*

Creating new content in GarageBand means "recording". And again, there are two different signals that we can record in GarageBand: MIDI signals and Audio signals.

Record a MIDI signal to a MIDI Track	Record an Audio signal to an Audio Track

I already explained the different anatomy of a MIDI Track and an Audio Track in the previous chapter. Now let's look again at each signal flow with a focus on the recording process to understand one very important fact:

> **Regions are recorded as a "dry" signal**

- ◉ The input signal (MIDI or Audio) will be recorded onto the Track Lane ❶. This is where the Region will be created.

- ◉ The incoming MIDI signal will be recorded as it is without going through any components, while the incoming Audio signal passes through two components ❷, the Input Source Selection (that determines which Audio Device will be recorded) and the Recording Level (that determines the level of the recorded audio signal).

- ◉ It is very important to understand (and to follow on the diagram) that all the signal processing on a Track is happening AFTER the Track Lane ❸ without any influence on the created (recorded) Region.

  - The sound of the selected sound generator ❹ that you hear while you are recording your MIDI keyboard will not be recorded, only the MIDI data of the notes you are playing (and additional controllers like Mod Wheel and Pitch Bend). That's why you can change the sound anytime after you recorded your MIDI Region.

  - The sound of the selected guitar amp ❺ that you hear while you are recording your electric guitar will not be recorded! You are recording your guitar "dry", the way it comes into your computer. That's why you can change the amp anytime after you recorded your guitar (which would not be possible if you recorded a guitar amp with a microphone).

  - Whatever signal you record with a microphone will also be recorded "dry" the way it enters GarageBand.

- ◉ Any Effect and Master Sends ❻ will not be part of what you are recording. They are not affecting the recorded Region.

- ◉ Also keep in mind that when you record an audio signal, the Volume and Pan controls on the Track Header ❼ have no affect on the actual recording. They control the signal after the recording. This is also a common misconception. Only the Recording Level slider ❷ controls the level of the recorded signal in GarageBand.

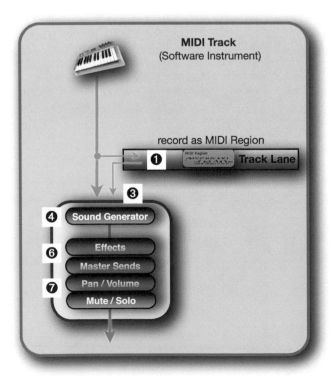

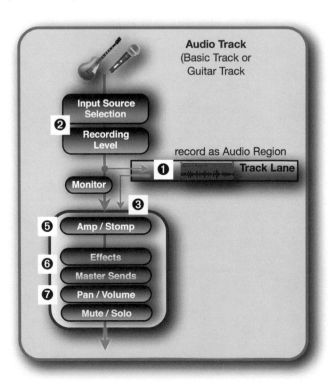

MIDI Regions

 Record New

The newly created Region will contain the recorded MIDI information and that is stored with your GarageBand Project.

 Import MIDI Files

If you drag a MIDI file onto the Track Lane, GarageBand creates a new MIDI Region at the time position where you dragged the file to. The MIDI information from the MIDI file will be extracted and placed on that new MIDI Region. That new MIDI Region with its content is now part of your GarageBand Project and saved with the Project File.

The MIDI File that you drag onto your Project stays untouched. The file itself didn't move, you only copied its MIDI content.

Audio Regions

 Record New

GarageBand creates two things.

- ☑ **Audio File**: The newly recorded audio signal is saved as a new Audio File. That Audio File is not visible because it is embedded in the Project File in the separate Media folder.
- ☑ **Audio Region**: This Region will be created "in front of your eyes" while you are recording. It will refer to its linked Audio File and the play instruction will initially be: "start the Audio File from the beginning and play all the way through".

 Import Audio File

The procedure is a little bit different when you drag an existing Audio File onto the Track Lane.

- ☑ **Audio File**: The Audio File doesn't have to be created because it exists already. GarageBand however copies that Audio file to the current Project File, to the same Media folder where it places the newly recorded Audio Files. Audio Loops are not moved to the Project's Media Folder by default!
- ☑ **Audio Region**: GarageBand creates a new Audio Region at the time position you dragged the file to. The length of the Region depends on the length of the original Audio File. This new Audio Region contains a link to the Audio File (its location in the Media folder) and the play instruction: "start the Audio File from the beginning and play all the way through".

Two things to keep in mind about Audio Files:

- The more audio you are recording or importing into your Project, the more the size of your Project File will increase. Setting the audio format to 16bit instead of 24bit for newly created Audio Files (select GarageBand ➤ Preferences ➤ Advanced ➤ Audio Resolution ➤ Good uses less space.

- Apple Loops are Audio Files that are not imported into the GarageBand Project File. This has a potential danger of breaking the link between the Audio File and the Audio Region if you move your GarageBand Project to a different machine, change the location or name of the original Apple Loop file. To embed those Audio Files into your Project, you have to save your Project with the "Save As..." command and check the "Archive Project" checkbox.

Now that we have a basic understanding of Regions, let's look at the steps of a simple MIDI Recording:

☑ Select the MIDI source you want to record.
☑ Select the MIDI Track you want to record to.
 • Optional: Set the sound on that Track. Remember, the sound settings will not be recorded!
☑ Place the Playhead at the position in your song where you want to record.
 • Optional: choose the Metronome, Count-in and set a comfortable playback mix for the other tracks.
☑ Start Recording

MIDI Source

I covered the topic of the MIDI Input in the <u>Hardware</u> Chapter and explained how to select an external MIDI Keyboard. However, you don't need an external MIDI Keyboard to record a MIDI signal in GarageBand. You have actually three input options:

 External MIDI Keyboard

The standard method is using an external MIDI Keyboard that is connected directly to the USB port, or via a MIDI interface that is connect to the USB port on your computer.

  MIDI Keyboard
 USB Keyboard

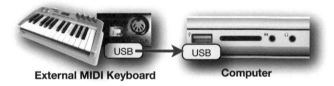

External MIDI Keyboard **Computer**

 **Mouse (onscreen)**

You can also use your mouse to play on a virtual Keyboard in GarageBand. This is very limited but gives you the option to quickly input some MIDI notes for those occasions when you don't have an external MIDI Keyboard available. The following commands will open a separate window with a software keyboard that you can click on with your mouse.

 Menu Command Window ➤ Keyboard
 Key Command **cmd+K**
 Once the window is open, you can also use the two buttons on that window to switch between the Keyboard window and the Musical Typing window.

Keyboard

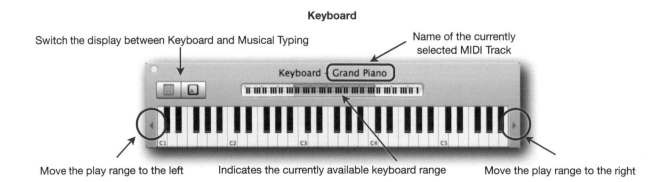

Switch the display between Keyboard and Musical Typing

Name of the currently selected MIDI Track

Move the play range to the left   Indicates the currently available keyboard range   Move the play range to the right

Computer Keyboard

Instead of using your mouse and clicking on a virtual keyboard, you can also use your computer keyboard to enter MIDI notes. This method gives you a few more options. Open the Musical Typing window with any of these commands:

- Menu Command Window ➤ Musical Typing
- Key Command sh+cmd+K
- Press the button on the Musical Typing Window

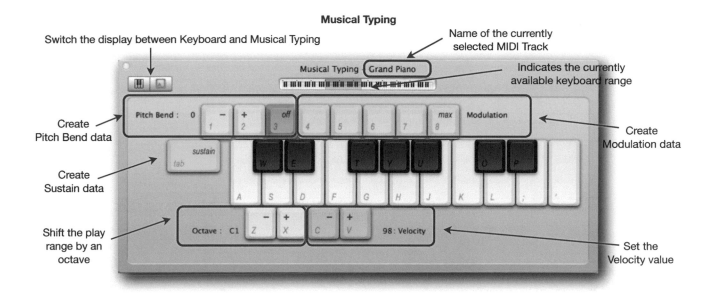

Musical Typing

Switch the display between Keyboard and Musical Typing

Name of the currently selected MIDI Track

Musical Typing : Grand Piano

Indicates the currently available keyboard range

Create Pitch Bend data

Create Modulation data

Create Sustain data

Shift the play range by an octave

Set the Velocity value

MIDI Track selection

To record on a specific MIDI Track, just select that Track in the Track Header and start recording.

You can only record one MIDI track at a time. GarageBand provides a Multitrack Recording feature but that applies to eight Audio Track pus one MIDI Track.

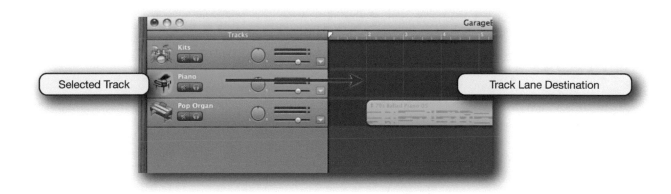

Selected Track

Track Lane Destination

MIDI Region Creation Process

Now let's see what is exactly happening during the recording process:

- When you start recording, GarageBand creates a new red Region starting at the Playhead position. That Region "grows" with the moving Playhead until you stop recording.
- If GarageBand doesn't receive any MIDI signal during the recording, the red Region will disappear. No Region has been created.
- If GarageBand received any MIDI signal during the recording, the following rules apply:
  - The left border of the newly created Region will be the bar at which you sent your first MIDI signal. For example, if you started recording at bar 1, but played your first note on the second beat of bar 3, then the newly created Region will start at bar 3.
  - The right border of the newly created Region will be at the end of the bar of your last MIDI signal. For example, if you recorded to bar 7 but your last played note was at beat 2 of bar 5, then the newly created Region will end at bar 6.
  - The newly created Region will change its color to green. The red color only indicates an ongoing recording.
- You can create an empty MIDI Region with a **cmd+click** on the Track Lane of a MIDI Track. The new MIDI Region will be one bar long.
- A newly recorded Region will be given the name of the Track it is recorded on.
- The MIDI Region displays the actual MIDI Notes on the Region. However this is only a rough indication to see where MIDI "activity" is and how much.

MIDI Region creation

► **Import MIDI File**

A few things to look out for when you drag an existing MIDI file onto the Track Lane instead of recording a new one.

A MIDI File has the file extension *.mid* but no further indication about its MIDI content. GarageBand reacts differently when creating the MIDI Region depending on the content of the MIDI files:

- **MIDI File contains one Region on a single Track**

  You can drag the File onto the Track Lane and GarageBand creates exactly that MIDI Region that was contained in the MIDI File.

  If you drag the File onto the un-assigned Track Lane area, then GarageBand will create a new MIDI Track before putting that MIDI Region on it.

- **MIDI File contains multiple Regions on a single Track**

  GarageBand seems to be able to extract only the first Region of such a MIDI File.

- **MIDI File contains multiple Tracks**

  This kind of MIDI file cannot be dragged onto a Track Lane. Instead, it has to be dragged onto the un-assigned area below the last Track in the Timeline Area. GarageBand will then create as many new Tracks that were contained in the MIDI File and put the Region on those new MIDI Tracks.

Although the process of recording Audio is similar to recording MIDI, you have to keep the previously discussed difference between Audio and MIDI Regions in mind:

☑ Choose which one of the two specific Audio Tracks you want to record.
  - Basic Track (Real Instrument) for recording signals through a microphone.
  - Guitar Track (Electric Guitar) for recording an electric guitar using GarageBand's amp simulation.

☑ Select the Input Source and adjust the Level in the Track Info window.
  - Optional: Set the sound on that Track. Remember, the sound settings will not be recorded!
  - Select if you need to enable Monitoring.

☑ Place the Playhead at the position in your song where you want to record.
  - Optional: Choose the Metronome, Count-In and set a comfortable playback mix of the other tracks.

☑ Start Recording

Audio Track selection

To record on a specific Audio Track (blue), just select that Track in the Track Header and start recording.

Single Track Recording

Selected Track — Track Lane Destination

Multitrack Recording

Record Enabled

You can only record on one (selected) Audio track at a time. However, you can enable the Multitrack Recording feature that allows you to record up to eight Audio Tracks plus one MIDI Track at a time.

  ⚲ Menu Command Track ➤ Enable/Disable Multitrack Recording
  ⚲ Key Command opt+cmd+R

If enabled, each Track displays a Record Enable button on the Track Header that can be selected for the Tracks you want to record.

Audio Source

I covered the topic of the Audio Input in the <u>Hardware</u> chapter.

When recording more than one track in Multitrack Recording mode, you have to make sure that you use an audio interface that provides multiple audio inputs. Each record enabled Track has to be set to a different input channel. If you select the same input for two Tracks, you will get an alert message

Can't enable Track for Recording
The input channel of this track is already in use. To record on this track, choose another input channel.

OK

Audio Region Creation Process

Whenever you are dealing with Audio Regions, keep in mind that "invisible" Audio File that it is representing. Let's pay special attention to that when we look at the creation process of an Audio Region:

○ When you start recording on an Audio Track, GarageBand creates a new red Region ❶ starting at the Playhead position. That Region "grows" with the moving Playhead until you stop recording.

○ That growing Region in front of you is a representation what happens in the background. While you are recording, GarageBand creates a new Audio File ❷ that is embedded inside your Project File ❸.

○ When you stop the recording, the red Region turns purple ❹, indicating that the recording process is finished and that the following things happened:

  • A new Audio File has been created inside the Project File ❸ with what you've just recorded.

  • The new purple Audio Region is now linked ❺ to that Audio File.

  • The new Audio Region is given the name ❻ of the Audio Track. Please note that every new Region you record on a Track will get that same name. You might want to properly rename the Region afterwards.

  • The Audio Region's initial "play instruction" for its linked Audio File is "*play the Audio File from the beginning* ❼ *and play it all the way to the end* ❽". Therefore the length of the newly created Audio Region represents the total length of the new Audio File.

○ When you delete that Audio Region (maybe you didn't like what you just recorded), then its linked Audio File will also be automatically deleted.

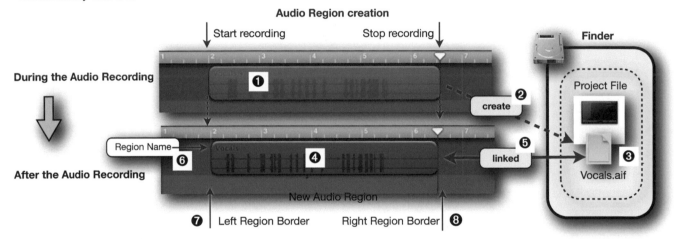

▶ **Drag in an existing Audio File**

Here is a slightly different procedure when dragging an existing Audio File into the Project.

○ A new Audio Region will be created with the name of the Audio File at the location where you dropped it on the Track Lane with the length representing the imported Audio File.

○ If the Audio File is a regular Audio File.

  • GarageBand makes a copy of that Audio File and places it into the Project File.

  • The new Audio Region has the color yellow and is linked now to that copied Audio File.

○ If the Audio File is an Apple Loop.

  • GarageBand leaves the Apple Loop file at its original location (you can copy it to the Project File too with the "Save as" command using the Archive option).

  • The new Audio Region has the color blue and is linked to that Apple Loop file.

The procedure we just discussed, recording a new signal and GarageBand creates a new Region, is just the basic procedure when there are no Regions on the Track Lane yet. However, what if there are already Regions on the Track Lane, how does GarageBand behave under those circumstances? The answer is, it depends. It depends on a few factors and you have to look at the big picture to understand and predict what will happen to your new recording (the new Region) and especially what will happen to your existing recording (the existing Region).

Three Recording Modes

GarageBand provides three different modes. Unfortunately, once you understand those modes, it is not as simple as selecting one of them from a popup menu. The actual mode that applies to the recording depends on a combination of various settings. Let's start first with the understanding of what those modes are.

Replace	**Create Takes**	**Merge**
The existing Region will be replaced with the new Region that contains the new recording.	A new Region will be added to the existing Region as a new independent "Take". You can choose later which one of those Regions (Take) you want to use in your Song.	The new recording will be added to the existing Region, they will be merged. This mode is only available for MIDI Regions.

Replace

The behavior in replace mode is similar for MIDI Regions and Audio Regions but the consequences are different.

➡ MIDI Regions

Here is an example that demonstrates what happens.

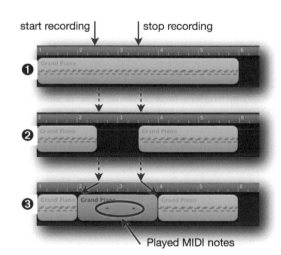

start recording | stop recording

Played MIDI notes

❶ The first screenshot shows an existing Region that starts at bar 1 and ends at bar 6. We will start the new recording on that same Track on the second beat of bar 2 and stop recording at the third beat of bar 3.

❷ If we do that, but we don't play any new MIDI notes on our keyboard, the following will happen.

- The exact range (from rec-in to rec-out) will be replaced with what we just played - nothing. The original Region is cut in two Regions. Please note that there is no rounding to the beginning of the bars.

- The previous notes of that section are deleted, cut out. However, you can bring them back with the Undo command.

❸ Now we do the same recording procedure, but this time we play two notes. You can see them as two little dots on the Region.

- This time, the newly created Region (with the two notes) will be rounded to the full bar. The new Region starts exactly on bar 2 and ends on bar 4. This is the same rounding behavior when you record a Region on an empty Track Lane.

- Again, the section of the existing Region we recorded over will be deleted. Due to the rounding which always makes the Region longer than the recorded section, more notes of the existing Region will be deleted.

➡ *Audio Regions*

I did a similar recording procedure but now with Audio Regions, recording an audio signal on an Audio Track. This time, we have to take into account that an Audio Region is fundamentally different from a MIDI Region.

❶ We start with a similar setup. The Audio Region is 6 bars long and we will record over that Region between beat 3 of bar 2 and beat 3 of bar 3.

❷ First, let's simulate the same what we did with the MIDI recording. Recording without playing anything. Here is the first difference. MIDI represents data and no MIDI data means no data and therefore nothing to put onto a Region. With audio, this is different. If you hook up a microphone to a track, record for a minute but don't sing into the microphone, technically you recorded something even though nothing audible was recorded (maybe picking up the sound of the air conditioner).

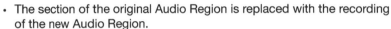

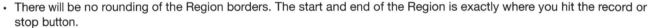

❸ In this screenshot, I made some noise in front of the microphone which is now recorded (and displayed on the Region) as a signal. GarageBand doesn't care what you recorded, the important thing is that you created an audio file which is represented by an Audio Region. In both cases the following applies:

- The section of the original Audio Region is replaced with the recording of the new Audio Region.

- There will be no rounding of the Region borders. The start and end of the Region is exactly where you hit the record or stop button.

- However, while MIDI data will be deleted when you record over it, with Audio Regions, no audio data will be deleted at all! This makes sense if you remember what an Audio Region is.

Here is a Recap:

🎤 **MID Region**	🎤 **Audio Region**
A MIDI Region contains the actual MIDI data, the musical Instruction.	An Audio Region contains a link to an Audio File with the instruction what section of that Audio File to play.

Here are the two Audio Regions again. Example ❹ is one Region with the instruction to play the Audio File (the file stored on your drive, shown here as a red waveform) from the beginning ❻ to the end ❾.

In example ❺, the original Region was recorded over (with a new Region in the middle). Here comes the important part. Nothing happened to the Audio File. Only the Audio Region changed. Now the first Region has the instruction "play the Audio File from ❻ to ❼. Then a new Audio Region takes over with its own instruction to play a different Audio File (not shown here). After that, the third Audio Region takes over. This one refers to the same Audio File as the first Audio Region ❹ but now with the instruction "play the Audio File from ❽ to ❾".

I hope this makes it clear that the Audio Region only changes the instruction for the Audio File but never alters the Audio File itself.

The only exception is when you delete the whole Audio Region in your Project. Then the Audio File will be deleted too. If nothing in your song refers to a specific Audio File anymore, then there is no use for it anyway.

Create Takes

In this recording mode the MIDI Region and Audio Region behave the same.

The concept is very simple and useful. When you record on tape, you only can record one "version" on a specific track. After you recorded a guitar solo, you had to decide if you wanted to keep it or record it again, which meant, delete the previous version by recording over it. You could only keep the last version unless you recorded on another track.

One of the advantages of hard disk recording is that you can record multiple versions of a guitar solo and keep them all. Then you can decide later which one you want to use at the end in your final mix, or different versions for different mixes.

The term "Take" is borrowed from film making where the camera man shoots different "takes" of the same scene, so the director can decide later during the editing process which Take he wants to use.

This is the basic procedure:

- ☑ You record a guitar solo on the guitar Track. GarageBand creates a Region for that recording.
- ☑ You record the guitar solo again on the same Track. Instead of replacing the first recording, it keeps it as "Take 1" and records the new solo as "Take 2". Although GarageBand uses Take 2 (the last recording) as the active Region, you can after that switch to Take 1 if you prefer the first solo.
- ☑ You could go on and record the guitar solo three more times. GarageBand just adds those recordings as "Take 3", "Take 4" and "Take 5" etc.

And here is how it looks like in GarageBand.

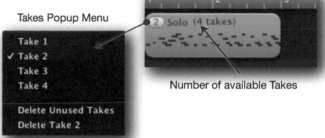

Takes Popup Menu

Number of available Takes

- The Region indicates in parenthesis next to its name how many takes are included in that Take Region. In this example "(4 takes)"
- The yellow number Tag indicates which Take is currently active (played).
- Click on that tag to open the Takes popup menu.
  - Select any Take to make it the active one.
  - Select "*Delete Unused Takes*" to delete all the Takes except the currently active one. For example if you decided that the current Take is the best one and you don't need the other Takes anymore (saves up hard drive space too).
  - Select "*Delete Take n*" to delete the currently active Take. For example, if the current Take is so bad that you definitely don't need it anymore.

➡ *Activate Take Recording*

To activate the Take Recording mode, you have to turn on Cycle Mode. Toggle the Cycle Mode by clicking on the Cycle button in the control bar or use the Key Command **C**. The yellow cycle bar will slide out underneath the timeline where you can edit the cycle range.

To link the Cycle Mode to the Take recording mode makes sense because you can record the same section a few times, play the solo part five times without interacting with GarageBand. After that you just select the best Take or record a few versions more.

- You record over an existing (regular) Region while in Cycle Mode and it will add the new recordings as Takes.
- You can even record over two separate Regions and they will be merged as one long Region (Take 1) with the new recording as Take 2.

Although Take Recording behaves the same for MIDI Regions and Audio Regions, always keep in mind what the Regions represent (containers for MIDI data vs containers for play instruction for a specific Audio File).

Merge

This recording mode is only available for MIDI Tracks and not for recording Audio Tracks!

It allows you to add the newly recorded MIDI signal to an already existing MIDI Region. This is especially useful when recording layered instruments or MIDI drums. You can record the bass drum and snare first and then record the section again to play the HiHat and so on. Every new note you record will be merged with the other MIDI notes on the existing Region.

Of course, this is very useful when you're in Cycle Mode, so you don't have to start and stop recording. You can use the Merge recording to start with a new Region (to fill it up), or add another layer to an existing Region.

➡ *Activate Merge Mode*

As I mentioned before, it is not as simple as selecting "Merge Mode" from a Recording popup menu. Instead you have to meet two conditions in order to record in this mode:

- ☑ Activate Cycle Mode
- ☑ Select the check box in the *GarageBand* ➤ *Preferences* ➤ *General* ➤ *Cycle Recording*

Overview

Here is a final overview of all the three recording modes and what setting has to be enabled

Record Mode	Cycle	Cycle Preference
Replace	-	-
Create Take	on	-
Merge	on	on

Multitrack Recording

In the Standard Recording Mode, GarageBand records on the Track that is selected, which means one track at a time. There is no need for a "Record Enable" button. Whatever Track is selected, that is the one that gets recorded on (Audio or MIDI).

But GarageBand also provides a Multitrack Recording Mode in case you want to record your vocals and your keyboard playing at the same time. You can record up to 8 Audio Tracks and 1 MIDI Track at the same time. This enables you to record a small band simultaneously.

- ☑ Enable Multitrack Mode. This adds a "Record Enable" button to the Track Header of each Track.
  - Menu Command Track ➤ Enable Multitrack Recording
  - Key Command opt+cmd+R
- ☑ Enable the "Record Enable" button on the Tracks you want to record (button turns red).
- ☑ Select the proper Audio Input in the Track Info pane for the selected Tracks (this requires a multichannel Audio Device).
- ☑ Start Recording as usual.

8 - Edit Regions ... on the Track Lane

We just learned step one, how to create a new Region. In this chapter, I cover the basic editing of the Regions, what we can do *with* a Region or do *to* a Region as a whole. The next chapter covers the editing of what's inside a Region.

Before we edit any Region on the Track Lane, let's make sure to recognize all the different Regions by their color code.

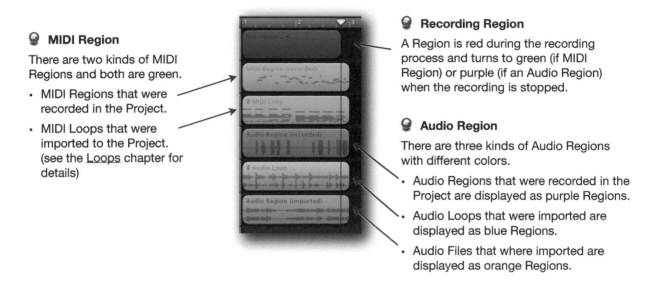

MIDI Region

There are two kinds of MIDI Regions and both are green.

- MIDI Regions that were recorded in the Project.
- MIDI Loops that were imported to the Project. (see the Loops chapter for details)

Recording Region

A Region is red during the recording process and turns to green (if MIDI Region) or purple (if an Audio Region) when the recording is stopped.

Audio Region

There are three kinds of Audio Regions with different colors.

- Audio Regions that were recorded in the Project are displayed as purple Regions.
- Audio Loops that were imported are displayed as blue Regions.
- Audio Files that where imported are displayed as orange Regions.

The Region editing on the Track Lane is basically the same for all the different Regions. There are only a few exceptions that I will point out later.

Before you apply any of the editing commands, you have to tell the computer what Region you want to edit by selecting it. This procedure is common to virtually all software applications: Any edit command applies only to the selected object(s).

Here are the basic commands for selecting Regions:

 Click on one Region to select a single Region. Selected Regions have a more glowing color.

 Sh+click on multiple Regions in a sequence to select them all. This also works for selecting multiple Regions on different Tracks. Click again to deselect individual Regions from that group.

 Click-drag an area around Regions ("lasso around them") to select them all.

 Click on the Track Header to select all the Regions on that Track.

Any edit you apply can be undone with the Undo command. You can apply this command multiple times to undo the last few edits in a sequence or use the "Redo" command to "redo the undo":

 Undo/Redo Menu Command Edit ➤ Undo or Edit ➤ Redo

 Undo Key Command **cmd+Z** or Redo Key Command **sh+cmd+Z**

Alignment Guide

Alignment Guides

GarageBand provides a feature that assists with any kind of movement of Regions (but also other Objects). The Region that you are moving will snap to any other Region in the Timeline Area to align with it. This works with both the beginning and ending of Regions. The alignments will be indicated with yellow Alignment Guides.

 Menu Command Control ➤ Show/Hide Alignment Guides

 Key Command **sh+cmd+G**

Regions on the Track Lane

Here are all the editing commands that you can apply to a Region. You are not changing the content (the actual music) of the Region but rather the arrangement and placement of the Region as a whole.

➡ Delete Regions

Let's start with an often used edit. You created a Region (recorded or imported) but you don't like it and want to get rid of it. You just delete the Region. There are two commands for deleting Regions on the Track Lane.

Standard Delete: This just deletes the selected Region(s).

 Menu Command Edit ➤ Delete

 Key Command delete

Delete and Move: This deletes the selected Region(s) and moves any existing Region at a later position on that Track to the left. How far they are moved to the left is determined by the length of the deleted Region(s).

 Menu Command Edit ➤ Delete and Move

 Key Command ctr+delete

➡ Move Regions

You can move a Region either to a new position on the same Track (horizontally) and/or to a different Track (vertically) by **click+dragging** the Region(s). Here are the rules and restrictions:

- MIDI Regions can be dragged vertically only to another MIDI Track (Software Instrument).
- Audio Regions can be dragged vertically only to another Audio Track (Real Instrument or Electric Guitar).
- When moving a Region on top of another existing Region, it will erase that Region or the overlapping part of it.

  Remember the procedure when recording "over existing Regions". The same rules apply when you move a Region over another Region. The shortened Audio Region will update its play instruction for the (unaffected) Audio File while a shortened MIDI Region will lose its MIDI notes for that section.

➡ Copy Regions

Opt+drag Region

There are two standard commands for copying Regions:

 Opt+drag the Region(s) to the new position.

 Use the Copy-Paste command either from the Edit Menu or use the Key Commands **cmd+C** (copy) and **cmd+V** (paste). The Region(s) will be placed at the Playhead position of the currently selected Track.

And of course, Regions can only be copied to the same Track Type (MIDI or Audio). The same overwrite rules apply.

➡ Split Regions

This command splits all the selected Regions at the Playhead position into two Regions, even across multiple Tracks. Splitting an existing Region is useful, when you want to move or copy only a portion of a Region or want to edit only a section of it (i.e. special quantize rules). The commands are:

 Menu Command Edit ➤ Split

 Key Command **cmd+T**

Please note

- Notes in a MIDI Region that extend beyond a Split point will be shortened so they end at the split point.
- The Split Command is not available for a Video Region on a Video Track because GarageBand can contain only one single Video Region.

➡ *Join Regions*

This command can only be applied to selected Regions on a single Track. Select one or multiple Regions (with or without gaps in between) and use any of the commands:

- 🔘 Menu Command `Edit` ➤ `Join`
- 🔘 Key Command **cmd+J**

Please note:

- • MIDI Regions: Creates a new MIDI Region containing all the existing MIDI data.
- • Audio Regions: GarageBand creates a new Audio File that is represented by the newly combined Audio Region.

➡ *Trim (Resize) Regions*

Drag the lower left or lower right border of a Region to shorten or lengthen the Region. The context-sensitive Cursor changes to the Resize Tool. Please note the different rules for MIDI and Audio Regions:

Trim Region

- 🔘 **MIDI Regions**

    Dragging the right edge of a MIDI Region will shorten it and it will look like you are deleting existing MIDI data. However, that MIDI information will NOT be deleted. The Region will just stop playing them but they are still there (like muted). Dragging the right edge of the Region to the right will reveal any existing MIDI information on that Region or just create empty space.

    The left edge of a MIDI Region has a restriction. You can drag it to the left as far as you want, creating empty space, but you cannot drag the left edge to the right beyond the first MIDI data!

- 🔘 **Audio Regions**

    Audio Regions have different trimming restrictions based on what an Audio Region is. We know by know (hopefully) that an Audio Region doesn't contain audio data, only the instruction to its linked Audio File, where to start playing that Audio File and for how long. Based on that concept, you can resize the left or right edge of an Audio Region freely, because you only change the play instructions. The only limitation is based on the Audio File that the Audio Region is representing (linked to):

    - • You cannot extend the left edge of the Region beyond the beginning of the actual Audio File.
    - • You cannot extend the right edge of the Region beyond the end of the actual Audio File.
    - • The Region cannot be longer than the actual Audio File.

➡ *Loop Region*

To "*loop*" a Region is the process of repeating the Region for a specific amount of time. You could accomplish that by copying the Region multiple times and place them one after another. The Loop command does exactly that, just in a more elegant way.

Move the mouse cursor over the right upper corner of the Region you want to loop. The cursor is context-sensitive, which means it knows where you placed it within the Region (in this case, the upper right corner). It changes to the Loop Tool. Dragging the Region with the Loop Tool to the right will lengthen the Region. This way you tell GarageBand up to what position on the timeline it should repeat the Region. This is the position where you release the mouse. The result looks like many Regions aligned in a sequence, but this is actually just one Region (plus its repetitions). A looped sequence doesn't have a separation line between the Regions and also no name.

Please note that If you change the length of the original Region (the first segment in the sequence), the section that repeats and the numbers of its repetitions (amount of Regions) changes to maintain the end position of the sequence.

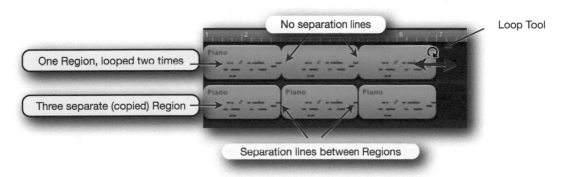

No separation lines — Loop Tool

One Region, looped two times

Three separate (copied) Region

Separation lines between Regions

Arrangement Regions

The Arrangement Track (with its Arrangement Regions) is a special tool for quickly working on the structure of your song. Instead of moving individual Regions around, this lets you apply commands to all Regions across the Tracks in a defined section.

Arrangement Track

Each Project can have only one Arrangement Track which is located at the very first Track in the Track Area. The Track can be shown or hidden from the Track Area with any of the two commands:

- Menu Command Track ➤ Show/Hide Arrangement Track
- Key Command **sh+cmd+A**

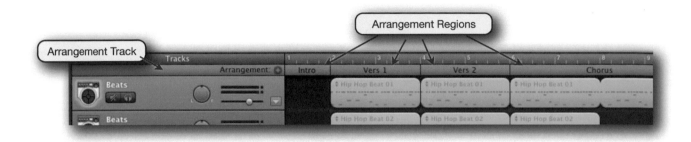

➡ *Edit Arrangement Regions* *(without affecting Regions on the Track Lanes)*

These are the commands that edit only the Arrangement Regions without affecting the Regions below. You use this to create the basic structure of your song.

- **Add Region**: Click the plus button in the Arrangement Track Header. The first Region starts at the beginning of your Song, any additional Regions will be added at the end of the last existing Arrangement Region. There are no gaps between Arrangement Regions.

Add Region

- **Name Region:** Double-click on the Region Name (it will be highlighted) and enter a name.

- **Resize Region:** Drag the boundary between two Arrange Regions. The context-sensitive cursor changes to a Resize Tool.

Resize Regions

➡ *Edit Arrangement Regions and all the Regions below*

Think of the Arrangement Regions as Macros or Placeholders. Whatever command you use on those Arrangement Regions applies to all the Regions (or section of the Regions) on all Tracks that fall inside the range of the Arrangement Region.

Make sure that no Track is locked when you apply any of the following commands or you will get an Alert Window giving you the option to unlock those tracks.

● **Select:** Click on an Arrangement Region to conveniently have all the Regions that fall inside its boundaries selected. If the Arrangement Region boundary falls inside an Audio or MIDI Region, then only that portion will be selected and any command will apply only to that portion of the Region. Please note that this procedure is not possible with any other command. It lets you edit a section of those Regions without splitting them first.

● **Move** an Arrangement Region and all of its Regions underneath by dragging the Arrangement Region along the Timeline. The other Arrangement Regions move out of the way to make space. Moving an Arrangement Region directly onto another Arrangement Region will change the context-sensitive cursor to a green circle with double arrows to indicate that both Arrangement Regions will swap their position when you release the mouse.

Original	Move - Swap	Move - Insert
	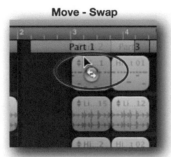	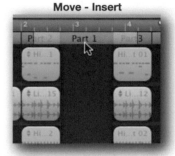
Three Arrangement Regions: Part 1, Part 2, Part 3	Move Part 1 on top of Part 2 will swap both selections indicated by the double arrow pointer.	Move Part 1 between Part 2 and Part 3 will move the Regions apart to make space for the insert.

● **Copy** an Arrangement Region and all of its Regions below by opt+dragging the Arrangement Region along the Timeline. The other Arrangement Regions move out of the way to make space.

Replace

● **Replace** an Arrangement Region and all its containing Regions by cmd+draggin any other Arrangement Region on top of it. If the Arrangement Region you replace and the one you replace it with have different length, then pay attention to the changing color bars. They indicate whether or not you fully replace Regions regardless of their length or if you end up having partial replacements.

● **Delete** an Arrangement Region. There are three conditions.

　📌　Press the delete Key once to delete all the Audio and MIDI Regions below a selected Arrangement Regions.

　📌　Pressing the delete key again (on the now "empty" Arrangement Region) will delete the Arrangement Region and move up all the Regions to the left by that amount to fill the gap.

　📌　Key Command opt+cmd+delete will delete the selected Arrangement Region and, at the same time, all the Regions that fall inside its boundaries. The remaining Regions to the right will move to the left to fill the gap.

Project with Movie Track

Be careful when you work on a Project that has a Movie Track, i.e. when you score music to picture. The Movie Region on the Track (the video clip) will not be included in the Arrangement Region. However if you have an audio track (dialog) of that video imported which is represented as an Audio Region on an Audio Track, then you cannot use the Arrangement commands. Because that Audio Region is also included in any copy, move or replace procedure, it will mess up that audio track (which should be locked to the picture without any changes on the timeline). Unfortunately, you cannot lock or exclude individual Tracks or Regions from those procedures. The only workaround is to move the movie's Audio Region temporarily all the way to the right (outside the area where you're moving stuff around with the Arrangement Regions) and then move it back. The movie clip starts always at bar 1 and moving its Audio Region to bar one restores their sync.

9 - Edit Regions ... in the Editor Pane

All those edits in the previous chapter apply to a Region as a whole. However, the real power unfolds when you start to edit the content of the Region, the "enclosed music" if you will. For that, you have to "open up" the Region and look inside. Whatever you find inside, that is the material you can edit.

 The button that opens up the Region is called the "Track Editor" button. However, you are not editing the Track itself but the Regions on that Track. The button toggles the Editor pane which is the window that slides out from the Control Bar to share the space with the Arrange window.

Open/Close the Editor with any of the following commands to display the detailed view of the selected Track.

- Menu Command Control ➤ Show/Hide Editor
- Key Command **cmd+E**
- Click the Editor button, the one with the scissor icon, on the left side of the Control Bar. The scissor turns blue when the Editor window is open.
- You can also **double-click** on a Region in the Track Lane directly to toggle the Editor pane.
- Once the Editor is open, you just click on any Region in the Arrange window to switch the displayed Track in the Editor window.

➡ *Interface Concept:*

As we know by now, the Arrange window ❶ lists all your Tracks in two sections, the Track Area ❷ with the individual Track Headers on the left that extend to their Track Lane in the Timeline Area ❸. On top of the Timeline Area is the Time Ruler ❹ which is tied to the Track Lanes.

Opening the Edit window ❻ will shrink the size of the Arrange window (they share the same space).

The Editor window acts like an Inspector window similar to the Track Info window. Remember, the concept of an Inspector window is to display content depending on the selection made in another window. Here, the content of the Editor window depends on what Track is selected in the Arrange window ❻.

The Editor window displays that single Track with more detailed information and functionality which allows you to edit the content of the Regions on that Track.

The Editor window is also divided into two section. On the left is the Track Header ❼ which provides specific controls for that Track. To the right is the Track Lane ❽ which is tied to its own Time Ruler above ❾.

The Track Lane in the Editor pane displays the same Regions that you can see on the selected Track in the Arrange window. It just provides you with an alternate view of the Regions that allows you to edit the content of those Regions.

That's it:

To edit the content of any Region on a selected Track, you just open the Editor window. This will display that Track (and all its Regions) in the Editor with its special editing tools. Of course the Editor and its tools will look different for MIDI or Audio Tracks.

Project Window without Editor pane

Project Window with Editor pane

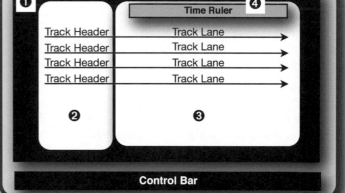

Interface

First, let's look at the basic window elements before getting into the details of the different Editor controls for Audio and MIDI Regions..

Project Window with Editor Pane

- This Project has four Tracks, the third Track is selected **❶**. This is the one that is displayed in the Editor window **❷**.

- On the left of the Editor window is the Track Header **❸**. As you can see, it is different from the Track Header on the Arrange window. Here it displays specific controls to edit the Region's content.

- On the right is the Track Lane **❹**. It functions similar to the Arrange window. It has its own Time Ruler and Playhead **❺** (which are linked to the Arrange window), scroll bars to zoom in and out and even the Grid button **❻** in the upper right corner. On this Track Lane, you can see the same Regions as on the Arrange window's Track Lane. Even the Region selection is linked. (on the screenshot, the second Region is selected **❼** and therefore displayed in a darker color).

Horizontal Zoom Slider

At the bottom of the Track Header is the Zoom Slider to adjust the horizontal zoom of the Track Lane. Remember, the Track Header itself is fixed and cannot be zoomed (same as with the Track Header in the Arrange window).

You can drag the Divider between the Arrange window and Editor window up or down to adjust how much of each window is visible.

Editor - Zoom Slider

Auto-scrolling (Lock Playhead)

If the Arrange Area shows only a portion of your song's length, then the Playhead will "disappear" when it reaches the right edge of the Project. You then have to manually scroll the Timeline Area to view that section. To avoid this constant maneuvering, GarageBand provides an "Auto-scrolling" feature. Now when you play your song, the Playhead stays fixed at the center of the Timeline Area and the Time Ruler with all the Track Lanes scrolls underneath the fixed Playhead. The little double-arrow icon in the lower right corner of the Arrange window lets you toggle between Auto-scrolling on **❽** and off **❾**.

Auto-scrolling On

❽

Auto-scrolling Off

❾

This has the same affect on the Editor window. When Auto-scroll is on, both Playheads, the one in the Arrange window and the one in the Editor window, will stay centered (lined up at the same position). Please note that the two areas still can have different zoom levels. This results in different scrolling speeds for the two areas (Arrange window's Track Lane and Editor window's Track Lane).

If Auto-scrolling is turned off, then both areas (Arrange window and Editor window) stay fixed and the Playhead moves, which requires you to use their individual scroll bars to move to the right position.

MIDI Region - Editor

First we look at the Editor window when a MIDI Track is selected. The specialty right there is the ability to have two different views. The Track Header has two big tabs at the top where you switch between the Piano Roll view and the Score view.

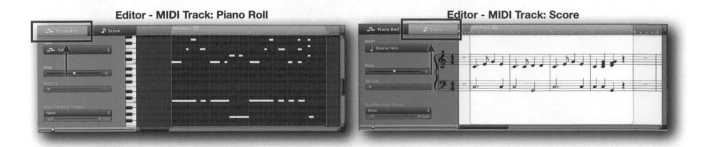

Editor - MIDI Track: Piano Roll   **Editor - MIDI Track: Score**

Piano Roll

This viewing method imitates the concept of a Player Piano where the music is stored mechanically on a Piano Roll.

➡ *Track Header*

You have only a few elements on the Track Header. However, it is important to understand not only "what" they are doing but also what they are doing "to whom". You can group it into three categories:

- Controlling display elements only
- Controlling Regions
- Controlling MIDI notes

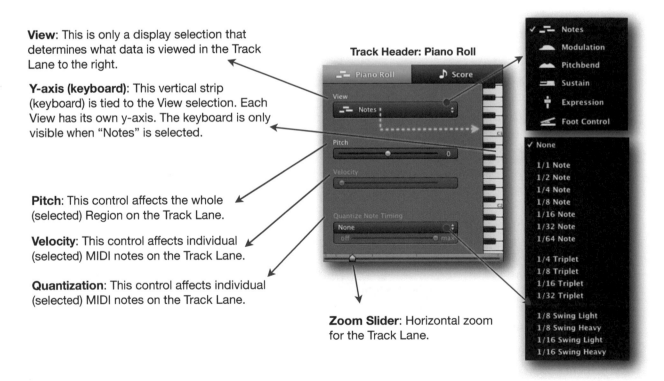

View: This is only a display selection that determines what data is viewed in the Track Lane to the right.

Y-axis (keyboard): This vertical strip (keyboard) is tied to the View selection. Each View has its own y-axis. The keyboard is only visible when "Notes" is selected.

Pitch: This control affects the whole (selected) Region on the Track Lane.

Velocity: This control affects individual (selected) MIDI notes on the Track Lane.

Quantization: This control affects individual (selected) MIDI notes on the Track Lane.

Track Header: Piano Roll

Zoom Slider: Horizontal zoom for the Track Lane.

The three controls Pitch, Velocity and Quantization are only used on MIDI notes data and therefore grayed out or not visible if the View is set to any other selection than "*Notes*".

MIDI Basics

To understand the various options on the View popup menu, requires a little bit of knowledge of how MIDI works. We touched on the MIDI <u>hardware</u> setup topic already. Now let's look at the software side of MIDI.

> The MIDI standard provides a unique way to transcribe music. If you look at western music notation, it's simply a standard for writing down music as symbols. These symbols represent all the various parameters that make up the music (pitch, rhythm, expressions, etc). It is a way musicians communicate with their music. MIDI is just a different language to describe the same parameters that make up the music. The MIDI language allows computers and electronic musical instruments to communicate with each other. GarageBand "speaks" MIDI language and can "translate" it into a visual (and audible) form so the user can understand and work with it (Piano Roll, Score).

Although GarageBand makes it easy to edit the MIDI notes by providing those common user interfaces (Piano Roll, Score), it helps to understand some basic MIDI principles. If you're new to this topic and want to understand MIDI a little bit better, I can recommend an excellent tutorial by Peter Schwartz "MIDI Demystified" (available at MacProVideo.com).

Here are just a few MIDI basics that you'll need in GarageBand.

Any musical instruction is called an "Event", regardless if it says "play the note C4", "press the sustain pedal", or "add vibrato".

☑ Note Position

Any instruction (those "MIDI Events") has to be placed on a Timeline. Each Event has therefore a time reference in your song. You can see those events on the Track Lane's Timeline, i.e. an event might be on the second beat of bar 4. If you want that event (i.e. Note) played later, then you just move it to the new position.

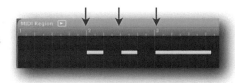

☑ Note (pitch)

This is the main information of a note event, its pitch. It is referenced to the vertical keyboard.

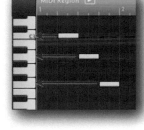

☑ Note Length (start to stop)

An additional bit of information for the note is, how long it should last. The length of a note, or duration, is either expressed in a standard musical notation with different symbols (quarter notes, eighth notes, etc) in the Score view or by the length of a line on the Timeline when looking at the Piano Roll view.

☑ Loudness (Velocity)

This is another bit of important information that belongs to the Note Event. "How loud should the note be played". In MIDI language this is called the "*Velocity*". Each MIDI note has an assigned velocity value that can range from 1-127. Musical notation is somewhat limited and provides only a few additional symbols (p, pp, mf, f, etc). On the Piano Roll view, most DAWs use a color code to make that velocity information visible. In GarageBand for example, the higher the velocity the brighter the color of that line which represents the note.

☑ Various Expressions (Controllers)

Any other instructions to play a note in a specific way exist as separate MIDI Events. There are many types but GarageBand lets you view and edit only five of the them, the most often used ones. If your MIDI controller generated those bits of data (when you used the pitch wheel or modulation wheel), then you can view them by selecting the appropriate view from the first popup menu in the Editor's Track Header. Not only can you edit those data elements (more vibrato, less vibrato), you can also create new ones.

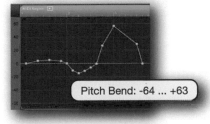

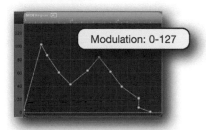

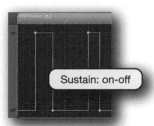

Editor Controls

View:

The View popup menu lets you choose to display the different types of MIDI Events on the Editor's Track Lane. The restriction is that you can view only one type at a time. These are the Event Types:

- **Notes**: This is the most commonly used view which displays all the MIDI Notes in a Region.
- **Modulation**: This is the type of data that is sent from the Modulation Wheel of an external MIDI keyboard. This data affects the vibrato in many synth sounds. The values range from 0 to 127.
- **Pitchbend**: This is the type of data that is sent from the Pitchbend wheel of an external MIDI keyboard. The value ranges from -64 (lower pitch) to +63 (higher pitch).
- **Sustain**: This is the type of data that is generated from a Sustain Pedal of an external MIDI Keyboard. It has two values, either on or off.
- **Expression**: This type of data is sometimes used to control the volume of a synth patch.
- **Foot Control**: This type of data is even less common. For example, an external Volume Pedal can be used to control specific parameters of a synth patch.

Y-axis:

As I pointed out, this area changes depending on the selected View. The most often used View is "*Notes*" and therefore most of the time you will see its y-axis, the vertical keyboard. A few specifics about that:

- The keyboard spans the whole 128 note range from top to bottom which exceeds the vertical zoom level. That's why this is the only view that has a vertical scroll bar. If you don't see note events, they might be out of view.
- You also can play notes on that keyboard by clicking on the keys.
- Clicking on a key will select all the Notes of that key in that Region.

Pitch

This slider applies a pitch offset to all the MIDI Notes in the selected Region(s). Move the Pitch slider or click on the number to enter a numeric value. Opt+click on the slider to reset it to zero. This pitch offset value (semitones) is displayed in the Arrange window as a number in the lower left corner of the Region with the Pitch offset. Maximum of 36 semitones (3 octaves) up or down.

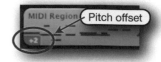

Velocity

The Velocity slider affects only the selected Note(s). If no Note is selected, then the slider will be grayed out.

Move the slider or click on the number to enter a numeric value. Opt+click on the slider to reset it to zero. If multiple notes are selected that have different velocity values, then the slider will change their values proportionally.

Quantize

The Quantize control has a few details you have to be aware of. I'll discuss that in the Track Lane section. Here is the basic concept of Quantization.

One of the main parameters of each note is its position. Where in time (when) should you play a specific note. When you play a part, then you can think of two positions for your notes:

- The position in time where you actually played the notes.
- The position in time where you wished the notes would have been played.

With a good musician both positions will be the same which means, he played the notes with precise timing. However, if you record a sequence of quarter note bass drums, you might end up having the notes played slightly before or after the beat, even if you wished you would have played them exactly on the beat.

This is where the Quantization comes in. GarageBand provides two parameters that can move notes to the position you wished you would have played them:

- **Quantization Grid**: The popup menu lets you choose a grid (time divisions) to which a note will be moved.
- **Quantization Strength**: This slider determines how strong (or how close) a note is moved to that division. "Max" means that the note is moved exactly to that division on the grid.

➡ *Track Lane*

Now let's look at the area where we can edit the MIDI data.

❶ Time and Value axis: The Timeline represents the time axis which functions the same way as in the Arrange window with the Playhead moving across. You can use the scroll bars at the bottom to move the Track Lane horizontally (remember the horizontal Zoom Slider on the left which sets the zoom level of the Track Lane. The Y-axis represents the values for the displayed MIDI Events. See the next page for details.

❷ Rename Region: Double-click the Region name, type a name and hit return.

❸ Region Play button: Click on the Region Play button to "cycle the soloed Region". GarageBand will play only that Region, everything else is muted. The Cycle function is temporarily activated for that.

❹ Grid button: This is the same function as in the Arrange window. If "Snap to Grid" is activated from the Control Menu, then the movement of the Regions, the Playhead or the Events in the Region are restricted to the grid chosen from that menu. Don't forget to also use the "Alignment Guides" when moving Events.

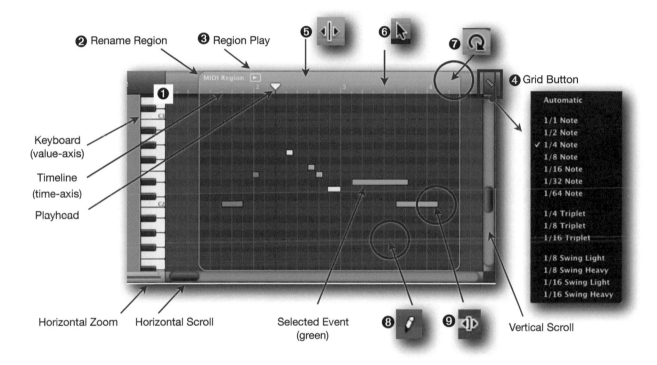

The Editor window makes use of the context-sensitive mouse cursor. This is a very efficient interface convention. Depending on the area of the Region you move the mouse over, the cursor will change its icon, indicating its current function when clicked or dragged along:

❺ Move: Click+dragging on the top portion of the Region lets you move that Region left or right. Pay attention to the Grid settings.

❻ Playhead Positioning: Moving over the area right below, basically on the numbers of the Timeline, changes the cursor to the standard pointer. This lets you position the Playhead by clicking or click+dragging.

❼ Loop: The area in the right upper corner changes to the Loop Tool. You can extend the Region as a looped MIDI Region the same way as in the Arrange window.

❽ Create: Holding down the command key while moving the cursor inside the Region will change the cursor to the Pencil Tool. This lets you create new Events (depending on the selected View.)

❾ Resize: Moving over the right edge of a note event changes to the Resize Tool. This lets you trim the duration of that note.

Here is how to edit the various elements on the Track Lane.

Editing Regions

The editing of whole Regions in the Piano Roll's Track Lane is limited. You can only Move or Copy a Region.

Editing Events

The Track Lane in the Editor window is nothing other than an x-y graph (remember that from math?). The Events are placed on that graph.

- **X-axis:** This is the time axis, referenced to the timeline. Every Event has its time reference on that timeline, displayed as Musical Time (bars and beats) or Absolute Time (min:sec) on the Time Ruler (change it on the LCD display).
- **Y-axis:** This displays the value range for the Event. Different Events have different units. The unit for Note Events are the actual notes (C1, C#1, D1, etc) represented by the musical keyboard.

The Events on a graph can be displayed in two forms: Lines or Dots.

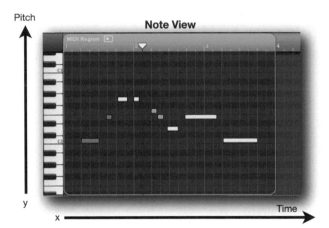

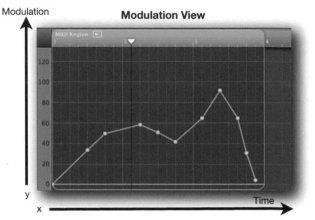

Lines are used for displaying notes. The vertical position represents the pitch and the horizontal position its start and stop time (duration of the note).

The brightness of a line acts as a third value axis, the Velocity value of each note.

Dots are used for discrete values of any MIDI Event other than Notes. GarageBand connects all those dots to form a continuous data stream.

The editing procedure of Events is straight forward:

- Select an Event by clicking on it or **sh+click** to select multiple Events.
- **Drag** around a selection of Events to select them.
- Use **cmd+A** to select all Events in a selected Region or all Events in all Regions if no Region is selected.
- **Click+drag** to move an Event in any direction. The yellow Tool Tip will display its current values.
- **Cmd+Click** to create a new Event.
- To delete a selected Event(s) use the Key Command **delete** or the Menu Command Edit ➤ Delete.
- For Note Events, you can also drag the edges to change their duration.

💡 Quantizing Event

Now let's have a closer look at the Quantize control. There are a lot of "if - then" conditions which determine the exact outcome of that action. You have to be aware of those conditions, otherwise the command you use might not give you the results you'd expected.

The quantize command affects the position of a note. GarageBand can only quantize Note Events, no other MIDI Event.

► Who

There are two answers to the question, who is deciding on the current position of a note. You do it yourself manually or tell GarageBand to position a note automatically based on your instructions.

Original Position	Quantized Position
Manually	**Automatically**
• You recorded the note (its the original position)	• You tell GarageBand to move the note(s) to a
• You moved the note (to a new position)	position based on your quantization instruction

► How

This following example demonstrates how quantization works.

A note is placed at its original position ❶. This is how you played it (or you moved it there). The note is not on a downbeat, just a little bit before the downbeat of bar 2. If you wanted to have it on the downbeat you could manually move it there. However, this is just too much work, especially if you have quite a few notes that need to be moved. Instead, you give GarageBand the proper instruction and let it move them automatically. Here is how.

You choose a timing grid (quantization grid) which is overlaid on top of the timeline and tells GarageBand to move any note onto the next closest grid line. In the example on the left, I chose a 1/4 grid ❷. That means there is a grid line on every beat (quarter notes). When I tell GarageBand to quantize that note to that 1/4 grid, it will move the note to the 4th beat of bar 1 ❸ and not to the 1st beat of bar 2. The reason is that the original position of the note is closer to the 1.4 grid line.

In the second example on the right, I chose a 1/2 quantization grid (half notes). The invisible grid lines appear only on every other beat ❹. Now if you instruct GarageBand to quantize the note ❶, it will be moved to the downbeat of bar 2 because this is now the closest grid line ❺ to the note.

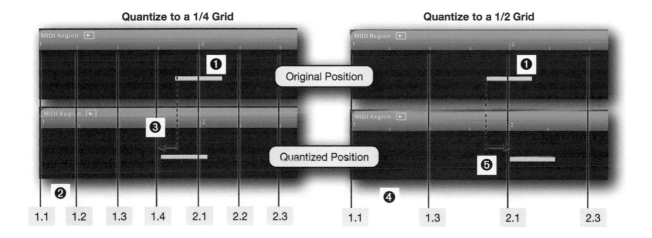

Quantize to a 1/4 Grid   Quantize to a 1/2 Grid

Original Position

Quantized Position

► How Much

The effect of quantization is like a magnet affect. The grid lines represent the magnets. Whatever grid line is closest to the note will pull it onto its line. This would be a full quantization. GarageBand provides a second control called the Quantization Strength. This value would determine how strong the "magnetic force" of the grid line would be. In the example above the strength would have been set to maximum because the note was pulled in all the way. If you lower the strength, then the note will move towards the grid line without ending exactly on the line. This is useful if you want to keep the original "feel" of the MIDI notes without ending up "too perfect" (too static or lifeless).

Quantization Strength

off

50%

max

► **Procedure**

Now that we understand the concept of quantization, let's see what the exact procedure is in GarageBand.

The final question is always, what is the current position of a note and what are the factors or procedures that determine that position (where a note is placed on the timeline).

- ☺ **Original Position**: We already learned that this is the position of the note as you recorded it. When you move the note manually to a new position, then that becomes the new Original Position. Please note that GarageBand always remembers the Original Position.

- ☺ If you did not use any Quantization commands, then the Original Position of a note is the **Current Position** of the note, the way you see it on the Editor's Track Lane.

- ☺ If you apply a **Quantization Value** to that note, then the note will be moved away from its Original Position based on the Quantization setting. This new position now becomes the Current Position of the note, the way you see it on the Editor's Track Lane. It functions like an offset to the Original Position.

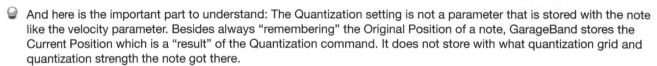

- ☺ And here is the important part to understand: The Quantization setting is not a parameter that is stored with the note like the velocity parameter. Besides always "remembering" the Original Position of a note, GarageBand stores the Current Position which is a "result" of the Quantization command. It does not store with what quantization grid and quantization strength the note got there.

- ☺ Every time you apply a different quantization value, which is a combination of the selected grid and strength, the Current Position gets updated. If you choose "no grid" or "0 strength", then the offset is zero and the note is back at its Original Position.

You can apply a quantization value on three different Levels

☑ Note(s)

Just select any note or a selection of notes and set the quantize values (grid and strength). And remember, the value that you saw on the controls when you selected the notes did NOT reflect their quantization setting.

☑ Region(s)

You can also set a quantization value for a Region or multiple selected Regions (make sure that no note is selected inside). In that case, the quantization value is applied to all the notes inside the Region (overwriting any previous quantization of single notes). And here is a big difference. The quantization value that is applied to a Region is stored with that Region and whenever you select a Region, the Quantization controls will display those settings. If you select multiple Regions that have different quantization values then the Quantization Grid menu will display "Multiple".

However, this doesn't mean that all the notes in that Region are quantized that way. If you now set a note to a different quantization value after you have set the quantization for the whole Region, then that value will overwrite the Region just for that note. Selecting a new setting for the Region again will overwrite the single notes position and so on. The rule is that the last applied quantize value determines the Current Position.

☑ "Future" Region(s)

If no Region and no note is selected in the Editor, then the Quantize Control is labeled "*Auto Quantize*". This means that whatever quantization grid you choose (quantization strength is not available) will be applied automatically to any newly recorded Region. All the notes in that new Region will be quantized, But remember, this will be applied after the recording, the Original Positions of the recorded notes are still remembered. Setting the Quantization grid to "None" will move the notes back to their original recorded position.

▶ Grid Menu

With so much detailed information, it is easy to lose the "big picture". Let's look at the various Grid menus again to make sure we clearly understand what they mean and what they do. The potential confusion is that the menu opens up in three locations looking exactly the same. However, there are two fundamental differences that can be easily overlooked.

We just discussed the position of a note, and that it is set manually (by the user) or automatically (by the Quantization controls). This is the distinction you have to keep in mind when you make a grid selection from any of those menus.

Project Window

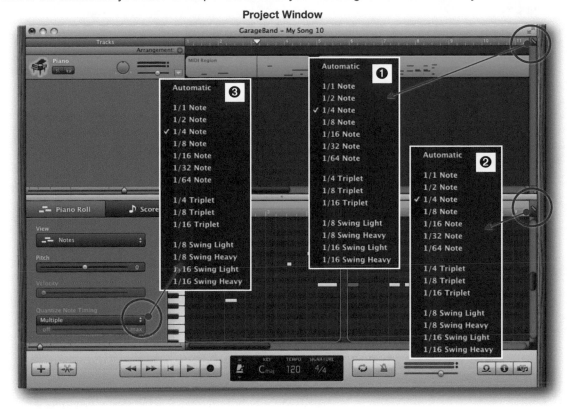

💡 Grid for manual placement (Song's Timeline)

The menu that opens with the Grid button in either the Arrangement window's Timeline ❶ or the Editor window's Timeline ❷ lets you select the grid that restricts the **manual** placement of any object on that Timeline and Track Lane. The object can be the Playhead, a Region or an Event inside a Region. It also restricts the trimming of those objects. That means, even resizing a Region or a Note is restricted to that grid. The grid can be set individually for both Timelines.

> This grid refers to the Timeline of the song. If you set it to 1/2, then you can place objects only on 1.2, 1.3. 2.1, 2.3 and so on. If you set the grid to 1/1, then you can place objects only on the downbeat of every bar, 1.1, 2.1, 3.1

💡 Grid for quantized placement (Region's Timeline)

The menu that opens up from the quantize section ❸ lets you select the grid that restricts the **automatic** placement of Notes performed by a quantize command.

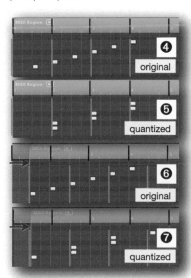

> There is one little detail about that quantization grid that you might never have noticed, but if you come across it, it could be quite confusing. It is the same behavior as in Logic Pro and many Logic users are not aware of it either.
>
> The Quantization Grid does NOT refer to your song's timeline. It is referring to the Region's own Timeline!
>
> In example ❹, the Region starts at the downbeat of bar one. When quantizing to a 1/1 grid ❺, the notes line up on the downbeats of each bar. In example ❻, all the notes are at the same original position again but the Region they belong to, starts at 1.3 of the Song's Timeline. Because the quantization grid follows the Region's Timeline (orange lines), when quantizing to 1/1, all the notes are on the downbeat of the Region's Timeline ❼ which has an offset of two beats to the Song's Timeline (black lines).

The moral of that story, make sure that your MIDI Regions always start on the downbeat of your Song's Timeline to avoid unexpected quantization results.

Score

The Score view is the second option that lets you display and edit the content of your MIDI Region. It uses standard Music Notion with notes, rests and other musical symbols, so you can interact in a more traditional way with your MIDI data. You can even print out the score (limited to one Track at a time).

➡ *Track Header*

The elements on the Track Header are similar to the Piano Roll view with a few exceptions.

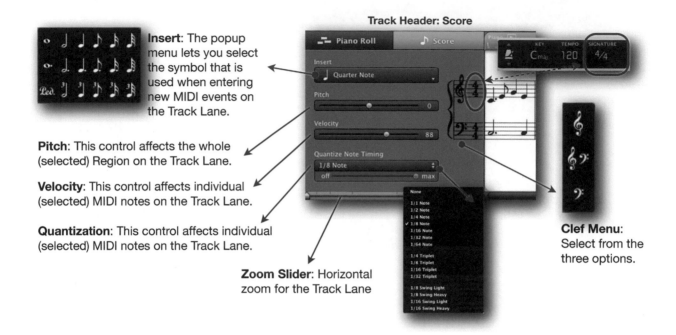

Insert: The popup menu lets you select the symbol that is used when entering new MIDI events on the Track Lane.

Pitch: This control affects the whole (selected) Region on the Track Lane.

Velocity: This control affects individual (selected) MIDI notes on the Track Lane.

Quantization: This control affects individual (selected) MIDI notes on the Track Lane.

Zoom Slider: Horizontal zoom for the Track Lane

Clef Menu: Select from the three options.

▶ **Same Controls as on the Piano Roll**

- 🌑 **Pitch**: The slider assigns a pitch offset to the selected Region(s). Remember, this is a playback offset that will not transpose the actual notes on the score. The offset (-36 to +36 semitones) will be indicated on the Region in the Arrange window's Track Lane.

- 🌑 **Velocity**: Sets the velocity for any selected Note(s). The score on the Track Lane itself doesn't reflect the velocity value of the displayed notes.

- 🌑 **Quantization**: This functions the same as in the Piano Roll view. Because the Quantization changes the position of the notes, this will affect the look of your score.

- 🌑 **Zoom Slider**: Zooms the Track Lane horizontally.

▶ **Score specific Controls**

- 🌑 **Insert**: This popup button opens a menu with various note symbols (and the Sustain Pedal symbol). The selected symbol will be the one that is used when you enter a MIDI note directly into the score on the Track Lane.

- 🌑 **Clef Menu:** Moving the mouse over the clef, will highlight that area with a little triangle at the bottom. Click on it to open a popup menu with three options: Single staff with treble clef, single staff with bass clef, double staff with treble clef and bass clef.

- 🌑 **Time Signature**: This is not a control, just a display. The Project's Time Signature (which can be set in the LCD Display) will be displayed in the musical staff.

➡ *Track Lane*

The Score's Track Lane also has many common elements of the Piano Roll view.

❶ **Timeline**: The Track Lane has only the horizontal axis, the Timeline, but no vertical axis. That would be the notation system itself. That system (the staff) goes through as one long staff with rests if there are gaps between Regions. One little difference on the Time Ruler is that it has dots instead of lines for the bar divisions.

❷ **Rename Region**: Double-click the Region name, type a name and hit return.

❸ **Region Play button**: Click on the Region Play button to "cycle the soloed Region". GarageBand plays only that Region, everything else is muted. The Cycle function is temporarily activated for that.

❹ **Grid button:** I discussed the different functionality of the Grid menu in the Piano Roll section. In the Score's Track Lane, that grid selection has the same function of applying an invisible grid that restricts the movement of objects (Regions and Notes) on the Track Lane. In the Score view, it has an additional function. The selected grid value determines the lowest possible displayed note value and by doing so "cleaning up" the appearance of the score without actually moving the location of the notes (no affect on the playback).

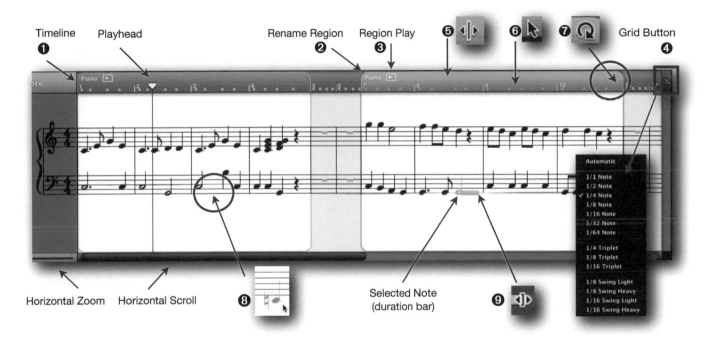

The Score view also makes use of the context-sensitive mouse cursor.

❺ **Move**: Click+dragging on the top portion of the Region lets you move that Region left or right. Pay attention to the Grid settings restriction.

❻ **Playhead Positioning**: The area right below, basically on the numbers of the Timeline, changes the cursor to the standard pointer. This lets you position the Playhead by clicking or click+dragging.

❼ **Loop**: The area in the right upper corner changes to the Loop Tool. You can extend the Region as a looped MIDI Region the same way as in the Arrange window.

❽ **Create**: Holding down the command key while moving the cursor over the score will add a gray "ghost" note to the pointer. The displayed note value (1/2, 1/4, 18) depends on the selection from the Insert menu in the Track Header. When you cmd+move the mouse, you will see what note (the pitch) will be inserted when you click the mouse.

❾ **Resize**: Changing the length of a musical note requires you to change it to a different note symbol. However, the Score view provides a different method. When you click on a Note(s), a Duration Bar will appear which is similar to the bar on the Piano Roll view. Now, when you move the cursor over the right edge of that bar, it changes to the Resize Tool which lets you drag the right edge to lengthen or shorten the note. The note symbol (and any necessary rests) will automatically be updated.

Editing Regions

The editing of whole Regions in the Score's Track Lane is limited. You can only Move or Copy a Region.

Editing Events

These are the available editing tools:

Select

- Select a Note by **clicking** on it or **sh+click** to select multiple Notes.
- **Drag** around a selection of Notes to select them.
- Use **cmd+A** to select all Notes in a selected Region or all Notes in all Regions if no Region is selected.

Move

- **Click+drag** to move a Note in any direction. The note will be updated in real time (and its surrounding notes and rests that are affected) during the move. You will also hear the sound of those notes played through the instrument while you are dragging it. You can move only vertically or horizontally at a time.
- Use the arrow keys on the keyboard to move a selected Note(s) left and right (change position) or up and down (pitch). The horizontal steps are determined by the Grid selection.

Copy a Note(s): **Opt+drag** the note(s). You can **drag** a whole group of selected notes at once by dragging one of the notes. All the selected notes will move as a group, even if the notes are not next to each other. You can move only up/down (set the pitch) or left-right (set the position) at a time.

Create

- **Cmd+Click** to create a new Note.
- **Ctrl+Click** anywhere in the score to open the Insert popup menu to select a note symbol. This saves you the trip to the Track Header to select it from the Insert menu.
- Besides Notes, the Pedal symbol is the only other MIDI Event that can be edited. When you create a new Pedal symbol, it always adds the "Pedal on" and "Pedal off" to the score which can be dragged independently.

Sustain Pedal

Edit

- The velocity value of a Note is not visible in the Score. To view or edit its velocity, use the Velocity slider in the Track Header for the selected Note.
- Change the length of a note by selecting it to make the Duration Bar visible. It represents the note's length which can be resized by dragging its right edge.

Duration Bar

Delete a selected Note(s) by using the Key Command **delete** or the Menu Command `Edit ➤ Delete` . The surrounding notes and rests are updated.

Print Score

GarageBand also lets you print the score of your Project, however only one Track at a time.

Whenever you are in the Score Editor, the Print command in the File Menu becomes active. Select the Menu Command `Edit ➤ Print` or use the Key Command **cmd+P**. The standard Print dialog window will open where you can choose the print settings.

GarageBand prints the whole song for that Track and automatically includes the following elements:

- *Tempo*: This is the Project's Tempo
- *Song Name*: This is the name of the Project
- *Track Name*: This is the name of the Track (Instrument)
- *Composer*: This is the name that you entered in the `GarageBand ➤ Preferences ➤ My Info ➤ Composer Name`

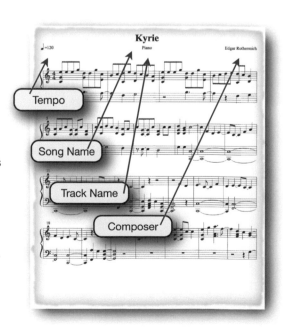

Audio Regions - Editor

Although the Editor window for Audio Regions looks pretty simple with just a few controls, it might be difficult to understand without some basic background knowledge about digital audio (WIKI MOMENT: Digital Audio, waveform).

I already discussed the two forms of capturing music.

Music **Written down as instructions** (Score, MIDI data)	**Music** **Recorded from a performance** (CD, audio file)

As long as music is written down, you can change it every time you perform it. If the band leader decides after the first evening to play the song xyz faster, one note higher or without the drummer, he just changes those "instructions" and the song will sound different on the second night. If you bought the CD of that song however, it will always sound the same as it was recorded. You cannot change it.

So far, this was also true for any recording in the studio. Once you recorded the performance of a musician on tape, you couldn't alter it, only manipulate what was printed on tape with added effects. I pointed out already that this limitation doesn't exist when you record MIDI data because you record "musical instruction" that can be altered any time.

This limitation with recorded music has been lifted over the last couple of years with the advancement in digital audio technology. While still not perfect, you can treat recorded audio material now almost as if it was a written score.

Here are the three main parameters that describe music. This is basically the instruction you give a musician: tell them **what** to play (pitch of the notes), **when** to play it (the rhythmical sequence) and **how** to play it (loud, soft, legato, etc).

Pitch	Timing	Expression
What note to play	**When** to play it	**How** to play it

GarageBand lets you alter the first two parameters, Pitch and Timing. When we look now at the various controls in the Editor window, we have to know first which of the two parameters they affect and then learn what the tools are and how they work.

💀 Audio Waveform

The main tool when editing audio in general is the waveform. This is a visual representation of the audio, "what the sound looks like".

It is a simple graph, where the x-axis (horizontal line) represents the time and the y-axis (vertical line) represents the amplitude of the sound in other words, how loud the music is at any specific time.

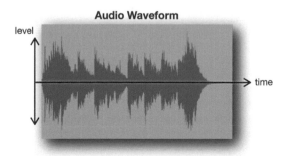

Audio Waveform

The more you work with audio waveforms, the better you will get at "reading" those waveforms. It takes a lot of practice, but you can figure out pretty fast how to recognize the musical content in those graphs.

➡ *Track Header*

The Track Header has only eight controls. I wished they were arranged differently to display which of the two parameters you are affecting.

◉ Activate Editing

The checkbox "Follow Tempo & Pitch" ❶ is the most important control. It turns this whole magic of messing around with recorded sound on and off for that track (affecting ALL Regions on it). If turned off, all the Pitch and Timing settings are ignored and the audio file is played back in its un-altered state. Please note that the settings are only disabled so you don't lose anything when you activate the checkbox again.

Remember that GarageBand distinguishes between three different types of audio files (indicated by their color code) There are a few things to pay attention to:

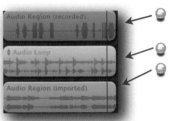

◉ **Audio Files recorded in your Project**. The checkbox is on by default for those Regions.

◉ **Imported Apple Loops**: The checkbox is also on by default.

◉ **Imported Standard Audio Files**: The checkbox is turned off by default. When turning it on for the first time, GarageBand performs an analysis of the audio file. It basically collects data which it needs to perform any audio manipulations.
Here is one restriction with imported audio files.

> **You cannot change the Pitch on imported audio files, only the Timing**

◉ Pitch Editing

It is very important to realize that there are three parameters that affect the pitch of an audio file once the checkbox for "Follow Tempo & Pitch" is activated. The controls are not very well laid out and that could cause some confusion:

☑ The Key Signature ❷

Once you have the Follow Pitch checkbox activated, you have to pay full attention to the Key Signature of your Project. This parameter is not visible in the Editor window only in the LCD Display when switching to Project.

LCD - Project

- Any Audio and MIDI Loop (that has pitch information) will be pitch shifted to that key. See the <u>Apple Loops</u> chapter for more details.

- Any audio file that you record in your current Project inherits the Project's key signature as its default key signature. Changing the Project Key Signature will pitch shift those audio files accordingly

☑ The Pitch Slider ❸

The slider lets you add an additional pitch offset. Audio Regions can be transposed up/down 12 semitones (one octave). The transposition value will be indicated in the Region with a semitone number ❹ in the lower left corner. Please note, this is a Region parameter not a Track parameter. It can be set differently for each Region on a Track (one reason why you might want to split up an existing Region into separate parts).

Timeline Area - Audio Region

☑ Automatic Tuning Slider ❺

This slider analyzes the audio file and tunes it if it was out of tune. This works only for "monophonic" (single notes) audio regions not for "polyphonic" (chords) parts or drums and multiple instruments. Adjust the amount of auto-tuning with the slider between 0-100. Setting the value too high could result in unwanted effects.

The "Limit to Key" checkbox adjusts the audio to the 7 notes of the scale that is set for your Project. If unchecked, the "chromatic scale will apply which means all 12 notes are available.

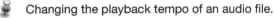

Time Editing

Time Editing of audio files means that you can pick notes inside an audio file and move them around like individual MIDI events. The computer compensates any time modification of the audio file so it will not be audible (hopefully). Of course that depends on how good the program is that performs that magic. If the modification is too extreme then you will start hearing audible artifacts and the quality of the audio file will suffer. All those edits are "non-destructive", meaning that the Audio File itself will not be altered.

Timing Editing of audio files is commonly used for:

- Changing the playback tempo of an audio file.
- Automatically Quantize an audio file.
- Manually shift events/sections horizontally inside an audio file.

Quantize Settings

- The popup menu lets you choose the grid you want to quantize the audio events to.

- The slider underneath lets you choose how close you want to move the audio to that grid. These are the same principles that I discussed earlier. (Quantizing Events)

This setting can be made individually for each Region. The current setting will be applied to any new Audio Region of the Track.

But wait a minute. Quantizing MIDI notes is easy to understand because they are single events that can be moved to a grid. But what about audio, there are no audio events. Audio is represented by a continuous waveform, so what is actually moved?

> **Manipulating Timing in an Audio File**
>
> This is an advanced editing technique which I cover in the chapter about Flex Time. Here is just the basic concept:
>
> In order to quantize an audio file, for example to correct the sloppy timing of a recorded live drummer, the audio has to be analyzed first. During that analysis, the computer tries to detect notes (just rhythmic patterns, not the pitch) and attaches Markers to those time positions in the audio waveform. Those Markers (similar to MIDI notes) can then be quantized which means moved to a timing grid. When those Markers are moved, that portion of the audio waveform gets moved too. Please note that not the whole audio file gets moved (shifted), only that little section of the audio around that Marker. Everything else stays as it is.

The handling of those Markers is different for the three types of Audio Files in GarageBand

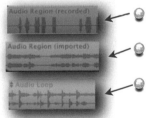

- **Audio Files recorded in your Project**. GarageBand has those files already analyzed automatically in the background and it has applied the Markers.

- **Imported Standard Audio Files**: Those files will be analyzed the first time you check the "Follow Tempo & Pitch" checkbox.

- **Imported Audio Loops**: Those files have their Markers already perfectly set. That's what makes them special Audio Loops. See the Apple Loops Chapter for details.

Changing Playback Speed

Once an Audio Track has the "Follow Tempo & Pitch" checked, all its Regions will follow any tempo changes you make in your Project.

Manually Shifting Section/Events horizontally inside an Audio File

I will cover this topic in the chapter about Flex Time. On top of the Track Header, you can see if Flex Time is activated for a Track by the squeezed waveform icon

➡ *Track Lane*

The same Region editing functions that you could do in the Arrange window's Track Lane can also be performed in the Editor's Track Lane. Please note that you have more editing tools available for editing Audio Regions than you have for editing MIDI Regions in the Editor.

Delete - Move - Copy - Trim - Split - Join

The Timeline and the Scroll Bars behave the same as in the Arrange window. Other features are:

❶ **Rename Region**: Double-click the Region name, type a name and hit return.

❷ **Region Play button**: Click on the Region Play button to "cycle the soloed Region". GarageBand plays only that Region everything else is muted. The Cycle function is temporarily activated for that.

❸ **Grid button:** This is the same function as in the Arrange window. If "Snap to Grid" is activated from the Control Menu, the movement of the Regions and the Playhead is restricted to the grid chosen from that menu. Don't forget to utilize the Alignment Guides, Menu Command: Control ➤ Show/Hide Alignment Guides.

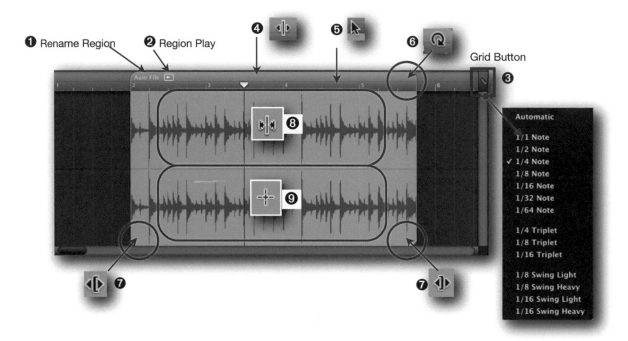

The Editor's Track Lane real power unfolds with the context-sensitive mouse cursor. Depending on the area of the Region you move the mouse over, the cursor will change its icon, indicating its function when clicked on or dragged along:

❹ **Move**: Click+dragging on the top portion of the Region lets you move that Region left or right. Pay attention to the Grid settings.

❺ **Playhead Positioning**: The area right below, basically on the numbers of the Timeline, changes the cursor to the standard pointer. This lets you position the Playhead by clicking or click+dragging.

❻ **Loop**: The area in the right upper corner changes to the Loop Tool. You can extend the Region as a looped Audio Region the same way as in the Arrange window.

❼ **Resize**: The area in the lower right and lower left corner changes to the Resize Tool. This lets you trim the size of the Region on both ends. Please note that you cannot extend the Audio Region beyond the limits of its referred Audio File.

❽ **Flex Marker**: The upper half of the Region changes to the Flex Marker Tool. I will cover that in the Flex Time chapter along with additional Track Lane features.

❾ **Crosshair (Marquee)**: The lower half of the Region changes to the Marquee Tool (that's the official name in Logic). It lets you draw a range on the Track Lane (not restricted to one Region). Hitting play, will play only that range. Copying will only copy that range. Delete will only delete that range. Clicking on the range will split the Region at the left and right border. Click+drag the range will move just that range.

Movie/Podcast - Editor

I'll cover the Podcast and Movie topic in a later Chapter. Here is a quick peak to see that the concept of the Editor window is also used for those types of Tracks, even though they don't have any audio or MIDI content.

- When a Movie or Podcast Track is selected, the Editor ❶ displays its content where you can view and edit it.
- The Editor is also divided into the Track Header ❷ to the left with some basic controls.
- Next to the Track Header is the Track Lane ❸.
- Instead of a Timeline that contains all the music, the Track Lane is arranged as a list that shows the Track's content, Chapters ❹ and its.

Editor Window - Movie

Editor Window - Podcast

10 - Apple Loops

Apple Loops are the type of tools/features that you can use immediately without knowing much about them. You are ready to go if you can answer the following four questions:

❶ **What are they** - pre-recorded music files

❷ **Where to find them** - in the Loop Browser

❸ **How to import them** - drag them onto a Track

❹ **How to use them** - move their Region to the right position and loop them

And that would be the end of the Apple Loops chapter. However, if you want to know a little bit more about Apple Loops and learn how to make the best use of them in your GarageBand Project, read on.

The Basics

> **Apple Loops are "special" audio files**

The reason these audio files are special is because they contain additional data that enables them to be used in your Project in a way that would not be possible with a standard audio file.

That raises two questions:

▶ **"What way"** is that? What you might want to use those audio files for?
▶ **"What data"** is necessary to make that happen?

➡ *How You Want to Use Them*

Let's look at it from a different angle. Instead of first showing you the features of Apple Loops, I'll give you two examples that demonstrate the limitations of standard audio files. Then we'll see how those "special" audio files, called Apple Loops, could lift that limitation. Here are three requirements for external audio files if you want to use them in your Project:

☑ Contain Music
☑ Easy to Loop
☑ Work in your Project

Audio File contain Music

Usually when you create a new song, you record your own music. That means you or other musicians play their instruments and you record the performance in GarageBand, which creates the Audio Regions or MIDI Regions. However, you have a problem if you need a rhythm guitar part in your song but you don't play the guitar, or you need a live drummer but you don't have a recording booth to record those drums.

With the wide spread popularity of DAWs, companies recognized that need and provided a new type of product.

Audio Files with pre-recorded music

However these were not your typical audio files that contain pre-recorded music like mp3 files from your favorite artist that you buy on iTunes. The new music files were meant to be used as building blocks in your song and therefore contain mostly single instruments playing repeatable musical patterns that you can use in your song. For example, an audio file of a great live drummer playing a basic groove on a great sounding drum set, recorded with expensive equipment. Or a strumming guitar pattern played by a top studio musician on his $3,000 Martin guitar through a $2,000 microphone, ... you get the idea.

You can buy those little "audio files" (or even better, they come free with GarageBand) and lay them into your project, mix them with your vocals and you've got yourself a great sounding song with just a few clicks. By the way, those audio files are licensed for this purpose and therefore legal to use in your song (read the fine print for details).

Audio Files must be easy to loop

Those new type of audio files, used as building blocks, have something in common. They are usually short, maybe only one bar or two, but usually not longer than eight bars. Most of them are generic musical patterns or phrases that can be repeated. For example, the drummer would repeat the same one bar groove throughout the eight bars of a verse (and later in the second and third verse again). Same procedure with the guitar player. The strumming might be the same one bar pattern throughout an 8 bar verses.

In GarageBand you would need only the audio file of that one bar which is represented by a one bar Audio Region. You then just copy that Region eight times. But Instead of repeating the same Region by copying it manually, you would use the more efficient Loop Tool by dragging the upper corner of the Region to the right and GarageBand creates those repetitions.

Audio Files must be properly truncated

However that only works if the audio file has been properly trimmed ("truncated"). Otherwise the music will not line up.

Here is an example of the same recording of a two bar drum pattern. Sample ❶ shows the original Audio File with silence at the beginning and end of the recording. The audio file in example ❷ has been trimmed so the file starts exactly at the first signal (downbeat) and ends exactly at the end of the second bar.

If you would place the un-trimmed audio file on bar one of your Project ❸ and loop it, the drum beat wouldn't line up at the first bar (due to the silence at the beginning) and the repeated Regions would never line up to the following beats of your song either.

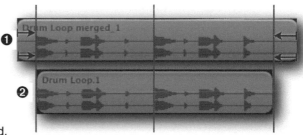

However, if you place the properly trimmed audio file on bar one ❹, the drum beat will perfectly start at bar one and each repetition lines up perfectly every two bars. That file is "easy to loop", you just place it at any bar in your song and loop it, no prior Region trimming required.

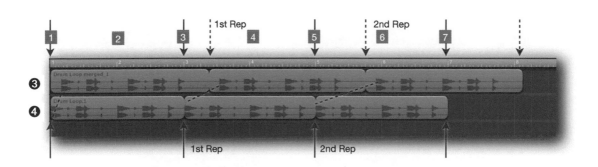

🌀 Audio Files must work in your Project

So the first two requirements we just discussed can easily be done with standard audio files, no need for a "special" audio file. So let's stick with our example and import the perfectly trimmed and "ready to loop" audio file and import it into a different Project.

What just happened?

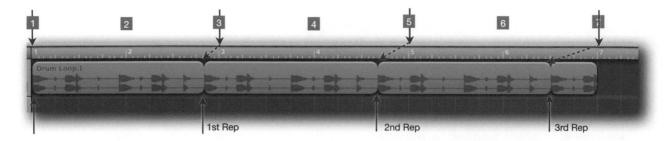

The drum groove still lines up perfectly on the first bar but now it is getting out of sync. Every two bars, the start of the repeated Region is further away from the bar it is supposed to be. We ignored one fundamental parameter of music. The Tempo. Taking a perfectly trimmed audio file and using it in a Project, only works if the music in that audio file was performed at the same tempo as the tempo of your Project. In the previous example, we were lucky that the drum beat was recorded at 120bpm and imported into our Project with a tempo set to 120bpm, perfect match. In this example, the same 120bpm audio file was imported into a Project with a tempo of 110bpm. The result, the drummer plays too fast.

And this is one of the first "specialties" of an Apple Loop. Regardless of its originally recorded tempo, Apple Loops can match the tempo of any Project. In our example, that would mean that the audio file would slow down the drum groove to play in the 110bpm tempo. But not only that, it has to slow down the tempo without changing its original pitch. And that is not necessarily an easy task.

But wait, what about the other example with the strumming guitar player. Even if the Apple Loop is able to match the different tempo, there is another important parameter in music that could be a problem. What if the guitar pattern was recorded in C and you import that audio file into a Project that is set to a different key like E?

To make a long story short, another requirement for the special audio file called Apple Loop is the ability to match the original key of the recorded audio file to the key of the Project. In other words, GarageBand must be able to transpose the audio file. This time it must make the change without affecting the tempo of the audio file.

Tempo Match - Key Match

So these are the two most important features to make an audio file work in your Project without the restriction of tempo and key. An Apple Loop provides those features, making it a "special" audio file that allows GarageBand to perform Tempo Match and Key Match.

But there is other data embedded in an Apple Loop. Let's look at the complete list.

Apple Loops - What's inside

➡ *Audio File*

The main content is the audio data. After all, it is still an audio file that looks like a regular audio file with a standard audio file extension (.aif, .caf) and it can be played by any audio application. They just ignore the additional information.

➡ *Loop Type*

This is a flag that is set to "Loop" or "One-shot". It tells GarageBand (or Logic Pro) whether or not it should apply the Tempo and Key Matching to that audio file.

So far we've discussed only musical patterns that are suitable for looping. However, there is also use for audio files with musical (or non musical) content that is not based on a rhythmical pattern. Long drones, atmospheric synth pads or short hits and stings. Even sound effects and spoken words are available as Apple Loops. They make use of the other Apple Loop feature, keywords. See below.

- ☑ **Loop** is used for musical pattern and is expressed by its duration in **beats**
- ☑ **One-shot** is used for non-pattern based audio files and is expressed by its duration in **min:sec**

➡ *Tempo Match*

Tempo match requires two components. First, it needs to know the original tempo the audio file was recorded in. Secondly, the audio file has to be marked with so called "Transient Markers". This is the same technology we discussed briefly in the Audio Editor when enabling quantization for Audio Regions. Those Transient Markers act like a grid that is "glued" on top of the audio waveform. When you slow down an audio waveform, the grid gets stretched and when you speed up and audio waveform you squeeze the grid.

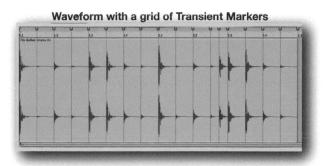

Waveform with a grid of Transient Markers

➡ *Key Match*

Key Match also relies on Transient Markers, plus, it needs the information of the key the audio file was recorded in. Now the process is just opposite of Tempo Match. This time GarageBand transposes the audio file based on the difference between its key and the Project key. Since the required pitch shift speeds up the audio file, it applies a reverse tempo change (with the help of the Transient Markers) to compensate. Now the audio file plays back at its original tempo.

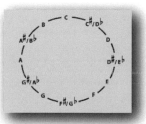

➡ *Keywords*

Apple Loops provide a set of Keywords (or Metadata, Tags) that function similarly to the tags that you use in iTunes. There you add Artist, Album, Genre, etc as keywords to your audio files and later can search for those keywords in your huge iTunes Library.

Apple Loops provides the following keywords that can be added to each audio file:

- ☑ **Genre**: Jazz, Blues, Urban, World, etc
- ☑ **Instrument Description**: This is a two part field, i.e. "Bass - Electric Bass" or "Bass - Acoustic Bass", etc.
- ☑ **Mood Description**: This category allows to select 8 mutually exclusive descriptions: Acoustic-Electric, Relaxed-Intense, etc but also a more practical descriptions like Part-Fill or Single-Ensemble.
- ☑ **Scale**: The Key information in the Tempo Match only provides the root note without determining whether the musical pattern is playing in a major or minor key. The Scale tag provides this additional information.

Here are the available values of the four category fields that an Apple Loop can be tagged with. These are the same fields that you can search for later in the Loop Browser when you're looking for a specific Apple Loop.

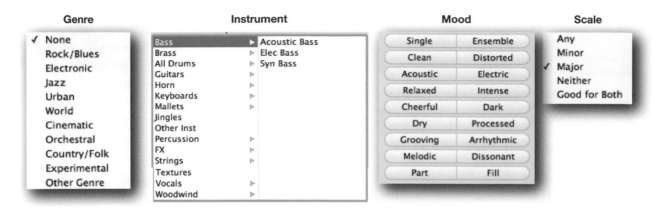

Remember, you can make any audio file into an Apple Loop by just using its tagging feature. If you have a huge selection of audio files, adding those tags lets you use the Loop Browser later as a powerful search engine without using the Tempo and Key matching feature.

➡ *MIDI Region + Channel Strip Settings*

This is an interesting type of content. Apple Loops are available for all different types of styles, genres, instruments and patterns. Many of them are recorded with live instruments but the audio file could also be based, for example, on the pattern of a synth bass played on a MIDI keyboard. Think about that recording process. Someone could use GarageBand, load a synth bass Instrument, tweak the sound, load a couple of plugins to fatten up the sound even more, record a 2 bar MIDI Region and bounce (export) that as a two bar audio file for an Apple Loop library.

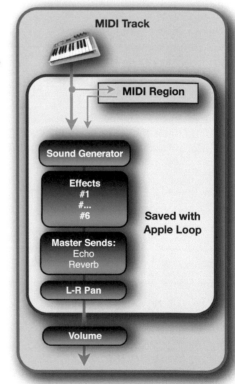

Apple Loops says, "wait a minute, what if along with that audio file, I let you store the MIDI Region, the setting of the sound generator plus all the used plugins with their settings and the left-right pan" that you just used. And that is exactly what happens. With such an Apple Loop, you would have the option to use the audio file on an Audio Track or drag it onto a MIDI Track and GarageBand would load the exact Software Instrument and all its plugins with the exact settings that were used when the Apple Loop was created and put the MIDI Region (the notes that were played) on that Track.

This has the great advantage that you not only can change individual MIDI notes but also tweak the sound or load a completely different Software Instrument to play the pattern. Besides that, the musical pattern is performed "live" with a Software Instrument so Tempo and Key Matching are not required. This has its advantages because it avoids possible problems like this:

 I haven't pointed out that the process of Tempo and Key mapping has some limitations. Depending on the source material and the amount of tempo change and transposition, this could produce some sonic artifacts that could degrade the sound quality quite a bit

This last category of what is inside an Apple Loop, the MIDI content, is very important.

So far I haven't mentioned that there are two types of Apple Loops. One kind has MIDI content and the other one doesn't.

Types of Loops

There are two types of Apple Loops and some confusion about their differences.

If you followed the previous section about the added content in an Apple Loop, then the distinction between those two Apple Loop types will be easy to understand, especially if you separate the various content into two groups:
The **Music** (content data) and the **Data about the Music** (metadata)

Official Icon:		
Official Name:	**Real Instrument Apple Loops**	**Software Instrument Apple Loops**
Alternative Name:	**Blue Apple Loops**	**Green Apple Loops**
I would call it:	**Audio Loops**	**MIDI Loops**
Content:	Contains **only** the Audio Data	Contains the Audio Data **and** the MIDI Data
Optional Content:	Loop Type, Tempo, Key, Keywords	Loop Type, Tempo, Key, Keywords

And here is what happens in GarageBand when you drag one of those Apple Loops into your Project.

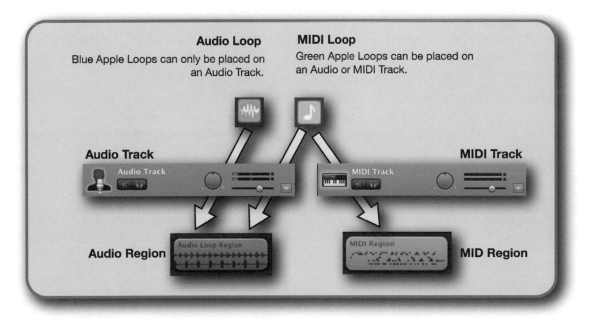

Audio Loops

Here are the procedures and rules regarding the Blue Apple Loops ("Real Instrument Apple Loops"):

- Blue Apple Loops can only be dragged onto an Audio Track (Basic Track or Electric Guitar Track). If you try to drag them onto the Track Lane of a MIDI Track, you will get a warning message on the Track Lane.

- A blue Audio Region will be created at the position where you dropped it with the audio content of the Apple Loop. Only Audio Regions from blue Apple Loops are colored blue, so you can tell them apart from other Audio Regions (purple: newly recorded audio files, orange: imported non-looped audio files).

- If you drag a Blue Apple Loop to the empty space below the Track Lanes (where it says "Drag Apple Loops here"), GarageBand creates a new Audio Track first (a Basic Track) and places the Audio Region on it.

MIDI Loops

Here are the procedures and rules regarding the Green Apple Loops ("Software Instrument Apple Loops"):

- If a Green Apple Loop is dragged onto an Audio Track, GarageBand will use its audio file and create an Audio Region. The new Audio Region will also be blue, indicating its origin from an Apple Loop (even if it was a Green Apple Loop).

- If a Green Apple Loop is dragged onto a MIDI Track, GarageBand will use its MIDI data and create a new MIDI Region, this time a green Region. But there is one extra procedure. The MIDI data in a Green Apple Loop also comes with channel strip settings for that MIDI data (Software Instrument settings ,Plugin settings, etc). However the existing MIDI Track has its own settings already. In that case you will get a Dialog window with two options:

  - OK: This option will only use the MIDI data and not the Channel Strip Settings from the Apple Loop. It will leave your current Track settings untouched but the loop will sound different because you didn't use its intended settings.

  - Create Track: This option will leave the current MIDI Track untouched and create a brand new MIDI Track with the Channel Strip Setting and the MIDI data from the Apple Loop. This ensures that the Loop will sound exactly like its audio file version.

- You can also drag a Green Apple Loop to the empty space below the Track Lanes (where it says "Drag Apple Loops here"). GarageBand creates a new MIDI Track with the stored Channel Strip Setting and places the MIDI Region there or it will create a new Audio Track with Audio Region. The behavior can be set in the Preferences window.

➡ About the color coded Regions

Blue Region: If you use the audio data of an Apple Loop (Blue Apple Loop or Green Apple Loop), then the created Audio Region will be blue to indicate that it comes from a Loop and might behave differently (Tempo Matching, Key Matching).

Green: Region: If you import the MIDI data of a Green Apple Loop, it will be converted into a green MIDI Region on the Track. This time however there is no indication if this MIDI Region was recorded new in your Project or came from an imported Green Apple Loop. Both have the same green color.

Orange Region: This color is for an Audio Region that is linked to a standard Audio File which was imported to the Project. However, there are Audio Loops which use only the Keyword tagging feature without the specification of the Loop Type "Loop" or "One-shot". Those audio files will be available in the Loop Browser as Apple Loops, but when you drag them onto an Audio Track, their color will be orange instead of blue.

Let's summarize what we've learned so far about Apple Loops:

- ☑ They contain musical patterns and phrases that are ready to use
- ☑ That music is stored as an audio file
- ☑ Sometimes the music is also available as MIDI data including sound settings
- ☑ The audio file can play in the current Tempo of the Project (Tempo Matching)
- ☑ The audio file can play in the current Key of the Project (Key Matching)
- ☑ The Apple Loops contain keywords that makes them easily searchable.

The last feature, the search of Apple Loops, is done in the Loop Browser. It is a separate window pane that slides out on the right side of the GarageBand Project window. That same window pane is shared with the Track Info window and the Media Browser which means you can view only one of those three windows at a time.

To open the Loop Browser, use any of the following commands:

 Menu Command Control ➤ Show/Hide Loop Browser

 Key Command cmd+L

 Click the Loop Browser button in the lower right corner of the Control Bar

Loop Browser Button

Window Elements

Here is an overview of the various interface elements on the Loop Browser.

Library Selection

Select from the popup menu which Apple Loops Library you want to search.

View Selection - Search

Select from three different views of how to search for Loops.

Search Criteria

Make the search selection.

Result List

Pick the Loop from the Results List. This list displays all the Loops that match the search criteria.

Refine Result List

Enter text to limit the Result List to those Loops that match that text string.

Adjust Preview level

Adjust the playback volume when previewing the Apple Loops in the Results List.

Loop Browser

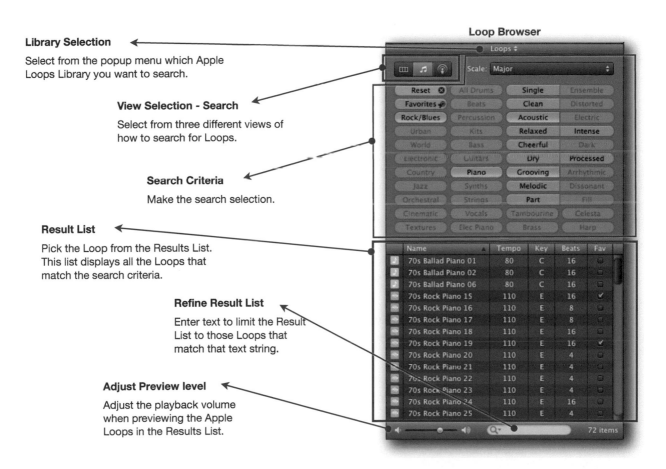

➡ Library Selection

The Header of the Loop Browser is actually a popup button. Its menu displays all the available Apple Loop Libraries that GarageBand can find on your computer. You can select the first item which searches for Apple Loops in all Libraries or select a specific Library to apply the search criteria to only those Libraries.

The menu has the following sections:

- **Show All**: Search in all Libraries.
- **My Loops**: Search only for Apple Loops that you created.
- **GarageBand**: Search only for Apple Loops that come with GarageBand.
- **"Additional Libraries"**: This section lists all the additional Apple Loop Libraries that you have installed on your computer. All the non Apple Loop Libraries that you've installed are listed under "Others".

➡ View Selection - Search

With these three buttons, you can toggle the different views of the main search section.

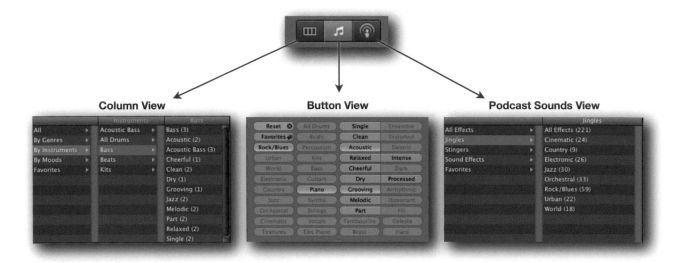

Column View	Button View	Podcast Sounds View

➡ Search Criteria

Before you use the Loop Browser to search for any Apple Loops, you have to be aware of how the search works so you understand what kind of search results or "hits" you will get.

Technically, you are applying a filter when performing a search in the Loop Browser. You are starting with all the available Loops on your computer and with each additional criteria, you filter out all the Loops that don't meet that criteria.

For example:

- Filter 1 - search only the "GarageBand" Library.
- Filter 2 - only Loops that are marked "Major Scale" in the Scale field
- Filter 3 - only Loops in the Genre "Blues"
- Filter 4 - only Loops with Instrument Description "Acoustic Bass"

The Loop Browser will show you (filter out) only those Apple Loops that meet "ALL" the selected criteria. In this case.

"Show me all the Apple Loops with Acoustic Bass in the Blues genre from the original GarageBand Library that are marked as played in the major scale."

The Loop Browser performs this as an "instant search" which means changing any criteria will instantly update the search results in the window section below.

Scale

The Scale popup menu is always visible and independent from the chosen search view. It lets you narrow down the search to find a musical pattern played in the major or minor key (or any, neither or good for both). Please note that this is not based on an analysis of the audio file. Instead, it is just a label entered by the creator of the Apple Loop so this search result is only as accurate as the original entry in the Apple Loop. This is also true for the other keywords.

Column View

Here you make one selection based on the three columns.

❶ Column 1: Lets you search in "All Categories, or just in the Genre, Instrument or Moods category. The fifth selection is "Favorites", which narrows the search to only the Apple Loops that you have flagged as Favorites (see below for the explanation).

❷ Column 2: This column shows you all the available subcategories in the selected category of Column 1.

❸ Column 3: This shows you the sub-sub-category available in the selected sub-category of Column 2. The number in the parenthesis tells you how many Apple Loops are found. Click on an item in that column to display those Loops in the Results List section below.

Column View

Button View

This view provides a matrix with selectable buttons.

If you look closely then you'll recognize the keyword categories. Select one Genre ❹. Select one or multiple Moods ❺ (these are the paired buttons that de-select each other) and select any of the Instruments ❻. The "Favorites" button ❼ limits the search to only your Favorites.

This search procedure is kind of "intelligent". Only the buttons that provide a potential hit will be highlighted. For example, if you selected "Urban", "Synth" and "Distorted" and none of the Apple Loops that meet those criteria have a keyword "Relaxed", then that button will be grayed out. You can always change the combination of selected buttons or hit the "Reset" button in the upper left corner to de-select all the buttons.

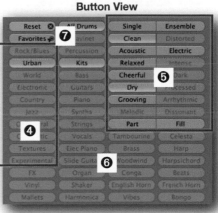

Button View

You can also re-arrange the Genre and Instrument buttons by dragging them to a new position (they swap places) or **ctr+click** on a button to choose a different selection from the popup menu. You can reset the buttons to their original position in the Preferences window
Preferences ➤ Loops ➤ Keyword Layout ➤ Reset

Podcast Sounds View

This is a questionable choice of label. "Podcast" just hints as to the potential use of those Apple Loops. What you really can search in this view are Apple Loops that are labeled as "One-shots" which are audio files that are not meant for looping. In the first column you have three categories of audio files that fall under that description:

- Jingles: These are short (professionally produced) music files that you can use as intros or musical beds in your Podcast or Movie Project.

- Stingers: Stingers are short musical events like orchestra hits, horn stabs or typical reaction stings used in comedies.

- Sound Effects: This are non-musical sound effects used for movie productions (background noise, door slams, animal noises, rain, etc).

Podcast Sounds View

This is also a column view. You select a category in the first column and then the second column displays all the hits in different sub-categories. The number in (parenthesis) displays the number of available Apple Loops in that sub-category. Select that sub-category to display the Loops in the Result List.

➡ Result List

The Result List displays all the hits, the Apple Loops that meet your search criteria.

It is a list view with six columns

- 💬 **Loop Type**: The first column displays the icon for the Loop so you know right a way if it is a Blue or Green Apple Loop. You can preview the Loop by clicking on the icon (it changes to a speaker icon). Click again to stop the preview.

- 💬 **Name**: This lists the name of the Apple Loop. The Loops are listed in alphabetical order and you can change the sort order with the little triangle button on the header.

- 💬 **Tempo:** This lists the Tempo of the Apple Loop. If the Loop is a "One-shot" type, then that field is empty ❶. You can hide this column in the GarageBand ➤ Preferences ➤ Loops ➤ Loop Browser ➤ "Display original Tempo and Key" .

- 💬 **Key:** This column lists the Key of the Apple Loop. If the field is empty ❷, then it is either a non-pitched loop (drums) or a One-shot type loop. You can hide this column in the GarageBand ➤ Preferences ➤ Loops ➤ Loop Browser ➤ "Display original Tempo and Key" .

- 💬 **Beats/Length:** This column can display one of two values, depending on the type of Apple Loop. If it is a "Loop" type Apple Loop, then the field will display the number of beats ❸ of that loop. If it is a "One-shot" type Apple Loop, then the field will display the length of that Apple Loop in min:sec ❹.

- 💬 **Favorites:** You can mark any Loop in the Result List as a "Favorite" by clicking on the checkbox ❺. As you've seen in the search criteria sections, this lets you later limit your search to only your Favorite Apple Loops.
  Please note that this tag is not stored with the Apple Loop. This information becomes part of GarageBands's Preferences file.

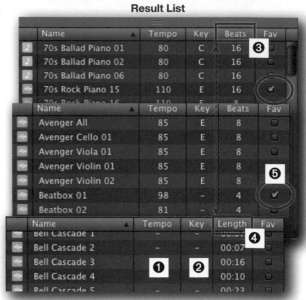

Result List

➡ Refine Result List

The Result List displays all the Apple Loops that meet the current search criteria. But you can add one more filter to that.

The search box at the bottom of the Loop Browser lets you filter the Result List to limit it to those Apple Loops which name matches that entered text.

The number to the right displays the total number of matched Apple Loops in the Result List

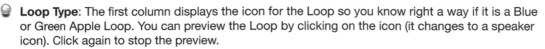

Name search

➡ Preview Level

The Volume Slider lets you adjust the level when you are previewing an Apple Loop.

Here are a few rules:

- When you drag an Apple Loop to a new Track, then the volume slider of the new Track will inherit the current value of this slider.

- Opt+click on the volume slider will reset it to 0dB.

- When the song is playing while previewing an Apple Loop, the loop will play in sync (starts on the downbeat).

- The Apple Loop will always be previewed in the Project's Tempo and Key (if the Apple Loops have Tempo Match and Key Match data).

Preview Level

Other Features

➡ *Loop Family*

Many Loops belong to the same family. They have the same Name with an incremental number at the end. To group similar loops makes sense. Remember our two examples with the drum groove and the strumming guitar pattern.

- 🔵 **Drum Groove**: Imagine the drummer plays slightly different variations of the same groove (HiHat, Ride Cymbal, etc) and also extra fills or groove variations that end with different fills. Now you could end up with ten similar Apple Loops. If you place those variations at the right place in your song then the drum track sounds more organic and natural because it varies instead of playing the same pattern throughout the whole song.

- 🔵 **Strumming Guitar**: You would have the same benefit if the guitar player would play different variations like light strumming or busy strumming and maybe a sustain chord for the end of a pattern.

But even if you have those groups available, it would still be a lot of dragging around between the Loop Browser and the Track Lane to experiment and find the right combination. For that, GarageBand has a very simple and elegant solution.

☑ You drag the first Apple Loop of that loop family onto your Track Lane, in this example a Piano loop.

☑ But instead of dragging the other Loops in that loop family also to the Track Lane, you just copy the same Region on the Track Lane to the position where you need that part played.

☑ A Region that belongs to a loop family (Green Loop or Blue Loop) has a little popup button in the upper left corner of the Region. Click on it to display a popup menu with a list of all the loops that belong to the same loop family.

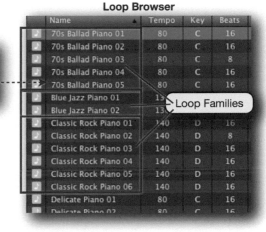

Loop Browser

"Loop Family" Region on a Track Lane

☑ Now when you create your arrangement of your song, you can quickly switch to a different variation of that Loop in any Region of that Track without going back to the Loop Browser.

➡ *Preferences*

The Preferences Window in GarageBand has a special tab for Loops with five settings.

- 🔵 **Keyword Browsing**: This restricts the search results only to those Apple Loops that don't have to be transposed more than 2 semitones. This guarantees that you don't wast your time trying loops that sound bad at the end as a result of a too extreme transposition.

- 🔵 **Keyword Layout Reset**: This resets the buttons in the Loop Browser's Button View to their original position.

- 🔵 **Adding Loops to Timeline**: With this option, GarageBand will always create an Audio Track with the Audio Region when a Green Apple Loop is dragged onto the empty space below the Track Lanes. **Opt+drag** a Green Loop to the empty area will always create an Audio Track regardless of this Preferences Setting.

- 🔵 **My Apple Loops**: This restricts the access to the Loops you are creating to only you. Anybody logged in on your computer as a different user can't use them.

- 🔵 **Loop Browser**: You can hide the Tempo and Key column in the Result List by un-checking this option.

GarageBand Preferences

We came across the "My Apple Loops" feature a few times already, so let's find out how to create your own Apple Loops. The procedure couldn't be more simple:

- ☑ Select a Region in your Project that you want to make into an Apple Loop
- ☑ Select the command "Add to Loop Library"
- ☑ A single Settings window opens up where you select the keywords
- ☑ Click "Create" and you're done

Details

◉ Select a Region

- You can select only a single Region. If you have more than one Region , then use the Join command to merge them first.
- An Audio Region will create a Blue Apple Loop and a a MIDI Region will create a Green Apple Loop.
- A Region has to be trimmed to exactly one bar (or a multiple) length to create a "Loop" type Apple Loop. Otherwise the created Loop will be a "One-shot" type Apple Loop.

◉ Select the Command

It is only available as a Menu Command Edit ➤ Add to Loop Library...

◉ Settings Window

▸ **Loop Icon**: the window will indicate with the Loop Icon ❶ if you are about to create a Blue Apple Loop or a Green Apple Loop.

▸ **Name**: Enter a name for your Apple Loop ❷.

▸ **Type ❸**: This is the important flag that tells GarageBand how to treat the Apple Loop when you use it in a Project:

- **Loop**: The newly created Apple Loop will store the Key and Tempo information of the current Project plus the Transient Marker Grid. Later, when you add that Apple Loop to any Project, GarageBand will perform the Tempo Matching and Key Matching.

- **One-Shot**: No Key or Tempo information will be stored with this type Apple Loop. GarageBand will use the Loop in any Project without any Tempo and Key Matching.

- If a Loop is not properly trimmed before opening this Settings window, then the selection automatically defaults to "One-shot" and is grayed out ❹ so you can' t overwrite it.

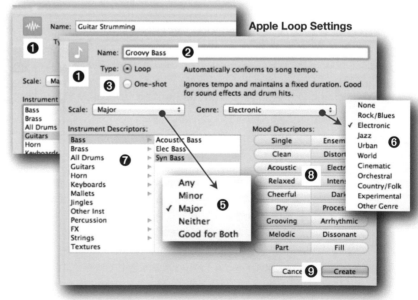

▶ **Keywords**: The next four sections (❺ - ❽) will assign the keywords to the Apple Loop. The Loop Browser can later search for those keywords.

- **Scale**: Select from the popup menu ❺.
- **Genre**: Select from the popup menu ❻.
- **Instrument**: Select the category from the first column ❼ and a subcategory from the second column if available.
- **Mood**: Click on up to eight mood buttons ❽. They come in pairs and are mutually exclusive.

💡 Create

When you click the Create button ❾, the Apple Loop will be created and placed in the following location on your hard drive:

`username/Library/Audio/Apple Loops/User Loops/SingleFiles/`

The new Apple Loop will be indexed and can be immediately searched for in the Loop Browser.

Indexing

The whole concept of search relies on one important procedure: Indexing. It doesn't matter if you search for Apple Loops in GarageBand's Loop Browser or do a Google search on the internet. It's a similar concept.

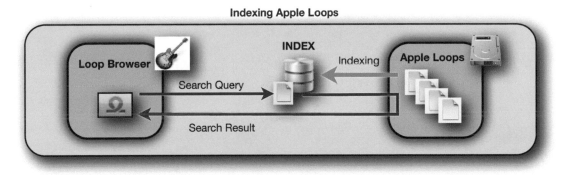
Indexing Apple Loops

All the Apple Loops have to be "indexed" first. This is a procedure of finding all the Apple Loops on your drive and listing them in a simple index file with all their information (metadata), similar to cataloging. Now when you do a search query in GarageBand's Loop Browser, it will, instead of searching all over your hard drive, just look at the Index file and send back the search results based on those findings. As you can see, if an Apple Loop isn't indexed then the Loop Browser can't find it

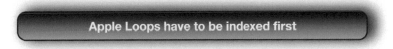
Apple Loops have to be indexed first

Loops will be automatically indexed when you install GarageBand, install new Apple Loops, and also when you create your own Apple Loop in GarageBand.

Add more Loops (or standard audio files) to the Loop Browser

- **Single file**: Drag the file onto the Loop Browser which opens the Apple Loops settings window.
- **Folder of files**: Drag the folder onto the Loop Browser. GarageBand will copy the folder into the same "User Loops" folder and index the files.

Update (Re-Indexing) the Apple Loops

Sometimes the index file gets corrupted. In that case you have to trash them and manually drag the Loop folders from the Finder over the Loop Browser to re-index the loops. However this is already a more advanced "surgery". If you are interested in learning more about Apple Loops you can go to my website to download my free "Apple Loops" manual from 2005.

http://DingDingMusic.com/DingDing/ManualsFree.html

11 - Advanced Features

Automation

Automation is a standard feature in all DAWs and virtually no mix is done without automation anymore. GarageBand has a limited implementation of that feature, but it's still very powerful and super easy to use.

Concept

Here is a quick look at the basic concept with a little bit of a math background (it looks scarier than it actually is).

➡ *Scenario* ❶

Real Life

You set the fader for the rhythm guitar track on your mixing board to 0dB. You start to play the project and throughout the 3 minutes of the song, you leave the fader at that position without changes.

Math Representation

You might remember from your math class that you could draw that as a graph. The x-axis represents the duration of the song (playing for 3 minutes) and the y-axis represents the position of the fader (the value of the volume).

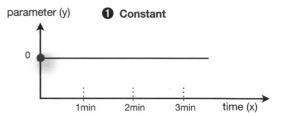

The Result:

> The parameter value (the Fader) stays

➡ *Scenario* ❷

Real Life

In real life you probably find that the guitar player moved a little bit too close to the microphone during the song at 1min and you have to gradually lower the volume fader to -10dB all the way to the 2 minute mark. At that point, the guitar player seemed to realize that and moved slowly closer to the mic, but this time a bit too close. You compensate that by raising the volume fader back up, all the way to +3dB by the time the song reaches the 3 minute mark.

Math Representation

The mathematical function is a visual representation of the movement I just did with the fader. The parameter value starts at 0 and stays at that value up to the 1 minute mark. Now the value decreases gradually to -10 and when the graph reaches the 2 minute mark on the time axis, it gradually increases to +3 when it reaches the 3 minute mark on the time axis

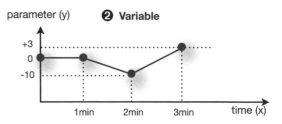

The Result:

> The parameter value (the Fader)   over time

What is Automation

If we look at the graph, it is telling us one thing:

> **"It describes the behavior of a parameter (the fader) over time (the length of the song)"**

And that is exactly how you can define mix automation. Instead of doing the movement manually with each pass of the mix, you describe the movement and let GarageBand perform it automatically:

> **Automation: Describes how Garageband changes the value of a Track Parameter during the song**

These are the few elements needed when using automation in your GarageBand Project

❶ Automation Lane (Graph Area)

> Instead of a graph, Automation is visualized right below the Track Lane in an area called "Automation Lane".

❷ Timeline (x)

> The time axis of the graph is already there. It is the Timeline of your current Project.

❸ Parameter (y)

> The Parameter in your graph would be any fader or control available on the Track that you want to automate (change during the song). For each parameter, you create a separate graph (separate automation).

❹ Control Points

> The red dots on the previous graph represented the values of the parameter at a specific time. In math class, these were the coordinates, but GarageBand calls them "Control Points" (other applications use the terms "nodes" or 'keyframes").

❺ Automation Curve

> When you connect the Control Points, you will get the resulting Automation Curve. This line represents the change of the parameter value over time, staying constant, going up or going down.

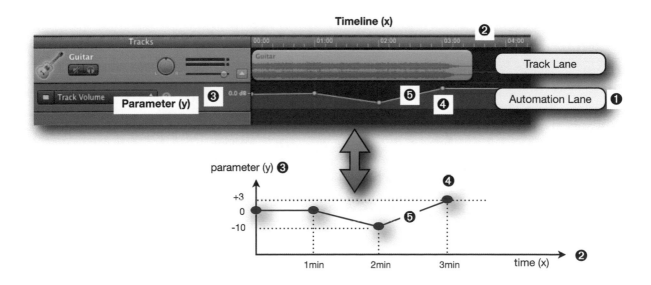

Automation in GarageBand

The implementation and use of automation in GarageBand is very easy. Just follow these four steps:

☑ Select the Track you want to automate

☑ Open the Automation Lane

☑ Select the Parameter

☑ Create/edit the Control Points and therefore the resulting Automation Curve

GarageBand only allows you to create and edit automation data "offline". That means you have to use your mouse to create and edit the Control Points and therefore the Automation Curve. It is not possible to "record" the movement of a fader as Automation data while the song is playing.

➡ *Automation Lane*

The Track Header of each Track (Audio, MIDI) has an Automation button in the lower right corner. This button functions as a disclosure triangle that toggles the Automation Lane. Please note, this doesn't turn the Automation on or off, just the visibility of the Automation Lane.

 You can also use Key Command A

Only one Automation Lane can be displayed per Track. But you can switch between the displayed Parameters. However, if you use a lot of Automation in your mix, you have to be careful because you can't monitor all the automation curves at once.

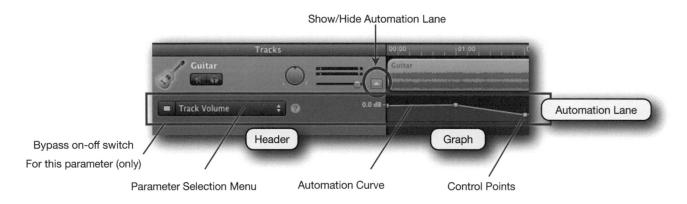

The Automation Lane is also divided into two areas, following the same interface elements of the Track:

💡 **Header**

- Bypass: This button turns the automation for the displayed parameter on and off (temporary disabled). The button uses the same Track color code (blue: Audio, green: MIDI, purple: Master).

- Parameter Selection: This is a popup button that opens a popup menu when you click on it. The menu displays all the available Parameter that you can automate (and add more to it). Select the Parameter that you want to display (and edit) on the Automation Lane.

- ?: The question mark button opens the GarageBand Help Center window.

💡 **Graph**

The Graph area displays the Control Points and Automation Curve. This is where you edit the automation.

➡ *Parameter Selection*

To select a different Parameter to be displayed on the Automation Lane, you click on the Parameter menu button ❶. This will open the Automation Popup Menu ❷.

💡 Automation Popup Menu

The content of this menu changes. As a default it displays only two parameters, the Track Volume and the Track Pan. Select one or the other to switch the Automation Lane to that Parameter.

At the bottom of the menu is the item "Add Automation..." ❸. This is a command that opens a separate window, the "Add Automation window" ❹.

💡 Add Automation Window

The content of this window is also dynamic.

- It displays all the available Plugins assigned to the current Track plus the Master Echo and Master Reverb, available in the Track Info pane ❺.

- If a plugin doesn't provide any parameter for automation ❻ then it is not listed.

- The plugins are displayed regardless of whether they are turned on or off in the Track Info pane.

- Next to the plugin is a disclosure triangle that reveals all the available Parameters ❼ for that plugin.

- Selecting any Parameter with the checkbox will add that Parameter to the Automation popup menu ❽.

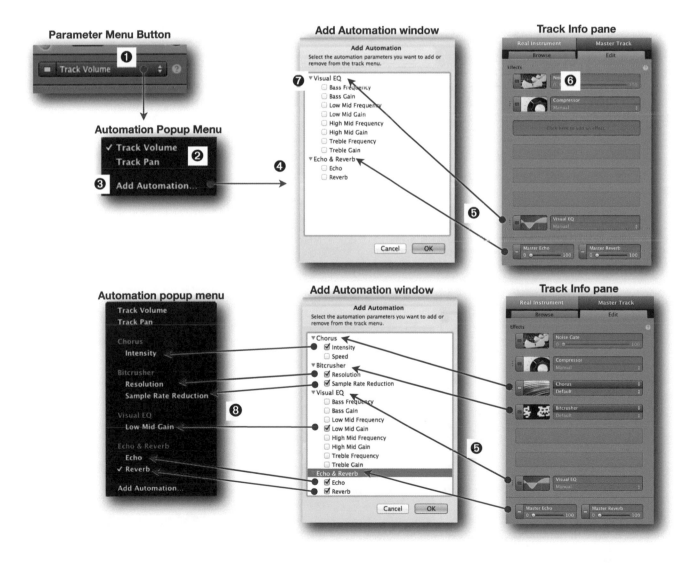

➡ *Creating an Automation Curve*

First of all, you cannot edit the Automation Curve directly. All the editing is done through the Control Points. All the Control Points are automatically connected via straight lines which results in the final Automation Curve.

▶ Who's in charge

Before creating some automation for a Parameter, you have to be aware of a specific "side effect".

Once you are activate the Automation for a Parameter (the button is lit), its control on the Track Header (or on the edit window for a Plugin) is dimmed, telling you that it is disabled, you cannot change it there anymore. Instead, the Automation is now in charge of that Parameter. However, the control is still moving, so you see the result of the Automation, even if the Automation Lane is hidden.

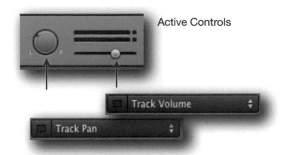 Active Controls

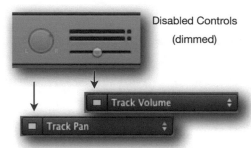 Disabled Controls (dimmed)

▶ Lock Automation (Control Points)

The Control Points on a Track are locked to the Timeline of the Track. However, if you created for example a special Automation Curve over the first eight bars with the Region of the Guitar Strumming and you want to re-use that Region later in the song, you just copy the Region. A possible problem is that you might need the same Automation performed over the copy of the Region. For that, GarageBand has a special mode. It can lock the Control Points to the Timeline of the Region instead of the Timeline of the Track.

 Menu Command Control ➤ Lock Automation Curves to Regions

 **Key Command** opt+cmd+A

Now, Control Points will be moved (and copied) with the Region, even to another Track. Deleting a Region will delete the Control Points too. This mode doesn't apply to the looped portion of a Region.

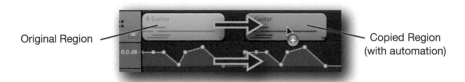

Original Region   Copied Region (with automation)

▶ Default Automation Curve.

If you open the Automation Lane for a Parameter the first time, it will look like this. Only one Control .

- 💡 **Automation off**: There is one Control Point at the beginning of the Song with the value of the current control set on the Track Header. Because there is only one Control Point, the resulting Automation Curve is one straight line. The graph however is dimmed because the Automation is still deactivated. You can change the control on the Track Header and you will see the Control Point (and the line) following the changed value.

- 💡 **Automation on**: When you turn on the Automation button for that Parameter, the graph becomes active. Now you can see the Control Point and the Automation better. The Automation is now in charge of that Parameter and the original control on the Track Header (or Plugin Editor window) will be grayed out and no longer responsive to your mouse clicks.

▶ **Add Control Points**

As I mentioned in the beginning, you cannot draw the Automation Curve directly. Instead you have to work with the Control Points to "outline" the Automation Curve you want to create. You can create and edit the Control Points freely with the standard editing commands (create, select, move, copy, delete) to shape and fine tune the final Automation Curve.

Add

Create a new Control Point by simply *clicking* directly on the line of the Automation Curve.

Select

To edit existing Control Points, you have to select them first with the standard commands. A selected Control Point looks a little bit thicker and brighter.

Selected Control Point

- *Click* on a Control Point to select a single one.
- *Sh+Click* a Control Point to select multiple Control Points (or deselect the ones that are already selected). Please note that the Control Points don't necessarily have to be next to each other.
- *Drag* around existing Control Points to select all of them in that range.

Move/Copy

The procedure for copying is the same as for moving Control Points, you just add the *option* key to the command.

- Single Control Point: just *click+drag* the Control Point vertically or horizontally.
- Multiple (selected) Control Points: *Click+drag* one of the selected Control Points to move the whole group.
- *Sh+drag* allows for a finer adjustment when moving vertically (change of value). You have to press the shift key after you start the movement to switch to "fine mode".

Delete

Use the *delete* key to remove any selected Control Point.

The Automation Curve will automatically update any changes with the Control Points, even while you're dragging the Control Point(s) around. A yellow Tool Tip will display the parameter value while you are dragging a Control Point.

▶ **Alignment Guides**

Guides

The yellow Alignment Guides, which are useful when moving Regions to align them to other Region boundaries in your Project, also work when positioning Control Points. Control Points, unlike Regions however, do not align to the bar and beat grid. Use the following commands to toggle the Guides:

 Menu Command `Control` ➤ `Show/Hide Alignment Guides`

 Key Command **sh+cmd+G**

▶ **Master Track Automation**

There are a few specialties about Automation on the Master Track:

Master Track Automation

- The Master Track doesn't have a Track Lane because you don't put Regions on that Track anyway. Instead, it always displays the Automation Lane.
- The Volume Parameter is always at 0dB when Automation is not activated for the Master Volume. Automating this Parameter is useful to fade your song in or out.
- The Automation Popup Menu has two extra Parameters besides the Volume: Master Pitch and Master Tempo.
- Master Pitch lets you automate pitch changes throughout your song. This will apply to Audio Tracks that have "Follow Pitch" enabled and MIDI Tracks (except the ones that have a percussion Instruments assigned to them).
- Master Tempo lets you automate tempo changes to speed up or slow down your song. The Tempo value in the LCD display on the Control Bar will update accordingly. Make sure that all your Regions can follow the tempo. The LCD indicates "auto" if there is Tempo automation programmed. Clicking on the Tempo will toggle the Master Track displaying the Tempo Automation Lane.

► **Dragging a Group of Control Points up-down**

There is one thing you have to pay special attention to when dragging a whole group of Control Points up or down to change their value. I mentioned earlier that you cannot move the Automation Curve directly. Instead, you have to drag the Control Points. This is also true when selecting a whole group of Control Points in order to move them all together. You have to click-drag one of the selected Control Points, which moves the whole group.

If you drag the group horizontally to change their position on the timeline, then it doesn't matter which Control Point you drag. However, if you drag the group vertically to change their value, then it does matter which Control Point you drag.

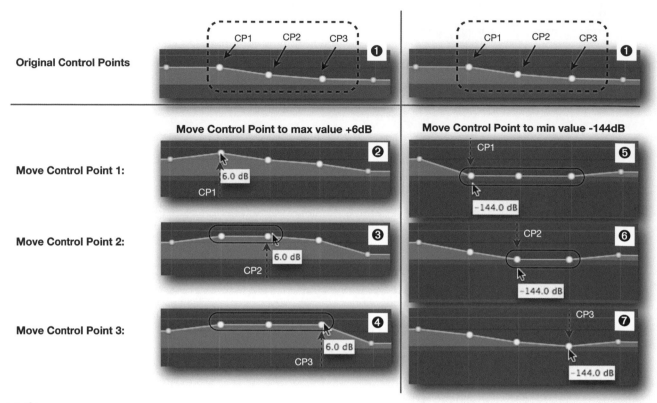

Example

Here you have an Automation Curve with five Control Points. Three of them are selected, displayed by their bigger, brighter dots. The first two screenshots on top are the same ❶. They show the original Automation Curve with the three selected Control Points labeled CP1, CP2 and CP3. They have three different values, 0dB, -10dB and -20dB. The next three rows show what happens when I move the selected Control Points by click-dragging CP1, CP2 or CP3 up or down. For each of those movements, I have two examples. The three screenshots on the left show the result when I move a Control Point all the way up (+6dB) ❷ ❸ ❹ and on the right you see the result when moving the Control Point all the way to the bottom (-144dB) ❺ ❻ ❼.

Result

Usually, the relationship between the Control Points in a group is maintained when you move a group vertically (in the example above 0dB, -10dB, -20dB). However this changes when any of the Control Points hits the maximum (+6dB) or minimum (-144dB) value.

- 💡 If you drag a Control Point to the maximum value, then any other Control Point that has a higher initial value will reach the maximum level before that and stays there. As a result, those Control Points end up now having the same value (0dB) ❸ ❹.

- 💡 If you drag a Control Point to the minimum value, then any other Control Point that has a lower initial value will reach the minimum level before that and stays there. As a result, those Control Points end up having the same value (-144dB) ❺ ❻.

As long as you drag the mouse up and down, their original difference will be restored. However, once you release the mouse, that value is now stored. For example, the original curve ❶ will be "squeezed" and becomes a flat line ❹ ❺. Only undo will recover the previous values.

We briefly touched on that topic already in the chapter about quantizing Audio Files and when discussing Apple Loops. Those discussions were based on the fact that both have their foundation in a fairly new technology called Flex Time (sometimes called Elastic Audio). Let's have a closer look.

Concept

Back to the original discussion about the two ways to record music. This time we will learn how to alter the timing of those recordings.

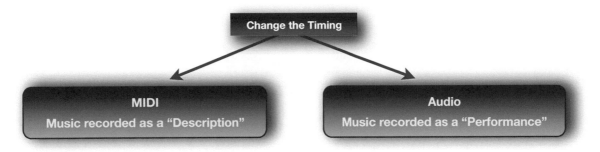

➡ *MIDI Recording*

Changing the Timing in a MIDI Region is easy. You open up the Piano Roll Editor and all the individual notes are there as single events. You can drag them manually to any position you want or apply a quantization command to have them automatically moved to a specific timing grid. Is it that simple.

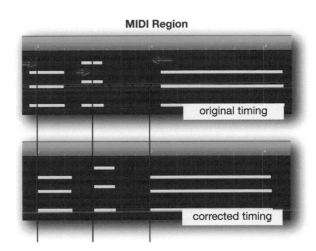

MIDI Region

original timing

corrected timing

➡ *Audio Recording*

Changing the Timing of an Audio Region (and therefore the audio file) was just not possible until the beginning of the era of digital audio. An Audio File is like a snapshot, a frozen event. You couldn't change the details in it. That snapshot is represented by the audio waveform where you can "see" the containing audio signal over time.

So how is it possible to change isolated notes or sections inside the waveform without affecting the rest of the audio file? This is were the Flex Time or Elastic Audio technology comes in.

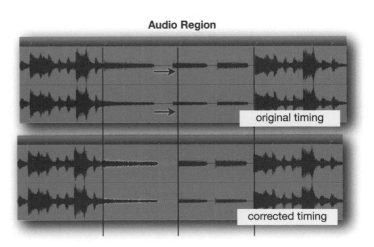

Audio Region

original timing

corrected timing

How the Magic Works

I will try to demonstrate how time alteration of an Audio File works. Once you understand the concept, then working with GarageBand features like Apple Loops, Quantize Audio and Flex Time makes much more sense.

❶ The Problem

We start with an audio file that has a note with a bad timing. For example, this could be the recording of a strumming guitar where the player hit the chord a little before the downbeat.

❷ The Preparation

Now imagine that we split the audio file exactly on that note, make another split on a note before and a split after that note. By making three splits on the audio file, we end up having created four files.

❸ The Operation

File 3 is the one that contains the note with the wrong timing. Let's assume the note is 10ms to early. Here is the first trick. We would squeeze (compress) that audio file so it is 10ms shorter. If we keep the right border of the file locked at its position, then the left border of the file will start 10ms later. The Result, the guitar chord which starts exactly at the left border of file 3 now plays 10ms later, exactly where we wanted it to be.

❹ The Clean-up

By making file 3 shorter, we left a gap of 10ms between file 2 and file 3. To fill that gab, we would take file 2 and stretch it by exactly the same amount of 10ms. This makes file 2 10ms longer. This time, we keep the left border of the file locked which means it ends 10ms later. That right border of file 2 touches now exactly the left border of file 3 and the gap is closed.

❺ The Achievement

By closing up the gab, we ending up with one continuous file when we merge the 4 individual files together again. The problem note is corrected by playing exactly on time and another important aspect: If we look at the area of the former file 1 and file 2, nothing has changed there. That means the content in the audio file before and after the corrected note stayed untouched.

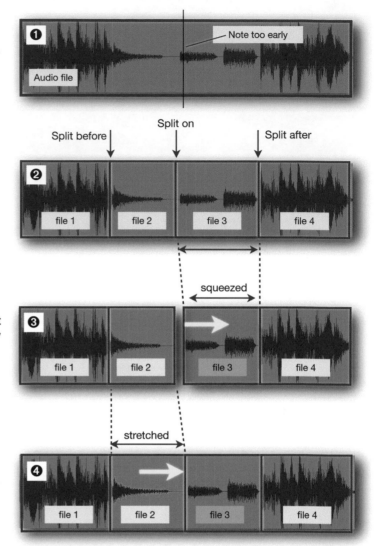

This was just a simplified example to demonstrate the procedure of the underlying technology on how to do time correction inside an audio file, which uses time expansion and time compression, a technology in digital audio.

Please note that when it is actually happening in GarageBand, all that splitting, stretching and squeezing is done in a non-destructive way. This means that the actual audio file isn't altered at all. All the audio file manipulation is done as a playback procedure and you can change it any time to get the best results.

Practical Use

So how is Flex Time done in GarageBand and how do we use it.

When we move an Event inside a MIDI Region in the Piano Roll Editor, we just move that event, it is right there, an individual horizontal line. As we have just seen in the example, in an Audio Region, we cannot grab an Event, there are no lines, only one continues waveform. Instead, in the waveform, we mark a position that we want to move, the position where we visually identified the troubled note. In the previous example I demonstrated that with a Split. This created a separate audio file that started at that troubled note. The newly created separate file would then be moved through stretching or squeezing.

But instead of splitting up the Region, we mark that position with a Marker, a so called "Transient Marker. In addition to that, to perform a timing change at that Transient Marker, we need two additional Transient Markers, one before and one after the main Transient Marker. They mark the boundaries for the time stretching and squeezing.

Here are the elements

- The center Transient Marker that will be moved ❶.

- Two Stationary Transient Markers mark the left ❷ and right ❸ boundary.

- The area of the waveform left ❹ of the center Transient Marker and right ❺ of the center Transient Marker are either extended or squeezed.

    Think of the center Transient Marker as a stick ❶ that is held in place by two rubber bands which are tied to a pole on the left ❷ and a pole on the right ❸. If you pull the stick to the right, then the rubber bands shorten on the right ❺ by the same amount the left ❹ rubber band extends. If you pull the stick to the left, then the rubber band shortens on the left by the same amount the right rubber band extends.

- The two areas outside that boundary ❻ are not affected by the squeezing and stretching and stay untouched.

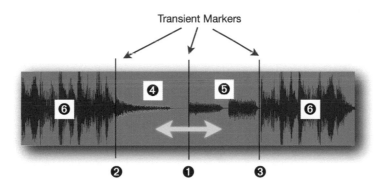

The key to a successful time correction lies in finding the best possible placement of the Transient Markers. In the example above, the right boundary marker ❸ is not a good choice. While we are moving the center Marker ❶ to the right, the right section ❺ is squeezed. If you look closely at the waveform, you will notice that there is a second Event (maybe a second guitar chord) that was played correctly in time. But now, by moving the chord at the center Transient Marker, we will move that second Event too. Fixing one problem, but creating a new one.

Here is a better choice how to set the Transient Marker in that case. We set the right boundary marker at that chord ❼. Now the area to the right of the center Marker ❽ includes only the problematic chord. The second chord (that shouldn't be shifted) which is at the position of the right Transient Marker 3, lies outside the boundary ❾ and is therefore not affected wherever or how much we move the center Marker.

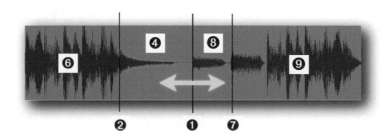

Transient Markers

If we understand the concept of timing correction in an Audio File so far, then we realize that the most important elements are the Transient Markers, or to be precise, the right placement of those Transient Markers.

The next question would be, who is in charge of setting those Markers. There are two mechanisms, automatic and manual.

➡ *Automatic Transient Markers*

In this case, GarageBand creates those Transient Markers automatically based on its own analysis of the Audio File. Here are the steps:

- 🔵 You have to tell GarageBand which Audio File it has to analyze.

  - Audio Files that you record in your GarageBand Project are automatically analyzed. The "Follow Tempo & Pitch" checkbox ❶ in the Audio Editor is activated for those Audio Regions.

  - Apple Loops have that checkbox checked when you import them to your Project. However, GarageBand didn't create those Transient Markers. They are stored within the Apple Loops which is one of the main elements that makes the Apple Loops functionality possible.

  - Standard Audio Files that you import into your Project have the "Follow Tempo & Pitch" checkbox unchecked. When you try to use a feature (i.e. Audio Quantize), a Dialog window pops up that reminds you that you have to have "Follow Tempo & Pitch" enabled ❷. When you click the checkbox for the first time for that Audio Region, GarageBand starts the analysis.

- 🔵 GarageBand starts the analysis.

  During the analysis process, GarageBand looks for significant points in the waveform. These are peaks (transients) that stick out in the waveform most likely caused by rhythmical patterns of the instrument (beats) or the beginnings of sections or phrases. It will display a window with a progression bar ❸ during this short process.

- 🔵 GarageBand now creates a Transient Marker at every peak it recognizes.

  Those Transient Markers are stored with the Audio Region in GarageBand and not with the Audio File. Remember, the Audio File stays untouched during those non-destructive edits.

Use for Transient Markers

The automatic Transient Markers (created by GarageBand or incorporated in an Apple Loop) are the bases for the following features:

🔵 **Audio Quantization**

Setting any Quantize value in the Audio Editor will shift the Transient Markers (and that portion of the audio) to that Quantization Grid.

🔵 **Tempo Changes**

Adjusting the Tempo of an Audio Region to the current Project Tempo also relies on the Transient Markers that get shifted to the tempo grid and result in stretching or squeezing of the audio file (play slower or faster) while maintaining the pitch of the audio file.

🔵 **Pitch Shifting**

While not that obvious, Pitch Shifting also depends on Transient Markers. Pitch change is achieved by speeding up or slowing down the audio file. That speed change must be compensated by an additional speed change with the opposite value (with the help of the Transient Markers).

➡ Manual Transient Markers (Flex Markers)

Flex Markers are manually managed Transient Markers.

With the automatic Transient Markers, you have no control on how and where they are created. You can only activate them and then have to rely on GarageBand's analysis process as to where it places them. With Flex Markers on the other hand, you have full control.

Flex Markers are Transient Markers managed by the User

The functionality of Flex Markers is based on the same principle as standard Transient Markers. Now that we have a solid understanding of that functionality, we can concentrate on the specific behavior of those Flex Markers.

The most important aspect to understand is that there is a hierarchy and interactivity between the Transient Markers and the Flex Markers. I try to demonstrate that in the following diagram. If you are not aware of that, then the results in your Garageband Project when using Flex Time could be confusing.

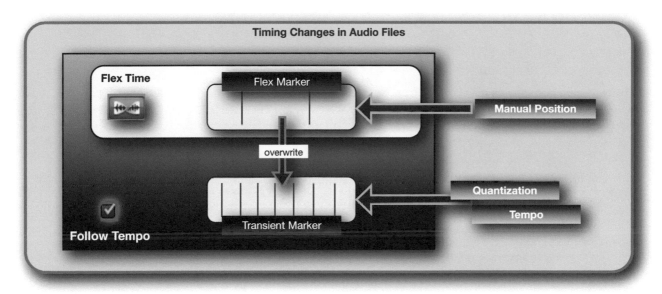

☻ The Systems

- *Follow Tempo*. This is the main system that enables the timing changes for the selected Audio Region. The checkbox enables or disables the function. It works like a bypass switch for the selected Region (not for the whole Track !)

- *Flex Time*. This is a system that provides additional functionality for timing changes. Please note that it is like a subsystem, which means it depends on the "Follow Tempo" system. Please be aware that Flex Time is a feature that can be turned on or off only for the whole Track not for individual Regions. However, if Follow Tempo is disabled on a specific Audio Region, Flex Time is disabled too for that Region, even if it is turned on for the Track. The blue waveform icon at the top of the Editor Header indicates if Flex Time is activated.

☻ The Markers

- The Transients Markers in the Follow Tempo system are automatically generated by the system.
- The Flex Markers in the Flex Time system are manually generated by the user.

☻ The Controllers

- The Transient Markers are shifted automatically by the Quantization settings and Tempo settings.
- The Flex Markers are shifted manually by the user.

☻ The Bully

Although the Flex Marker is technically just another Transient Marker that follows the same principle for altering the timing in an Audio File, it has priority over the existing Transient Markers. If you move a Flex Marker over an area where there are Transient Markers (which unfortunately you can't see), then those Transient Markers will be deleted. That area then can no longer be controlled by the Follow Tempo features like Quantization. Be careful, you could technically "wipe" out all the Transient Markers of an Audio File, leaving it unable to be quantized again!

If you need a moment to digest that "big picture", don't worry. It seems that the developers themselves were a little bit confused by stating something in the following Dialog window that is not correct.

Turn off Follow Tempo

As I pointed out, Follow Tempo can be turned on or off individually for each Audio Region. When you turn it off by unchecking the checkbox, you will get a Dialog window describing the consequences of that action: "...*you can no longer make timing edits on this track*". While the first part is correct, the second half of the sentence is not, because the Follow Tempo checkbox affects only the current Audio Region and you can still make timing edits on other Audio Regions that are activated on this Track.

By the way, if you select multiple Regions and they don't have the same checkbox setting (either all on or all off), then the checkbox for "Follow Tempo & Pitch" has a dash.

All Region are off: All Region are on: ☑   Some are on, some are off: ⊟

Turn on Flex Time

▶ If Follow Tempo is disabled when you try to create your first Flex Marker, then you get a warning that you have to turn on Follow Tempo first. That makes sense because, as we have seen on my big picture diagram, Flex Time doesn't function without Follow Tempo.

▶ If Follow Tempo is enabled and you create your first Flex Marker, then the Flex Time will be turned on for the whole Track.

▶ There is one special situation. If you've already created a Flex Marker on a Region but have turned off Flex Time, then GarageBand will notice and present a Dialog window with the following option.

- **Continue**: Flex Time will be turned on (now you can see the Flex Time edits) and you can go on and add more Flex Markers.

- **Reset**: This will delete all existing Flex Markers on ALL REGIONS ON THAT TRACK. (If you get the Dialog window again when you try to create the Flex Marker, just hit Continue).

Please pay close attention to the blue Flex Time button. It has three stages.

❶ This is the default icon when Flex Time is off and no Flex Markers have been set yet.

❷ Once the first Flex Marker has been set on any Region of that Track, then Flex Time will be enabled. The icon has a frame around it, indicating that there are Flex Markers and the waveform icon is twisted, indicating that Flex Time is enabled

❸ Once the icon indicates with its frame that Flex Markers have been set, then you can click on it to toggle Flex Time on or off. This state displays that there are Flex Markers (icon with frame) but Flex Time is disabled (waveform not twisted).

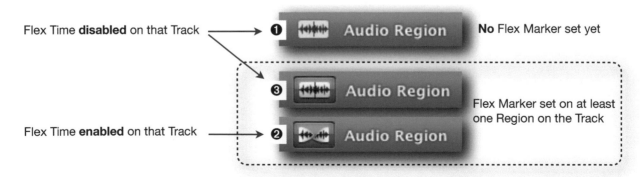

Flex Time

Once we are clear about the distinction between Transient Markers vs Flex Markers and Follow Tempo vs Flex Time, its time to finally find out how to create and edit those Flex Markers.

Creating Flex Marker

Remember from the chapter about the Audio Editor that the mouse is context-sensitive, it changes its appearance and functionality based on where you move it. Moving the mouse over the upper half of the Audio Region will change it to the Flex Marker Tool. This is the tool to create and edit the Flex Markers. You will see the Flex Time icon in the Track Header change when you create the first Flex Marker.

Click anywhere on the waveform to create a Flex Marker.

Flex Tool

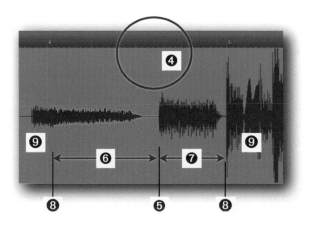

▶ **Restriction:**

❶ If the Timeline of the Audio Editor displays bars and beats, then the placement of a Flex Marker is restricted to the current grid selected in the menu under the Grid Button.

❷ Switch the Timeline to display Absolute Time in min:sec to place the Flex Marker freely inside the waveform.

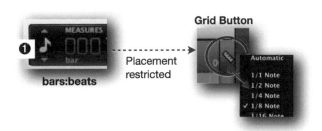

Flex Marker Visibility

It seems that Markers are kind of "shy" in GarageBand. They are hiding constantly. All the Transient Markers that are created by GarageBand through the analysis are not directly visible at all. And now the Flex Markers are visible but only if you are moving the mouse over that area with the Flex Marker Tool ❸ (in the upper half of the Region). If you move away, the Flex Marker disappears ❹.

The only direct visual feedback of whether there is a Flex Marker or not is the colorization of the waveform. The waveform to the left of the now invisible Flex Marker ❺ has a light glow ❻ around it and the waveform to the right has a darker glow ❼. This is the color code that indicates which section of the waveform is stretched (lighter glow) and which one is squeezed (darker glow).

The colored waveform indicates also where the Transient Markers ❽ are for the left and right boundary. The waveform outside that boundary to the left and to the right have the regular colored waveform ❾.

☻ Move the Flex Marker

Moving the Flex Marker is as simple as dragging the handle on top of the Flex Marker Line. As you move, you will see three things

- ☑ The waveform underneath the Flex Marker moves along with it. Remember the analogy with the stick and rubber band.
- ☑ The waveform to the left and to the right of the Flex Marker is not only moving, it is also changing color based on the color coded glow that indicates which part gets squeezed (compressed) and which part gets stretched (expanded).
- ☑ A third indicator becomes visible at the time ruler, a gray bar. That indicates how far you've moved the Flex Marker from its original position.

Here are three screenshots that demonstrate what happens. Once you try it out in your Project, then you will realize that it is not that complicated and actually a pretty nice interface for visualizing such a complex procedure.

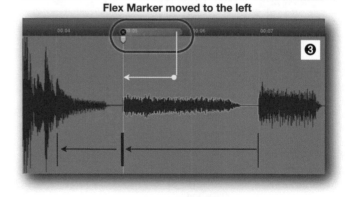

Original Flex Marker position ❶

Flex Marker moved to the right ❷

Flex Marker moved to the left ❸

❶ This is the original position of the Flex Marker, the way you would see it when the Flex Marker Tool is moved close to that Flex Marker (the Flex Tool is not visible in these screenshots).

❷ When you drag the Flex Marker to the right, you will notice the gray bar on the Time Ruler extending to the right. The waveform changes its shape and color accordingly

❸ When you drag the Flex Marker to the left, the gray bar in the Time Ruler extends to the left with the Flex Markers and the waveform inside the boundaries change their shape and color accordingly.

During the procedure, pay attention to the waveform outside the invisible boundary. It is not moving, the audio outside the boundary is not affected at all.

➡ How far can you move?

The boundaries where the stretching and squeezing happen are set by the two invisible Transient Markers (left and right of the Flex Markers). But be careful when you move the Flex Marker beyond that position, you will DELETE that invisible Transient Marker (use the Undo command). You might want to do this on purpose however if you want to increase the affected range.

If one of the boundaries is another Flex Marker, then you cannot move the center Flex Marker beyond that point. You would have to delete that (boundary) Flex Marker first.

☻ Delete a Flex Marker

Just click on the 'X' above the Flex Marker handle.

Here are three waveform examples that show the level of difficulty when it comes to finding peaks for possible placement of the Flex Markers.

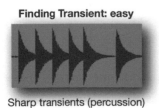

Finding Transient: easy

Sharp transients (percussion)

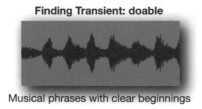

Finding Transient: doable

Musical phrases with clear beginnings

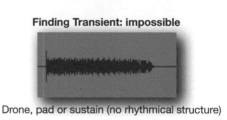

Finding Transient: impossible

Drone, pad or sustain (no rhythmical structure)

Groove Track

Groove Track is a special Quantize feature. The regular quantize feature is great because it corrects all the tracks so they have a perfect timing. However, if every Track is "perfectly" quantized, it could lead to a static or "lifeless" feeling. Even the best musicians are not always 100% perfect in their timing, there are slight variations, the "human touch".

Groove Track - Timing that isn't right but "feels" right

You might listen to a groove of a great drummer and the way he plays feels perfect. You load it into your Project and if you look at that audio file in the Editor, you would see that his timing isn't perfect. If you play it together with the other Tracks in your Song which are 100% quantized, they won't play tightly together. The solution would be to quantize the drum groove too. Although this would match all the tracks to a "perfect timing", you would have sucked out the "feel" of the drummers performance.

And this where the Groove Track feature comes in. Instead of using a perfect grid of 8th notes or 16th notes from the quantize menu, GarageBand lets you choose any Track as the quantize reference. GarageBand analyzes that Track and extracts a "custom grid" that matches exactly the performance on that Track.

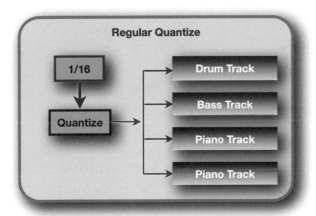 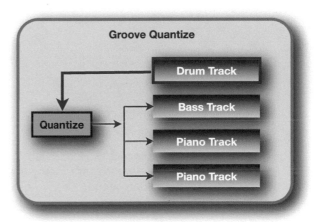

🌀 Activate Groove Track

The Groove Track feature is not activated through a Menu Command or a Key Command, it is "hidden" in the Track Header. Move the mouse cursor over the left side of any Track Header and a Star will slide out.

- 🌀 Click on the star of the Track that you want to use as the Groove Reference.
- 🌀 This opens a Dialog Window telling you what kind of preparation GarageBand has to do first.

    It has to analyze all Audio Tracks, not only the reference track. Even if it doesn't tell you, we know by now that it must create Transient Markers on all audio files that don't have any. It is the same analyzing process used for the "Follow Tempo" feature to create the Transient Markers.

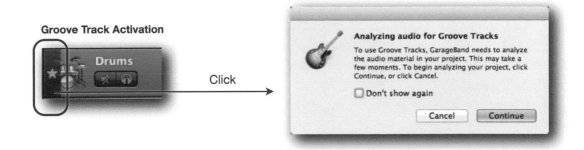

- We also learned in the Flex Time section that you have to turn on "Follow Tempo" so GarageBand can perform the timing edits with those Transient Markers. That is what the next Dialog window will tell you. If you click *Continue*, it will turn on the *Follow Tempo* checkbox for any Region that didn't have it on.
- Now Groove Track is activated.

When the Groove Track turns on, the Project window will slide to the right to display a section to the left of each Track Header. The section can display four states:

Groove Track enabled

Yellow Star: This is the Reference Track.

Checkbox checked: All Regions on this Track will follow the Reference Track.

Checkbox unchecked: None of the Regions on this Track have any quantize settings.

Checkbox with a hyphen: Groove Track is disabled but there is at least one Region that has a different quantize setting. If you click the checkbox, then the Track will be enabled and those individual quantize settings will be replaced with the Groove Track settings.

As always, there are a few details you have to pay attention to when Groove Track is activated:

- All the MIDI Tracks will automatically be activated: If any MIDI Region had a quantize setting before, then that will change to the "*Groove Matching*" setting. Please note that if you deactivate Groove Track, the previous quantize setting on that Region will be restored.
- Audio Tracks with Apple Loops or Audio Files that have been recorded in that Project will automatically be activated (checked).
- Audio Tracks with imported Audio Regions will not be activated yet (unchecked). "*Follow Tempo*" however will be checked by the prior analysis process so they are ready for Groove Track. You just have to check it manually.
- The Referenced Groove Track doesn't have to be an Audio File, it can also be a MIDI Track.
- If a Track is enabled (checked) to be quantized by the Groove Track, then all of its Regions will change their Quantize Setting. Instead of a value from the Grid, it displays "*Groove Matching*". This option is grayed out because it is controlled by the Groove Track checkbox on the Track Header. The quantize strength slider is still active. Any prior quantize setting will be restored when you turn off the Groove Track checkbox for that Track.

Track Editor - Quantize Setting

Change the Reference Track

Just drag the Star to a different Track.

Turn off Groove Track

Click on the Star and the whole section on the Track Header will disappear.

Rewire Applications

Rewire is a special protocol (communication language) that enables two DAWs (from different manufacturers) to "play together". (WIKI MOMENT: ReWire)

► **Host and Client**

- One of the DAW functions as the **Host**, that's the one that has to be launched first.
- The second DAW recognizes the launched host and starts itself as a Rewire **Client**.
- Both applications are communicating now via the Rewire protocol.
- The Rewire protocol provides a list of different data types that can be transferred between the DAWs. However not every DAW supports the full protocol of each data type.

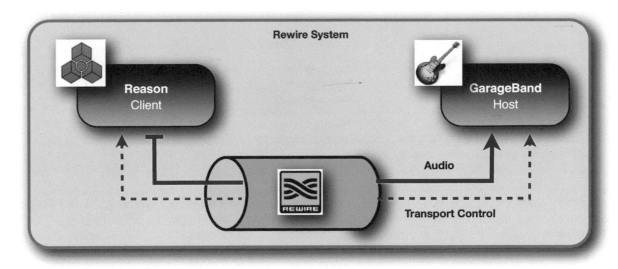

► **GarageBand Setup**

- GarageBand can only function as the Rewire host and has to be launched first.
- Lets assume Reason is the second DAW that acts as the client.
- This setup provides two Rewire features: Synchronized Transport Control and sending Audio Transfer. The audio (master out only) from the client to GarageBand.

➡ *Synchronized Transport Control*

Using any controls on GarageBand will control Reason and vice versa. This includes the transport buttons but also the Cycle Mode, Cycle Range, Tempo setting and moving the Playhead.

➡ *Audio from Reason acts as a GarageBand "Rewire Track"*

GarageBand receives the master audio out from the client. Think of if as if that signal is available on an additional "invisible Rewire" Audio Track in GarageBand.

- Soloing any other Track will also mute that "Rewire Track".
- Any Volume Automation on the Master Track will also affect the "Rewire Track"
- Exporting (mixing) the GarageBand Project to a new audio file will include the "Rewire Track".

Final Touches

Before exporting the final Project and sharing it with the world, there are a few final touches to consider, starting with the Level.

⚲ Master Volume

It seems that the GarageBand documentation is not entirely correct regarding the Master Volume. Every Track has a Volume Slider on the Track Header to adjust the Tracks level. As we discussed in the Automation chapter, when you activate the Volume Automation for that Track, the Volume Slider is controlled by the Automation and cannot be controlled with the mouse anymore.

The Master Track is different. First of all, it doesn't have a Volume Slider on its Track Header, but it has Volume Automation.

Master Volume

The Control Bar at the bottom of your Project window has a Volume Slider and that could lead to confusion. This is not the "**Master Track Volume**"! The Master Track does not have a volume slider. This slider is the "**Master Volume**" that is placed in the signal chain after the Master Track's Volume Automation. It is the last checkpoint where you can set the overall volume before it is sent to your speakers (or exported). You can monitor the level of your "final signal" with the Master Level Meter. Above the slider.

Before you export your song make sure that the level is not too low, but also not too high which results in clipping and possible distortion of the signal. The signal should not hit the red Clipping LEDs. If it happens, lower the Master Volume.

⚲ Fade Out

It is always a good practice to fade out your song at the end to make sure that the end of the song is completely silent and nothing gets cut off.

You can create a Fade manually on the Master Track's Volume Automation Lane or use a Menu Command and GarageBand automatically creates a Fade Out on the Automation Lane for you. It will add four Control Points, 10s, 7s, 4s and 0S before the end of the last Region in your Project, gradually lowering the Volume.

Fade Out

Create an automatic Fade out with the Menu Command
Track ➤ Fade Out

You can use the command again if you change your song with an earlier ending. Hit the command again and it creates a new Fade Out at the new position. Using the Fade Out command again after you extended your song's length doesn't seem to work properly in the current version.

⚲ Normalize

There is a common function in digital audio that ensures that a signal hits the maximum level but doesn't go over it. This process is called "*Normalize*". I It is like a little built-in guard that looks at your Audio File which is created during the export and at the end decides how much the level has to be raised in order to hit maximum level without clipping. This is done before the exported file is created. This export feature can be activated in the Preferences:

Preferences

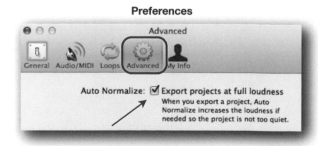

GarageBand ➤ Preferences ➤ Advanced ➤ Auto Normalize

● Output Format

If no audio compression will be selected during the export configuration, then the default file format will be aiff in 44.1kHz with a resolution of 16bit or 24bit. This depends on the Preferences Settings
GarageBand ➤ Preferences ➤ Advanced ➤ Audio Resolution. 16bit if set to "Good" or "Better" and 24bit if set to "Best".

● Notepad

This is a GarageBand feature that I haven't mentioned so far in the Manual. It is a built in Notepad. This is a little floating window (always on top) that can be toggled with any of the two commands.

 Menu Command Window ➤ Notepad

 Key Command opt+cmd+P

Of course you can use it throughout your Project to write down any kind of notes (What mics were used, who was the guitar player, reminders, anything). For the export it is useful when dealing with alternate mixes. Most of the time, you won't just make one mix of your potential hit song. You might try different versions. If you make those alternate mixes from one Project File, then you can make notes about those different mixes. Whatever adjustments you make a for a different mix, write it down in the Notepad.

● Computer overload

The advantage and convenience of using DAWs is that they do everything "in the box". However that box has its limitations. If you use too many Tracks with too many effect plugins that need a lot of processing power from your computer, then you might hit the ceiling where you've used up all the available processing power of your computer. There are two indications during playback:

☑ You will hear drop outs or distorted sound while playing your song.

☑ The Playhead turns red.

The export process is an "offline" process, so GarageBand is not playing back your Project while exporting it. While this overload problem doesn't affect your export procedure, it is a good idea in that situation to "freeze" some Tracks to lower the burden on your computer. (see the chapter about Locking Tracks)

What will be exported

Before you choose any of the export commands, you have to tell GarageBand what you want to export.

▶ **Tracks**

All Tracks are included in the export except the muted ones (with the Mute button or with an active Solo button). This way you can quickly export different versions of your song that include or exclude specific Tracks/Instruments.

▶ **Length**

The length of the exported song depends on a specific hierarchy.

- As a default, the exported Project starts at the beginning and ends about a second after the end of the last Region in your Project.

- If you put the the End-of-Project Marker exactly at the end of the last Region then the song ends exactly there. The end of song marker is positioned at bar 33 when opening a new Project. It can be placed between bar 8 and bar 9999 but cannot be placed before the end of the last Region. Otherwise, it only determines how far to the right you can scroll your Project.

End-of-Project Marker

- The best way however is to use the Cycle Range. When activated (visible), then GarageBand exports the exact length of the yellow Cycle Range. In case there is an effect still going on after the last note of your song, i.e. the tail of a Reverb or a Delay, you can set the end of the cycle to make sure that it is not cut off. It is also useful when you want to export only a section of the song that doesn't start at the beginning.
One exception is when you have a movie in your Project. In that case the export starts at the beginning (0:00) and ends with the last Region (regardless of the Cycle Range).

End of Cycle Range ↓

Share Menu

As long as you work on your Song inside GarageBand it just resides there and cannot be accessed or played by any other application (i.e. iTunes). It is like your band rehearses their material in their garage and nobody has heard their songs yet on CD or on stage.

There are only two exceptions.

- Logic Pro can open up a GarageBand project but just to continue to work on that Project.
- When you save a GarageBand Project, you have the option to let GarageBand save a mix of the current state of your Project embedded with the Project File. That audio file can then be accessed by other iLife applications (i.e. iMovie). Think of it as a "Rough Mix" of your song, not the finished product, just work in progress.

But know let's assume your Project is ready to be released to the world.

The process is called "mix down", "export" or "bounce", where GarageBand plays your song and saves it as a new Audio File. This is an "offline" process which means Garageband doesn't play the song in real time while "recording" it to the new file. It just calculates everything and creates that new Audio File.

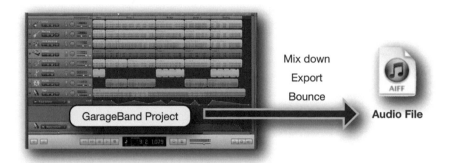

Instead of just one "Export" command, GarageBand provides a variety of commands that are tailored to what type of Project you are working on and where you want to export it to. All those options are listed under the Share Menu.

You have a total of five export destinations for your Project. Each one has its own command with specific settings for that destination. These are the destinations:

 Export your Project (Song, Ringtone, Podcast, Movie) and import it directly to your iTunes Library.

Export your Project (Podcast, Movie) and open it in the iWeb application to post it on your website.

 Export your Project (Movie) and open it in the iDVD application to prepare it for a DVD.

 Export your Project (Song, Podcast, Movie) straight to your Disk, anywhere on your hard disk.

Export your Project (Song) and burn it directly onto a CD.

Pay attention to those Menu Commands, they change slightly, depending what kind of Project you are currently exporting.

Export

➡️ *Send to iTunes*

This command involves two steps. It creates the new Audio File of your Project and then automatically imports it to your iTunes Library. The file itself will be stored in the `username/Music/iTunes/iTunes Music/Import` folder.

You can send any type of Project to iTunes (Song, Podcast, Movie). The command in the Share menu will change from "Song" to "Movie" (if the Movie Track is visible) or "Podcast" (if the Podcast Track is visible).

When selecting the command, a Settings Sheet will slide out from the top of the GarageBand Project to set the configurations for the exported file. The window is divided into an upper and lower section.

- 🎙 **Upper section ❶**: You have four fields to add information (called tags or metadata) to the new Audio File. As a default, it takes the information that is entered in the "My Info" tab in the Preferences window ❷. The four tags will be embedded with your AudioFile and show up in iTunes ❸ in addition to the Tempo information and the name of your Project that will become the name of the new Audio File.

- 🎙 **Lower section ❹**: This section looks different depending on what you export, a Song, Podcast or Movie. For a Song, it displays only a checkbox with the label "Compress" ❺. If unchecked, your song will be exported as an uncompressed aiff file in CD quality (44.1kHz, 16/24bit). If you check the box, then the window extends with more options to configure ❻. For a Song Project, you can choose between the mp3 or AAC format with more detailed settings about the quality (and therefore size) of your exported Audio File. If you export a Podcast ❼ or a Movie ❽, then the lower section with the configurations are different and provide specific settings for that exported Project.

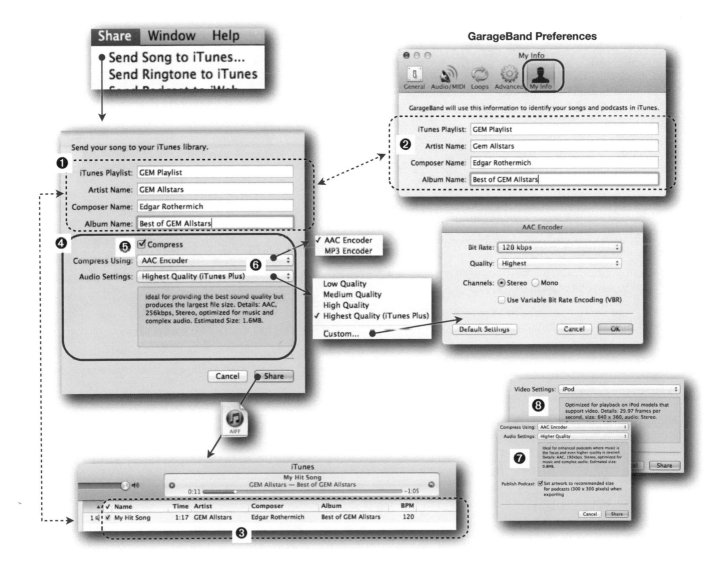

➡ **Send Ringtone to iTunes**

In GarageBand, a Ringtone is not really a different Project. Even a Podcast or a Movie Project can be saved as a Ringtone (the audio portion of it). The only requirements is that it cannot be longer than 40s. Just set the Cycle Range to less than 40s and you are good to go. If not, then you will get an Alert window that lets you adjust it for you.

When you choose the "Send Ringtone to iTunes" command, the audio file will be created right away with no further configuration options. The file will have the extension .m4r and will show up in the "Tones" section in your iTunes sidebar.

➡ **Send to iWeb**

This command lets you send a Podcast or Movie Project to the iWeb application. This application however is discontinued by Apple and no longer part of the iLife suite. So this feature might not be available in a future GarageBand version.

The configuration sheet lets you choose the compression format (mp3 or AAC) and audio settings for the exported Audio File. Click on the Share button to start the export process. When done, the iWeb application opens with a newly created Page that contains the exported Podcast or Movie.

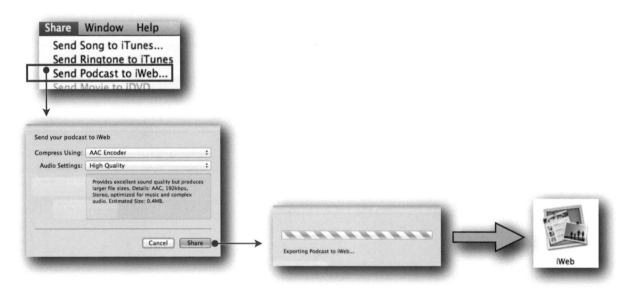

➡ **Send to iDVD**

Although the iDVD application is still part of the iLife suite, its days may also be numbered.

When selecting this command, your Project (Movie Track with a video must be visible) will be exported and opened in a new iDVD project. There you finish the DVD authoring process and burn a standard Video DVD of your Movie.

➡ Send to Disk

This is the basic export command. The Settings Sheet with all the configuration options is similar to the other Share commands. The difference is that here you don't "hand it over" or "share" it to another app. That's why the window doesn't have a "Share" button, it has an "Export" button. That button opens a standard Save Dialog window, where you can select any location on your drive you want to save the new Audio File to.

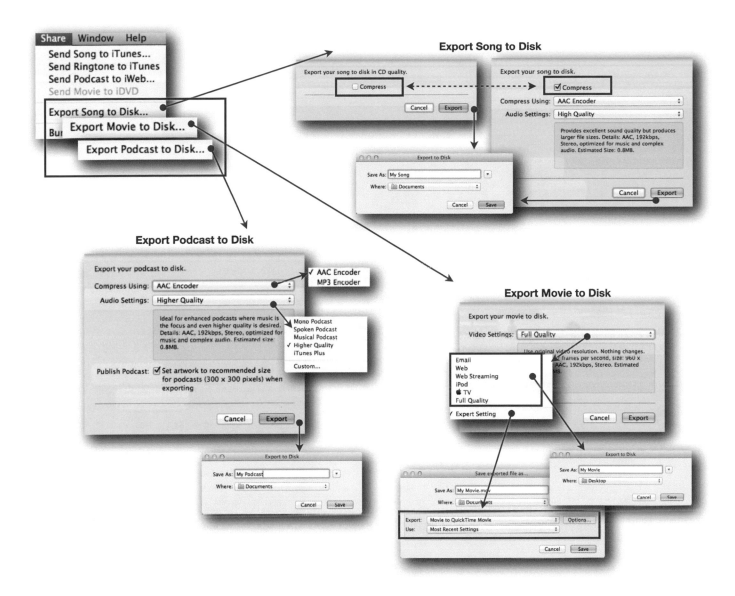

➡ Burn to CD

You can export any GarageBand Project and burn it directly to an Audio CD (it will ignore the movie if available).

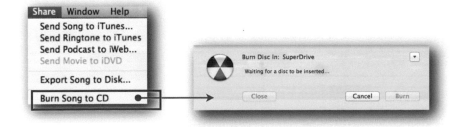

Podcast and Movie

While the most common use for GarageBand is to work on an audio-only Project, GarageBand also provides features that lets you create a Podcast or score a Movie. Some of those features are not even available in other DAWs.

Please note that there is no separate Podcast or Movie Project. What makes a Project a Podcast or a Movie Project is that you use the Podcast Track or Movie Track in your Project and add specific media and information to it. However, there is one minor restriction. Once you start, for example, with a Movie Project, switching to Podcast will delete all your movie related information and vice versa.

Movie Project

The only criteria that makes a GarageBand Project a Movie Project is that you added a video file to your Project. You can have two different approaches.

Add a movie to an existing Project: Any time while working on a music-only Project, you can make the Movie Track visible and add a video to it.

Start with a new Project: You can start with a brand new Project, using the Movie Template ❶ from the Project Chooser. This will open a new Project with the Movie Track ❷ visible and the Media Browser ❸ open to select a video file and you are ready to go. The Editor Pane ❹ is also visible, displaying the Movie Track specific editing tools.

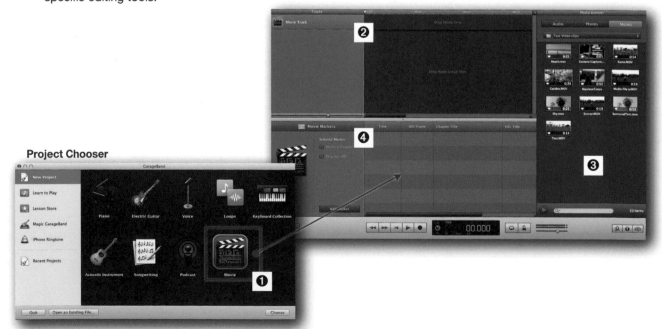

➡ Search for a Movie

Although you can drag a video file directly from the Finder onto the Movie Track, using the built-in Media Browser is more convenient for a couple of reasons.

Media Browser

Open the Media Browser with any of the three commands:

- Menu Command Control ➤ Show/Hide Media Browser
- Key Command **cmd+R**
- Click on the Media Browser button in the right lower corner of the Control Bar

Using the interface of the Media Browser:

- Selecting the Movies tab **❶** displays all the locations (folders) on your hard drive that contain video files showing only the video files in that location and leaving out any non-video files. For example, selecting "iPhoto" displays only the video files in your iPhoto Library and not the pictures. Searching for those video files manually among thousands of images in your iPhoto library would not be that easy otherwise.

- Please pay attention to the divider line **❷**. If you drag the line all the way up, then you will see a popup menu that lets you select any of the folders with video content. If you drag the divider line down, then the various folders are displayed as a list view **❸** with a scroll bar if the list is longer than the available space.

- The containing video files of the selected folder will be displayed as little thumbnail images **❹** with the information of their length. This helps you find the right video.

- You can even enter a specific name in the search box **❺** at the bottom to filter the displayed files if the folder has lots of video files in it.

- You can preview the video files in the Media Browser by selecting a video and clicking the Play button **❻** in the lower left corner or just **double-click** on a file.

- When you preview a video, the Media Browser changes its view to a little video player **❼** that lets you watch that video. This Player has the standard QuickTime controls on the bottom **❽**, even the volume control. Click on the video frame **❾** to return to the standard Media Browser view.

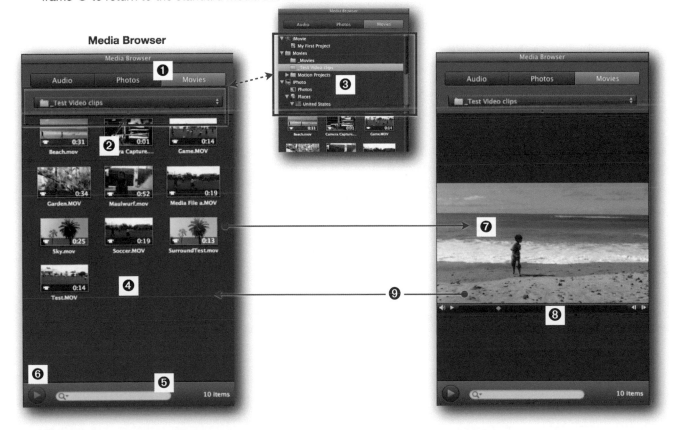

Media Browser

➡ Add a Movie

Before you can add a video file to your Project, you have to make the Movie Track visible. Use either of two commands:

- Menu Command Track ➤ Show/Hide Movie Track
- Key Command **opt+cmd+B**

With the Movie Track visible, you drag a movie from the Media Browser (or Finder) onto the Movie Track or anywhere in the Timeline area. Two things will happen:

☑ **Video**: GarageBand places the video on the Movie Track starting at the very beginning of your Project. It automatically converts the video file if necessary to the proper format. Please note that you cannot move or edit the video on the Movie Track in any way. During the import, GarageBand shows a progression bar while creating the thumbnails. These are the little images that display the video as a filmstrip ❶ on the Movie Track. The Resolution of those images can be set in the GarageBand ➤ Preferences ➤ Advanced ➤ Movie Thumbnail Resolution ➤ Low/High

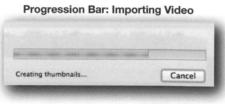

Progression Bar: Importing Video

Creating thumbnails... [Cancel]

☑ **Audio**: If the Video contains an Audio Track, then GarageBand will create a new Audio Track (Basic Track) below the Movie Track with an (orange) Audio Region ❷ that represents the audio track of the video file.

▶ **Viewing the Movie:**

Now when you play your GarageBand Project, you can view the imported video at the same time. You can do this in two places:

💡 **Thumbnail:**

The Track Header of the Movie Track displays only one element and that is an active thumbnail of your video ❸. You can watch the video on this little mini display while you are playing the Project.

💡 **Movie Window:**

When you move the mouse over that thumbnail, a little icon ❹ appears on the thumbnail. Click on the thumbnail to extract it to a separate floating Movie Preview window ❺.

- This is a floating window that always stays on top of the Project window.

- **Click-drag** the window to move it around and **click-drag** the corner to resize it.

- Moving the mouse over the window reveals its control bar ❻. That control strip represents the length of your Project (not the movie). The handle inside the strip is the playhead which is linked to the Playhead in the Timeline Area. You can drag it to position it. The number on the left is the current position of the Playhead and the number on the right is remaining time to the end of the project. Please note that this relates to the End-of-Project Marker, ❼ and not the end of the video itself.

- Click the X in the upper left corner to close the window and return to the mini display on the Track Header.

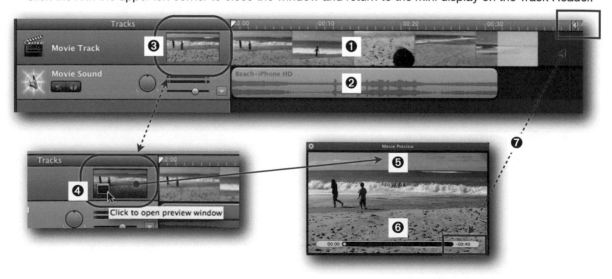

➡ Track Info

The Track Info window provides only five text fields. That information will be embedded with the file as tags (metadata) when you export your Project.

- **Title**: Uses the Project Title as default, but you can overwrite it.
- **Artist**: Uses the info from the Preferences window, but you can overwrite it.
- **Composer**: Uses the info from the Preferences window, but you can overwrite it.
- **Parental Advisory**: Select from the three options in the popup menu
- **Description**: Enter any text that describes the Movie Project. This text will end up in the "*Comments*" field when exporting the movie to iTunes.

Track Info window

➡ Track Editor

The Track Editor for a Movie Track lets you manage Markers and Chapters. These are common on DVDs when watching a movie. But it is not that widely known that those Chapters also can be embedded in a video file and to be used in the QuickTime Player or when watching a video in iTunes.

▶ Create Movie Markers/Chapters

Position the Playhead in your Project where you want to create a Marker and click the "*Add Marker*" ❶ button. This will create a line in the list to the right. Each Marker is represented by a single line that has five fields (five columns).

- **Chapter**: Selecting the checkbox "*Marks a Chapter*" ❷ makes the selected Marker a Chapter Marker. It will get a yellow diamond that is also visible in the Time Ruler ❸.
- **Time**: This is the position of the Marker. Click on the field to enter a new time if you want to move the Marker.
- **Still Frame**: This will display the video frame at the Marker position.
- **Chapter Title**: You can enter a name for that Marker.
- **URL**: You can assign a web address to a Chapter. The "*Display URL*" ❹ checkbox makes that URL visible in the video ❺.
- **URL Title**: Enter a name that is displayed for the web link ❺.

Delete a Marker by selecting its row and hit the delete key.

After you export your Movie Project, you can open it up in the QuickTime Player (or iTunes). There it has a little chapter icon ❻ in its control section that opens the Chapter window ❼. It displays the Chapters that you created in GarageBand. Click on any to jump right to it.

Podcast Project

Although you can use any DAW to record a Podcast, GarageBand provides unique features that let you do all the recording plus the preparations with artwork and chapters to create a professional Podcast. This is called an "Enhanced Podcast" that contains artwork, chapters and hyperlinks that are synced to the audio file. (WIKI MOMENT: Podcast)

This section lets you only create an audio podcast. You have to use the Movie Track if you want to create a video podcast.

➡ Create a Podcast Track

Again, the only criteria that makes a GarageBand Project a Podcast Project is that you show the Podcast Track in your Project and add the specific content to it. These are the two approaches.

📌 **Add podcast content to an existing Project**: Any time while working on a music-only Project, you can make the Podcast Track visible and start adding the podcast specific content to it. Use the Key Command **sh+cmd+B** or Menu Command `Track ➤ Show/Hide Podcast Track`.

📌 **Start with a new Project**: You can start with a brand new Project, using the Podcast Template ❶ from the Project Chooser. This will open a new Project with the Podcast Track ❷ visible. This time however, the template will include three additional Tracks ❸, two for recording the voices and one for adding Jingles (little music cues). The Track Editor ❹ and the Media Browser ❺ window are open again this time. This time, the Media Browser has the "*Photos*" tab pre-selected.

➡ Search for Images

The search functionality in the Media Browser is the same as I just explained in the Movie section. This time, you are using the Pictures tab to search for images that you want to use in your Podcast as artwork for Episode and Chapters logos.

GarageBand supports the standard graphics file formats like JPEG, TIFF, PNG, and GIF.

➡ Podcast Elements

The elements in the Track Info window and Track Editor window are similar to the Movie Project. So instead of explaining them again, let's look at an example of a Podcast Project to discuss those elements.

💡 Global Settings

The Track Info ❶ window provides the same fields that let you enter the metadata about your podcast. In the Track Editor on the left is an area where you can drag an image for the *Episode Artwork* ❷. This is the image that is displayed in iTunes or your iPhone for that specific Episode of your podcast, your current Podcast Project.

💡 Podcast Track

The Podcast Track functions differently than a Movie Track. Instead of dragging one video file on it that is represented by one single Video Region, here you can drag multiple images on that Track, each displayed as an individual gray Region ❸. Those Regions represent the chapters in your Podcast and when you play the podcast, the thumbnail ❹ on the Track Header functions like a movie (more like a slide show), changing to the Region's image when the Playhead reaches the next Region (with a different image). You can also open the thumbnail again as a separate Preview Movie window by clicking on it.

💡 Chapter List

Each Region on the Podcast Track is displayed in the Track Editor as a line in the Chapter List ❺. It has the same columns as in the Movie Track and you can edit the fields the same way. The *Still Frame* field is now the *Artwork* field containing the Region's artwork.

There is one extra checkbox "Display Artwork" ❻ to enable/disable the display of the current image for that Podcast Region.

The other Tracks in this example have the following content. One Audio Track for the main voice, the host ❼ with all the Audio Regions for that recording and a second Audio Track for the Guest ❽.

The last Track is another Audio Track that contains various music cues ❾ like opening and closing music and various transition effects between the Chapters. You can add as many Tracks as you need to create your special Podcast.

► **Podcast Region**

Here are a few rules regarding the handling of Podcast Regions

- You can move and trim the Regions in the same way as MIDI or Audio Regions.
- Regions don't have to be connected.
- You can create a new Region without an image with a cmd+click on the Podcast Track.
- You can edit the Artwork with the Artwork Editor.

Artwork Editor

► **Artwork Editor**

Double-clicking on any Artwork in the Track Editor (Episode Artwork or Chapter Artwork) will open the Artwork Editor that lets you adjust the visible area of your image.

- The square box in the center marks the area that will be displayed in the Podcast.
- Drag the image to position a specific section of the image inside the "visible" square.
- Drag the zoom slider to resize the image against the "visible" square.
- Click "*Set*" to use that setting.

Ducking

This is an automatic level control feature that is often used with voice over recordings like news or documentary films. Here is the concept.

You have Track A, the voice recording of a reporter and Track B, continuos background music. The movie starts with the music playing full level. When the reporter's voice comes in, you have to lower the background music and when the reporter pauses, you can bring the music back up. However, instead of doing that manually, you use an effect that is doing that automatically. That effect is called "Ducking" which is also useful in Podcasts and that's why GarageBand provides an elegant interface to use that feature. It automatically lowers the volume of any Track (B) whenever there is a signal on any other Track (A).

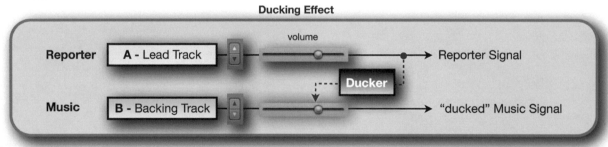

Ducking Effect

Turn Ducking of/off:

 Menu Command Control ➤ Ducking

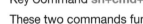 Key Command sh+cmd+R

These two commands function as a remote control to turn the actual Plugin on/off that provides that functionality, the "Ducker". It is located under the Edit tab of the Track Info window for the Master Track. Here you find the same user interface elements as with any other plugin slot. Click on the image to open the Plugin Editor to adjust the Ducking settings.

Ducker Plugin

Ducking Controls

When Ducking is turned on, all Track Headers in your GarageBand will display an additional Ducking Control that has two arrows. Clicking on the upper arrow makes it a "yellow" Lead Track (the reporter, Track A), clicking on the lower arrow makes it a "blue" Backing Track (background music, Track B). Click again (no arrow has any color) to disable ducking for that Track.

.

Magic GarageBand

The Magic GarageBand feature is like having your own band of professional musicians to jam along with in nine different musical genres. Let's have a look behind the curtain and see how this magic with its beautiful and simple interface is done.

The Concept

The nine musical genres are nothing other than nine different GarageBand Projects that are loaded in the background when you select a specific Genre. All those Projects are created with Apple Loops. So after all, you are still working on a GarageBand Project, the Magic GarageBand page is just a different user interface. Here are the elements.

▶ **The Genres**

First you select what musical genre you want to play with.

▶ **The Song**

Selecting a genre will load a GarageBand Project in the background. This is a song constructed with professionally recorded Apple Loops (mostly played with live instruments) and a full song structure with different sections and not just a 4 bar loop.

▶ **The Band**

Your band has five members (represented by five Tracks of the GarageBand Project). Drums, Bass, Guitar, Keyboards and a Melody Instrument. Each musician will bring a variety of instruments to the session to change the sound (i.e. Electric Bass, Acoustic Bass, Fretless Bass). You also can mix the levels of the instrument, "telling" each musician how loud or how soft to play or to pause all together.

▶ **The Featured Artist - You**

Now it's your turn to join in on the band. You can choose an instrument based on the selected input. This could be a MIDI keyboard using any of the GarageBands sound modules, an Electric Guitar or any acoustic instrument including your vocals using a microphone as an input.

▶ **The Purpose**

You can use your Magic GarageBand for different purposes:

- Just play along with the band for fun.
- Practice your improvisational skills over a specific section.
- Record a track with your performance to check how you are doing.
- Go to the next level and open the song in GarageBand which reveals all the Tracks and their Apple Loops. Now you can work on the song without any restrictions. Add new band members (Tracks), change the song structure and record more of your own material.

Now let's go through the interface elements to find out how to work the magic.

➡ Select the Genre (Project)

Because Magic GarageBand is after all just a GarageBand Project, it makes sense that you start in the Project Chooser. Open it with the Menu Command `File` ➤ `New` or the Key Command **cmd+N**.

Selecting "Magic GarageBand" in the sidebar will display all the nine Genres as album covers in the window pane next to it. Moving your mouse over a Genre reveals the word "Preview" with a tiny Play button. Click on it to preview that song.

Double-click on a cover or just click on the "*Choose*" button to open the selected Genre. This will open the Magic GarageBand window, presenting the band on a stage.

➡ Setup the Band

◉ Select the band member

In the upper section of the window, the Stage, click on any instrument to select it. A spotlight will shine on it ❶. That musician is now "listening" to you for whatever changes you want him to make.

◉ Select the instrument

Below the Stage is the Configuration area ❷. It displays all the alternate instruments that you can choose to play the part. Selecting "*No Instrument*" will remove the instrument from the stage ❸. You still can select that spot on the stage later and assign an instrument to it again.

◉ Adjust the level

A selected instrument displays a little black window with a disclosure triangle ❹. Click on it to reveal the instrument's controls ❺. You can set the level, mute it or solo it.

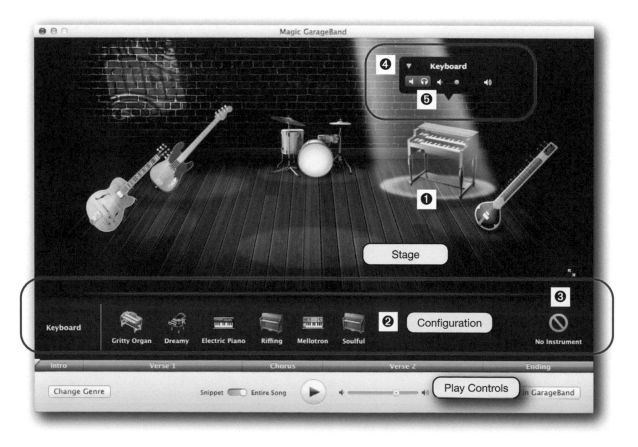

➡ *Setup your Instrument*

🔵 Select your Spot

There is one extra spotlight ❶ at the center stage and that is for you. Click on it to setup your own instrument.

🔵 Select the Instrument

When you select your spotlight, the configuration area below the stage ❷ will now display the options for your own instrument.

Input Selection: The popup menu on the left ❸ lists all the hardware input options where you select what signal you want to feed into GarageBand. MIDI Keyboard, Built-in Microphone, Line-in or any connected USB audio interface.

Tuning: The Tuning fork ❹ button has two functions. It changes the rest of the configuration area to the right. If the currently selected input is a MIDI keyboard, then it will display the notes you are playing and also the current chord symbol. If you selected an audio input, then it displays a tuner.

Instrument Selection: The displayed instrument selection (fork button has to be off) also depends on the selected Input. When MIDI is selected, then you choose from various sound modules. If an audio input is selected then you can choose from different Electric Guitar settings or generic audio settings. Basically what you see here are just various Instrument Settings. The last icon on the list is a Customize button ❺ that opens a menu ❻ to choose any Instrument Setting available in GarageBand.

🔵 Adjust your level

If you select your own instrument, the same control window will popup next to your instrument. In addition to level, mute and solo, this window has an input level meter ❼ where you can monitor the level of your signal.

💀 Reset Instrument Selection

Clicking on the stage (not on any instrument) will switch the configuration area to display only two big buttons ❽. "*Start Over*" will choose the default Instruments for the Genre and "*Shuffle Instruments*" will randomly select Settings for each Instrument.

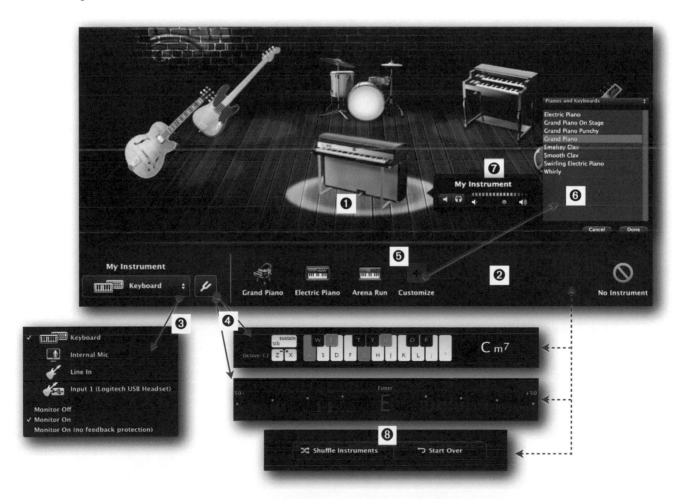

➡ *Let's Play*

The third section of the Magic GarageBand window at the bottom displays the various controls to play with your band.

⚉ Time Ruler

This section functions like a Time Ruler with a moving Playhead ❶. Instead of displaying bars and beats, it shows the structure of the song similar to the Arrangement Track.

⚉ Entire Song / Snippet

Now you have to decide if you want to play the entire song or practice on a section of the song. If you set the switch ❷ to "*Snippet*", then a section will turn yellow ❸. Now instead of cycling the whole song, GarageBand will only cycle the selected section. You can click on a different section or sh+click to select more than one section.

⚉ Transport Controls

- Click the Play button or use the space key to start and stop the song.
- Return sets the Playhead to the beginning of the song or the beginning of the selected section.
- Drag the Playhead to any position in the song.

⚉ Record

You can record only one track in the current song. However, GarageBand uses the "*Take*" mode which allows you to record multiple versions and later use the little Take number ❹ to switch between the different Takes.

GarageBand uses a visual ❺ and acoustic count-in when you hit the Record button. The recording starts either at the beginning of the song or the beginning of the selected section. You can also "punch in" to start recording anywhere while the song is playing by clicking the Record button. The recorded Region ❻ will be displayed below the Arrangement Region in green for MIDI or purple for Audio (and red while recording).

⚉ Other Controls

The slider for the Master Volume ❼ sets the overall volume.

The "*Change Genre*" ❽ button closes the curtain on the stage to let you select any other of the nine Genre songs. You will lose any settings and recordings at that moment.

The "*Open in GarageBand*" ❾ button opens the current song (including your new recording) as a new GarageBand Project to work further on that Project.

Learn to Play

GarageBand provides Piano and Guitar Lessons in the form of interactive videos that are integrated into Garageband. This makes it a unique feature that is definitely not found in any other DAW.

Guitar and Piano Lessons
as interactive Videos

The Project Chooser provides two separate items in the Sidebar for those Lessons:

Lesson Store

This iTunes like interface lets you download individual lessons from Apple directly into GarageBand.

Learn to Play

This is the place that lists all the downloaded lessons and lets you play them,

There are three types of lessons:

▶ **Guitar Lessons**: 20 free lessons (Basic, Rock, Blues)

▶ **Piano Lessons**: 18 free Lessons (Basic, Pop, Classical)

▶ **Artist Lessons**: 23 Lessons ($4.99 each) where artists like Sting and Norah Jones teach you how to play one of their songs.

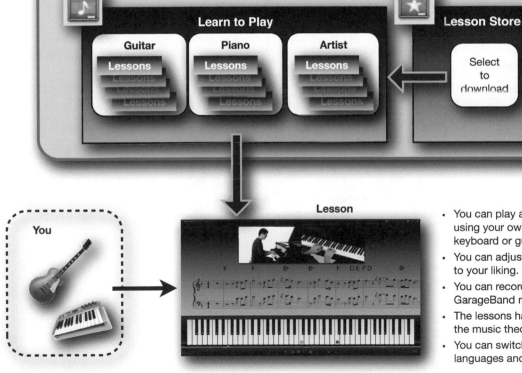

- You can play along with the video using your own instrument input (MIDI keyboard or guitar).
- You can adjust the Tempo of the music to your liking.
- You can record your own playing and GarageBand rates your performance.
- The lessons have a built in glossary for the music theory background
- You can switch between 5 different languages and 14 different subtitles.

Conclusion

This concludes my "GarageBand 11 - How it Works" manual.

You can find more of my "Graphically Enhanced Manuals" on my website at: www.DingDingMusic.com/Manuals

Subscribe to my mailing list for updates and future releases: subscribe@DingDingMusic.com

All the titles are available as pdf downloads from my website, as printed books on Amazon.com and as Multi-Touch eBooks on Apple's iBookstore.

(languages: English, Deutsch, Español, 简体中文)

If you find my visual approach of explaining topics and concepts helpful, please recommend my books to others or maybe write a review on Amazon or the iBookstore. This will help me to continue this series.

Special thanks to my beautiful wife Li for her love and understanding during those long hours of working on the books. And not to forget my son Winston. Waiting for him during soccer practice always gives me extra time to work on a few chapters.

More information about my day job as a composer and links to my social network sites: www.DingDingMusic.com

Listen to my music on www.SoundCloud.com/edgar_rothermich/

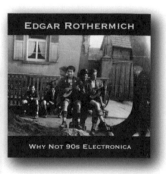

To contact me directly, email me at: GEM@DingDingMusic.com

Thanks for your interest and your support,

Edgar Rothermich